PUT A SHARK IN YOUR TANK

Signature Innovators Edition

Volume 2.1

Published by Best Seller Publishing®, Pasadena, CA
Best Seller Publishing® is a registered trademark
Printed in the United States of America.

ISBN 9798675451289

This publication is designed to provide accurate and authoritative information with regard to the subject matter covered. It is sold with the understanding that the publisher is not engaged in rendering legal, accounting, or other professional advice. If legal advice or other expert assistance is required, the services of a competent professional should be sought. The opinions expressed by the authors in this book are not endorsed by Best Seller Publishing® and are the sole responsibility of the author rendering the opinion.

Most Best Seller Publishing® titles are available at special quantity discounts for bulk purchases for sales promotions, premiums, fundraising, and educational use. Special versions or book excerpts can also be created to fi t specifi c needs.

For more information, please write: Best Seller Publishing®
1346 Walnut Street, #205
Pasadena, CA 91106
or call 1(626) 765 9750
Toll-Free: 1(844) 850-3500
Visit us online at: www.BestSellerPublishing.org

WHY EVERY TANK NEEDS A SHARK

Many years ago, Japanese fishermen had a big problem with the fish they were delivering to their customers.

By the time the fishermen made it back to land with the fish they had captured, the fish were dull, tired, lazy, lethargic – they lost their fresh taste.

After many years and tons of lost fish, the fishermen discovered the best method of delivering fresh fish was to place them in a tank – along with a small shark.

During the trip from the deep blue sea back to the mainland, the small shark would eat a few fish.

BUT the rest of the fish who **survived** would make it back to the mainland fresh, energetic, lively and amazingly tasteful because they were challenged in the tank.

The shark **challenged** the fish in the tank, so they constantly had to move around to stay alive – **the sharks kept the fish fresh.**

The same is true in business:

"Man thrives, oddly enough, only in the presence of a challenging environment."

– L. Ron Hubbard

YOUR BUSINESS IS YOUR TANK.

There are many moving parts in your tank.

Finance, marketing, database, management, public relations, websites, sales, merchandise – they're all vital to your wealth and keep your tank lively.

So, if this tank is your business, what does it look like?

Is your business lazy, lethargic and in need of new life?

Is a lack of funding keeping you from moving forward?

Have the no's and naysayers left you feeling defeated?

Are you struggling to express your idea, service or product?

Do you feel stuck in your business?

Are you "swimming" with the wrong fish?

Who's in YOUR tank TODAY?

What Does A Shark Look Like To You?

A shark is a mentor, a coach, someone with an unbelievable Rolodex, who will fast-track your success. A shark gives you direction, real-world experience, and will take your business and life to levels that you could never achieve on your own.

A shark pushes you to perform at your peak.

Without a shark, you might make a lot of wasteful mistakes – but having one on your team brings you certified experience and creates a **FASTER PATH TO CASH**.

Both Kevin and Loral have created thousands of multi-millionaires by using their proven wealth strategies … and now they're going to teach you how to **Put A Shark In Your Tank** in a never-before-seen workshop.

In this day-and-a-half intensive workshop, you will learn what it takes to attract a shark and why you need them – their money, their experience, their mentorship and their Rolodex.

Loral and Kevin do it themselves.

They use sharks EVERY DAY for their personal businesses, which is why they have such extreme results.

In the past 26 years, Kevin has launched more than 500 products with sales of more than $4 billion worldwide (*yes, billion with a "B"*). In the past 2 decades, Loral has created thousands of millionaires by showing them how to monetize the skills and resources they already possess.

So, we'll be honest with you…

If You Don't Have A Shark In Your Tank… Your Tank's In Trouble.

Think about it: Where would you be 3, 6, or 12 months from now if you brought a shark into your world RIGHT NOW, and started making the steps TODAY to take your business to the next level? Never underestimate the value of a mentor and coach who's already done what you're aspiring to do!

Who knows, you could become a shark yourself…

The good news is that Kevin and Loral have already done this – quickly.

Through their teachings, Loral has created millionaires in a matter of *months*, and Kevin has created them in a matter of *weeks*.

The key person of influence (KPI) is the leader in any given industry. The KPI is the leader of the business world, the leader of automobile dealerships, or the leader of selling hats—you name it. In other words, being the KPI is the go-to person. The crazy thing? Anyone can be a KPI. Any entrepreneur can be a KPI; any doctor can be a KPI; any salesperson can be a KPI; anyone can be a KPI. People just have to follow five steps, and then they will be well on their way.

What comes with being a key person of influence is value, ideally a massive amount of money, and being the leader in a field. A KPI is the person who comes up in conversations when it comes to a certain product, business, company, industry, or field. This is the person who others seek out, the go-to person. Being a KPI is how I got on *Shark Tank*. I tell the story of how I got on this ABC television (TV) show, because I had become a KPI but didn't even know how I did it. A lot of people asked me—and continue to ask me—how I got on *Shark Tank*.

Here's the story: I got a phone call from Mark Burnett's company. Burnett is a television producer. He produced shows such as *Survivor* and *The Voice*. His office called to set up an appointment. Burnett was starting up a new show and wanted me to go to Los Angeles to talk business. I was curious as to how Burnett's company found me, and why they reached out for my services. They told me it was because I was a key person of influence. Because I was all over the Internet, as a result of everything I was doing.

It was 2008, and I had been in the business at that point for 25 years. I started in 1984. I had created huge brands. I helped build fitness experts Tony Little and Jack LaLanne. I helped build FoodSaver and the NuWave Oven. I worked with people such as professional boxer George Foreman and his cooking products. The problem for me was that everybody knew the brands, which was good for business, but didn't know my actual personal brand. Consumers knew about the FoodSaver, they knew about Tony Little, and they knew about Jack LaLanne, but not everyone knew I was the guy who was behind all these people. Nobody knew me.

I made a conscious effort at that point to build my brand, and that's what I had to do. I wanted to become the go-to person in the industry to get the hot products along with the phone calls. I helped build Tony Little's business, but everyone was calling Tony Little. They weren't calling me. What's wrong with that picture? Well, I invested millions and millions of dollars of my own capital into Tony Little, and then he gets the phone calls. Shame on me for doing that, right?

I decided to build my brand, and that's when I came out with my book, *Key Person of Influence*. I published. That's one of the five steps—publish. The other four are focusing on pitch, products, profile, and partnerships. I go into greater detail about each step in my book, *Key Person of Influence*. I promoted myself by doing radio talk shows, TV shows, trade journals, speeches, etc. This is how I got on *Shark Tank*.

In 2008, Burnett was looking for "sharks," and that's when the phone rang from his company. It all plays perfectly into the story about how I got the phone call and how I consciously said—and this is before I used the term key person of influence—"I'm going to build my brand. I need to be the go-to guy." This book, if I hadn't met my co-author Daniel Priestley, could have become *How to Become the Go-To Guy,* because that's what I was looking to do. Daniel eloquently created a five-step system called the "Key Person of Influence." That's when we co-authored the book, and I launched *Key Person of Influence* in the United States.

Synopsis: "Becoming a KPI" explains how Kevin Harrington became a key person of influence, yet he didn't even know how he did it at the time. Becoming a KPI is how Kevin got on the hit show *Shark Tank.* Kevin talks about how he became the go-to guy, a KPI, in an untouched market at the time. Anyone can become a KPI, and it doesn't matter what industry a person is in. There is a KPI in every industry.

In 1984, I started the business of obtaining customers on TV. I was watching television, the Discovery Channel, and then the channel went dark for about six hours. I called the cable company, just in case there was a problem. They told me there wasn't, that the Discovery Channel was an 18-hour network. That's when the light bulb went off. This is downtime. They put no value on it. Instead of showing something during this time, bars were just put up on the TV screen.

At that time, I was thinking about what I could put in place of that downtime so I could sell something, make money, to obtain some customers. I created and invented the whole concept of going to TV stations and buying huge blocks of time to utilize the remnant downtime. In all these years of me doing this, no one has challenged the idea that I was the person who did it, created it, and invented the infomercial in 30-minute blocks.

I was buying big blocks of time. Why? Because I wanted to get customers. I wanted to obtain customers. How do you obtain customers? A lot of ways, but you ultimately have to get some form of media. How does it start? There are two metrics that you have to be looking at when you're obtaining customers. First, what does it cost? That is called the cost per order (CPO). Second, what is your average lifetime revenue value (ALRV) or average order value (AOV)? Thess are the two metrics you need to be looking at when you are trying to obtain customers.

The cost to obtain the customer obviously has to be less than the cost you are going to receive in income from the customer. The bottom line in obtaining customers: You have to set up the system. You have to set up testing. You have to set up as many sources of obtaining customers as possible. I was in the TV business, but I didn't just get customers through TV. My company got customers through TV; we got customers through radio; we got customers through the Internet; we got customers through retail stores; we got customers through international distribution; we got customers through home shopping channels, etc. The first thing to do when you are going to obtain customers is make a laundry list of every possible area where you can get these customers.

That's how I go about getting customers. Today, some people who are into the digital space are basically just getting customers on the Internet. You can focus in certain areas, and today some of these other areas that I mentioned have become really expensive. It's tougher to make money on TV. While we used to start on TV, the cost to get customers has become too high, so we now have made a switch to digital. When you talk about the Internet, there are many different ways to obtain customers, from Google AdWords to Facebook to social media, etc. You can even do a whole dropdown on the entire digital space.

The bottom line is that a lot of people do not realize they have to be sophisticated from a business analysis standpoint to set up a business. You need a marketing plan to obtain customers. You can also obtain customers with public relations and influencers.

With all the ways you can get customers, you need to focus on two numbers: your customer acquisition cost (CAT) and AOV. Those numbers have to work. Now, you can use TV, you can use radio, you can use the Internet—all these different media. Of course, referral is also a big source. Customer service is also crucial in the business world. A business can't have bad customer service and also get customers, after all, and that is especially true in this electronic day and age.

Synopsis: "Obtaining Customers" maps how Kevin Harrington went about obtaining customers in 1984. The chapter explains how Kevin saw a hole in the television industry, how this industry had a need, and how he filled that hole. In the process, Kevin found out how to obtain customers in a market that was not yet there, and one that he eventually created and mastered. There are many ways to obtain customers, and this chapter discusses certain metrics that people need to be monitoring every step of the way.

TABLE OF CONTENTS

Foreword by Kevin Harrington..iii

1. **The New Infrastructure**
Digital Sales and Marketing of the Modern Era
By Steven Alvey...1

2. **The "R" Stands For What?**
PR Means More Than Just Public Relations
By Michele Zabriskie...15

3. **The American Dream**
A New Movement for Homeowners Across the Nation
By Peter Magana..25

4. **The Chief Human Officer:**
*Combining Neuropsychology and Organizational Framework for
    Sustainable Results and Meaningful Impact*
By Dr. Aimée V. Sanchez, Ph.D...39

5. **Monetizing My Degree**
From Full-Time Physician to Medical Mogul
By Dr. Draion Burch 53

6. **Realigning Life**
A Record-Breaking Journey from Shopping Carts to Aspirations
By Stuart Burrell 67

7. **Against Myself**
From Mindsets to Self-Help Groups
By Beth Underhill..79

8. On The Liberation of Souls
The Seven Rays of Divine Unfolding Light
By Sh'Ari Shemoth 89

9. Conquering Global Markets
Taking Your Message International
By Carmen Ring 103

10. Resolution
Engaging with and Supporting Children Today
By Rize McGill 115

11. The Wildest Desert Poppy
Perfume is the Most Intense Form of Memory
By Sharon Farsijani 127

12. Balancing The Bazaar
A Lifelong Journey through Hospitality
By Lori McNeil 141

13. The Power of Resilience
Helping Children Bounce Back and Move Forward
By Kate Lund 153

14. Keep Singing
Leading with Harmony during Times of Dissonance
By Brenda Bowers 165

15. The Web Surfer
How I Got My Ph.D. from the School of Hard Knocks
By David Stewart 177

16. Unleashing Latent Potential
Are You Planning to Fail or Preparing to Succeed?
By Karl Shaikh 185

17. Amazing Wiser Visor
Helping Prevent Accidents and Saving Lives by Keeping the
  Glare Out of Your Eyes
By Annie Lane.. 201

18. Creating Chapter 2
My Best Compliment?
By Troy Aberle.. 209

19. Defeated By The Impossi-Ball®
Lessons Learned by a Patent Attorney
By John Rizvi 223

20. Becoming Your Own Shark Through Crowdfunding
Attracting Millennials and Other Aspiring
  Entrepreneurs to a New Lifestyle
By John Galley and Adam Ackerman 235

21. Truly "Successful Habits of The Rich!" ™
Helping Americans with Their Finances
  in an Improving Economy
By Ray A. Smith.. 247

22. Million-Dollar Marijuana Invention
The No. 1 Selling 2017 Harvest Product
By Wade Atteberry.. 257

23. Day Camp Horror
Itching for $UCCE$$
By Steven Greenspan.. 269

24. Fresh Off The Boat
From $600 to $1,710,000 on eCommerce
By Ellen Lin 279

25. Surviving The King
Mastering the Five Channels
By Jason Hall 287

26. Off The Dry Teet
A Long and Endlessly Winding Journey
By Dimitry Boss 297

27. Rich Niche
Identify Your "Niche" in Real Estate and Build
an Eight- or Nine-Figure Business Around It
By Cheryl Spangler 309

28. The Best-Kept Secret In Business Today…
How to Use the Most Successful Marketing Strategy
Ever Created to Build the Right Business for You!
By Dan Olsen 323

1

THE NEW INFRASTRUCTURE

Digital Sales and Marketing of the Modern Era

By
Steven Alvey

"Goodness, Rick. I don't know what to say…" It's 1995. You're seated at a bar with your best buddy, Rick. He's just been laid off. You ask, "What are you going to do?"

Rick takes a sip of his beer, shrugs, and says, "Sell RC cars."

You blink at him. "Sell… RC cars…?"

Rick sets down his glass and inhales, ready to elaborate. You lean in closely. It's loud in the bar and you probably misheard him. "Yeah. I like RC cars. Figure I'll start a business." He  says this last bit with another shrug and a casual wave of his hand—in the same way someone might declare they think they'll take a bath or go for a walk.

Knowing the answer, you ask, "Have…have you ever done anything like that before?"

"Nope."

"Do you have, like, a business plan? For the bank?"

"The bank?" Rick looks confused.

"Yeah," you say, "for a business loan."

"Nah, not getting loan. We've got a few thousand in savings and a couple low-interest cards."

"But… where are you going to get your inventory? How are you going to advertise? Where are you gonna open up shop? What are your startup costs?" You count the objections on your fingers as you list them.

Rick nods his head and smiles knowingly as though he's heard each one before. "Well," he pulls a pen from his shirt pocket and begins writing on a napkin. "I think I'll have to start off by drop shipping until we've got more capital for inventory. So I'll decide on around a dozen RC cars, maybe from US suppliers, maybe from China, and just fulfill each order manually as they come in."

He continues further into the specifics, "I'll buy a domain for twenty bucks, I'll pay a guy in Indonesia a hundred bucks to set up an eCommerce store for me and pay another guy fifteen bucks for a quick logo. I'll create product listings for those dozen RC cars I picked, with stock images and descriptions and all that."

Rick's plan doesn't end there. "I'll spend around $500 on search advertising and another $500 on native ads on social media, targeting people who like RC cars and sending them through a funnel of products, add-ons, upsells, and so on, to maximize my average order value. We'll put maybe another $500 into retargeting ads so we can follow the non-buyers around as they browse the web. Oh, and I'll use PayPal and Stripe for accepting payments."

Just as you're about to ask him what half of those words mean, he holds up one finger as though trying to remember something. "Oh yeah," he returns the pen to the napkin. "And I'll add a 5% coupon pop-up with an email opt-in so I can capture everyone's email address and market more products to them in the future. So… another twenty bucks for the email marketing software, then."

He holds up a napkin covered with scribbled writing and diagrams. "Should be able to get started within a week for under $2,000, give or take." He smiles and takes another sip.

You stare open mouthed.

It sounds absolutely insane.

And it is insane...because it's 1995.

The Times, They Are A-Changin'

Yes, that conversation would have seemed insane in 1995. Not only because many of the words would not have existed, but also because the chances of someone succeeding in starting a business with little or no capital and no business background would be non-existent. Even ten years later, in 2005, the likelihood of success would have been slim, despite the words being more familiar. The tools, venues, and tutorials just didn't even exist in 2005 that enable so many to start a business at the drop of a hat today.

Today, it's a whole new ball game. Anyone can start a business, from anywhere in the world, in a short amount of time and succeed. I know this first hand because I was in a situation similar to Rick's in 2016. I hadn't been laid off, but had decided to leave the Air Force after a decade-long career.

I had just returned from my third and final trip to war, my enlistment was ending, and I didn't want to be away from my wife and four children again. So I turned down an $80,000 reenlistment bonus and a $70,000 salary, and I started an online business (lead generation software). I did it with no starting capital (we were broke), very little outside funding (had a line of credit around $4,500 from PayPal Credit), and no business experience or degree.

Within six months, we successfully launched the business and made a splash in the marketplace. Within 13 months, we crossed the infamous "six figure" mark in gross revenue. A year later, we tripled that. I went on to speak from stage at live entrepreneurial events, to be endorsed by a Shark from Shark Tank, and I even had the privilege of lecturing about online startups at the United Nations.

It was hard, even hellish but, man, was it exciting! We tried the entrepreneurial experiment and succeeded. It was an incredible, surreal feeling. And it definitely could not have happened in 1995. But, what's incredible isn't my story. What's incredible is the fact that my story isn't unique—not at all.

People all over the world are starting online businesses every day. Some of them are recent high school grads. Some of them have just been laid off. Some of them are retirees who need more income. The only thing they have in common is that almost none of them have degrees or experience in business. It's not just "the Internet" in its broad sense that made this possible. It's the plethora of new, always-improving tools, venues, and strategies that anyone can grasp and leverage—provided they have time to watch a few 30-minute YouTube videos on each topic. And, it's not just online businesses that benefit from this. Brick and mortar businesses are suddenly able to withstand competition, stand out from the crowd, and increase their foot traffic with the art of digital marketing and online sales.

The list goes on and on. In this chapter I'd like to present you with a few super important things you need to understand if you want to leverage digital marketing and sales to start a business or grow an existing one. Specifically, I will be breaking down what I call "the new infrastructure" of online business.

Lead Generation and the Death of the Website

Do you remember the old days? The days when businesses would send people to "a website"? Visitors were expected to be impressed by a cliché looking "home page" with a sliding header, some general points about your business, and a few links at the top like, "about us," "contact," and "blog". And then, hopefully, some tiny percentage of those visitors would click around for a while in that dull gray wasteland, possibly read your "FAQ," and someday end up calling your business or making a purchase.

Oh, what strange and dark days those were…

Fast forward to today, and the online business world finally has its head on straight. Here's what they learned and what you need to understand:

You do NOT send traffic to a "website."

The old practice is now a waste of resources. Today, you send traffic to a landing page (depending on the purpose, it might also be called a lead page, squeeze page, opt-in page, etc.) You need to have a nice, clean, simple landing page with a very clear offer or proposition. The simpler and clearer, the better. And you usually don't go straight for a sale on this page; you're trying to generate a permanent lead, so you can market to them for free from that point forward.

Let's say you're a chiropractor. Rather than send someone to your website that nobody wants to browse (sorry not sorry), you create a slick looking landing page with a faded white stock photo background (e.g. a person lying down and someone's elbow digging into their back). There's a simple headline: "Want to Eliminate That Back Pain? Here's How…" followed by a small paragraph saying "This little-known technique can blah blah blah" (you're the chiropractor, you figure it out.)

To the right of that headline and paragraph, your audience will find a three-dimensional image of a booklet that contains your little technique. This is called a lead magnet. It's what they want. And to get it, they just need to click that big blue button underneath and enter their email address, phone number, etc. (you decide what type of lead info you're collecting.)

Get it? Targeted traffic that you know is interested in your product or service, sent to a simple, attractive landing page with a clear proposition and free offer, and finally a lead capture form. That's it. That's the future of lead generation. Don't worry about the HOW's, like "how do I build the page? How do I create a lead magnet?" and so on. We'll get to that later. First. Let me share what happens after they fill out your lead capture form and hit that submit button.

Funnels and the "Other" Death of the Website

Two things happen after a person becomes a lead, and they both happen around the same time: (1) they are redirected to another page, and (2) they get an email from you. Let's start with that first one. Rather than immediately sending people to a download page to deliver the free gift, it's now time to instantly monetize your leads. You see, your landing page wasn't just a landing page. It was the first page; the entry point of a funnel.

Funnels have ultimately replaced websites today. You're basically guiding people through a series of opportunities or offers in an attempt to present more value and make more money. If we were to stick with our chiropractor example, we could make this a simple two-page funnel. After signing up for that booklet, the lead is then redirected to an appointment booking page. The end.

But let's switch to another example now. Let's say we've just started a business selling robot vacuum cleaners. That first page, the lead page, might include a free e-booklet about dust and air quality. After signing up for that lead magnet, your new lead would then be redirected to a sales page. This is where you try to sell the vacuum. They'll see a clear headline, "Reduce Dust and Pet Hair by 72% on Autopilot," a sales video that makes the pitch, some sales copy where you go over the pain points, the solution, the benefits, and finally, an order form.

You've seen these a thousand times, right? Of course, a majority of people won't buy in that moment. But that's okay! You can market to them later; you captured their email on your lead page. Nonetheless, a certain percentage of them WILL buy—and those purchases will offset the cost of the paid ads you used to get your traffic!

Sounds good. But it's not good enough. After purchase, let's redirect them to another offer: an upsell. People claim to hate this, but they're kidding themselves. When's the last time you walked into an electronics store and found it totally empty, with just one single product sitting in the middle of a bare floor? Never. That would be crazy, and you'd be crazy too if you didn't add more value for customers and increase your revenue by offering them upgrades, add-ons, and accessories relevant to what they just bought.

That is what a funnel is and that is how you instantly monetize your new leads and convert them into customers (an important psychological transformation in your relationship). However, don't overdo it. A main, core offer and then an upsell (or two), which is relevant to that first purchase, is generally enough. You'll have plenty of opportunities to sell to them later. This brings us to that second thing that happened right after they signed up on your lead page.

Email Marketing: The Tree That Grows Free Money

Remember that "thing" you were supposed to do? You know, that e-booklet on back pain or air quality you promised all those leads you'd send them for free? Well if you forgot to do it, from all the excitement of selling them stuff in your funnel, don't worry! Your email automations took care of it! It was delivered automatically to their inbox; but that's not the only thing that happens automatically.Before even setting up your ad campaign or sending traffic to a page, you'll need to set up an email automation series. This should consist of a couple different sequences. First, there's your welcome sequence. This is where you introduce yourself and your brand. Over the course of 2-3 emails, you want to establish some rapport, some affinity, and some memorability. This is your chance to make yourself stand out in your lead's mind as someone different from all the others. Keep selling to a minimum during these first emails and try to throw some free value their way. This is also a good time to get them to connect via other channels like Facebook Groups or YouTube subscriptions.

Next, there's the "second chance" funnel-specific sales campaign. This is where you overtly make an attempt to sell them those things they didn't buy. Get them to reconsider the paid offers in your initial funnel. Elaborate in your emails on why they need what you're offering. If it's time-sensitive, mention that and use scarcity in your email copy.

After that, it's time to start general cross-selling. If you have other products, services, or solutions, sell those via email. If you don't have anything else to sell, try becoming an affiliate for relevant offers from others in your industry. If you're a business coach, in this sequence, you could then go and become an affiliate for a bookkeeping service, a CRM platform, or any number of tools that might be helpful and relevant to your leads. Do a 2-4 day promotion sequence for each of these offers, stick your affiliate link in the bottom of each email, and boom! Free money.

You should have at least a couple weeks' worth of emails preloaded as automations in your email marketing platform. This is an easy way to increase the lifetime value of each lead on complete autopilot. Of course, you shouldn't be selling something in literally EVERY email you send. Some of your emails need to be for offering value and maintaining good will. So how do you offer value and good will? Where do you send them? Remember that thing we keep saying is "Dead"?

The Resurrection of the Website (Cue Zombie Music)

Okay, so in a sense, websites did in fact die a while ago. To be more specific, they died in so far as they are useless for the role in which people were trying to use them. Make sense? Entrepreneurs thought those cliché old websites were where money was made. They thought they were the place to send traffic. They thought people would organically come across these websites and browse and read about their business. And once upon a time, that might have been true. Today, it simply is not.

So why resurrect the website? What role is there for it? There's a few. First off, you want your homepage to be similar to a landing page (like the one discussed earlier) in so far as it directs all traffic to a very specific lead-generating offer. You'll notice we do this in our business at Warlord.io—the main focus of the homepage is a valuable offer. It's okay to fill the rest of the page out with some of the traditional old website stuff (info about your company, etc.) but the star of the show needs to be a specific lead-generating offer.

Second, there's content marketing (or more specifically, a blog). And I don't mean the old 2011 "let's write a ton of blog content so that our site gets ranked higher in Google and attracts organic traffic" kind of blog. Sorry, that ship has sailed. On the contrary, every blog post you have should feature a specific, measured purpose that indirectly sells something, solidifies your reputation as an expert, or fills some other very specific purpose. This is useful for two reasons. First: it gives you non-salesy content that you can link to in your email marketing when you want to send out non-salesy emails from time to time, offering gratuitous value to your email list. Second: when people DO reach your site—either organically from browsing the interwebs or because they were already leads or customers of yours—it reinforces the image that you are "the real deal." That last purpose is very important and, even if you hate blogging, you should at a minimum have a half dozen blog posts so there's actually something there. By way of offering a tip: you can turn off the dates on your posts so nobody knows they're just static content pieces from several months ago.

If you're a huge fan of writing and pumping out non-stop content, then by all means, go for it. I just want to emphasize that (A) it's not necessary, and (B) you can accomplish the above two goals by having a pretty minimal amount of content. Bottom line: there is still a place for "the website" in a modern business; but the role has drastically changed and it takes a backseat to landing pages and funnels.

But "How" Do I Do This Stuff?

First, let's recap what we've learned. The entire infrastructure of online business has changed dramatically. Today, rather than sending traffic to a "website," you need to send it to a short and sweet landing page. This isn't a "popular trend" or "style." This is a logical development that was arrived at because of actual data and facts.

When you send a person to a clear and simple page with ONE specific action you want them to take, you will have a much higher rate of conversion than sending them to a general website. This means better

ROI on paid ads and better ROI on whatever time or effort you put into non-paid traffic (social, content, SEO). This is a fact and you need to be using this approach in your business. Ideally, this will be a lead-generating page—so you can market to them for free from that point forward.

The next part of the new infrastructure is "the funnel", a series of offer pages to which your landing page was the entry point. This is where you attempt to generate revenue, gain clients, etc. The final part of the infrastructure is automated email marketing. This is where you establish your brand, build relationships, take a second swing at selling what you hoped to sell them in that initial funnel, and then move on to cross-selling, affiliate promotions, and so on.

Behind all of that, much less important, is the tired old "website." This should act as yet another web property that directs people to a specific offer or funnel, and it should have some minimum amount of content that lends credibility to your brand—on the off chance anyone ever happens upon it. The role has changed. A lot. But it's still there and somewhat important. In the words of Miracle Max from *Princess Bride*: it's only "MOSTLY dead."

And now we come to that question: How?

If you're new to online business, there's a bit of a learning curve when it comes to establishing this new type of infrastructure (slight understatement). Assuming you already have an offer of some sort, you'll need the following:

- Landing page software and some time to learn how to use it (or outsource it).

- You'll need to learn high-converting copywriting (or outsource it).

- Email marketing software and a sequence of well written and strategically thought-out email automations (or outsource it).

- You'll need to link the pages of your funnel together and integrate them with payment platforms, tracking systems, and your email platform (or outsource it).

And if you don't have an offer or existing business yet, then of course you'll have to focus on creating one, deciding on your unique selling proposition (USP), branding, and so on (connect with me online and ask me about my branding secrets.) If all of that sounds overwhelming, it should be. It's a lot of stuff, and even the people who figure it out on their own usually don't pull it off very well. The success rate in online business is frighteningly low for lone wolves. The people who do succeed, on the other hand, all tend to have one interesting thing in common.

A Business Coach & Saint Thomas Aquinas

Can you smell a shameless pitch coming your way? Well you smelled right! Look, at some point, at the beginning of your online business journey, you need to make a call: do you get a coach or do you go it alone?

There's one thing all successful entrepreneurs have in common. They chose to get a coach. The same goes for people trying to lose weight, right? It's often a personal trainer that makes the difference (even if that trainer doesn't reveal much that the client didn't already know). How about fighting alcoholism, improving your grades, fixing your golf swing, saving your marriage?

For some reason, with the help of others, we tend to successfully do those things that we "can" but inexplicably "won't" do on our own. Why? Simple: as Saint Thomas Aquinas, the greatest philosopher in the history of the world tells us, mankind "is naturally a civic and social animal." We were designed to thrive with others. And you will thrive if you get a business coach to guide you through the process of starting or growing a business online. That's where I can help.

I don't like to brag, but it is a fact that I have some of the best performance rates in the industry when it comes to funnels, conversion rates, and email marketing. There's a reason I've been endorsed by some of the biggest names in business. There's a reason I've been invited to speak to and train entrepreneurs all over the country. It's because I'm damn good at what I do. Here's what some entrepreneurial legends have had to say about my expertise:

"Steven knows a thing or two about beating the odds...I highly recommend you reach out to Steven Alvey today."

- *Shark Tank's* Kevin Harrington

"His training and consulting are, quite frankly, worth a king's ransom...It is absolutely crucial that you work with Steven Alvey, right now."

- Brian Tracy

"Steven is a killer marketer who really knows how to sell...if you have a chance to learn from him, take it!"

- Laura Casselman, CEO of JVZoo

"Steven Alvey is a force to be reckoned with... I've never seen anything like it."

- Omar Martin

"I learned more about email marketing from 30 minutes with Steven Alvey than I have in a whole year."

- Ope Banwo

"Steven Alvey has created a whole new level of conversion... it's the stuff legends are made of!"

- Paul Counts

"Steven Alvey has a mastery of digital sales and marketing that few others have achieved. It's absolutely incredible."

- JOHN THORNHILL

Okay, okay, enough. I'm blushing. Bottom line: I know that you can kill it online. Whether it's starting a new business on a shoestring budget or 10Xing an existing one, you can do it. And I want to help you do it. Head over to StevenAlvey.com and get in touch. Tell me you read this chapter and let's talk about how you're going to take over the world.

Steven Alvey:

Steven Alvey helps people "sell more and sell better." He is an internationally recognized sales and marketing expert who specializes in conversion maximization and customer value maximization (a fancy word for getting each customer to spend more money with your business).

He has been endorsed and praised by famous entrepreneurs like Brian Tracy, who said "it's absolutely crucial you work with Steven Alvey right now", Shark Tank's Kevin Harrington, who said "Steven knows a thing or two about beating the odds", and Entrepreneur on Fire host John Lee Dumas, who says "give him a holla and you'll be prepared to ignite." He's also been featured on the cover of Home Business Magazine.

When he's not improving businesses and empowering entrepreneurs, Steven enjoys raising chickens and growing tomatoes on his acreage in the Midwest where he lives with his wife Emily and their seven children.

Yes... seven.

StevenAlvey.com

2

THE "R" STANDS FOR WHAT?

PR Means More Than Just Public Relations

By
Michele Zabriskie

A t 10 years old, I knew that I wanted to be in the business of helping businesses get their message out. When I was in fourth grade, our teacher told us, "Hey, you guys are old enough to start thinking about what it is you want to do when you grow up." My teacher gave us the homework assignment which we would address the

next day. During my childhood, my mother was a stay at home mom, and normally she was home when we got back from school. When I returned home that day, I mentioned my homework and explained in 10-year-old language what I wanted to do. My mom just smiled and said, "Hey, you'll have to tell your dad when he comes home from school."

At the time, I really only knew where he worked; I had no idea nor had I ever really thought about what he did for a living. As it turned out, that's exactly what he did and had been doing for most of his career. He started in the direction of writing at a young age and worked on his high school paper. This helped land him a job at the newspaper, where he met my mother, who was working there too. Not only do I get the media background from both of my parents but even my grandfather was a reporter for the local newspaper. I also had some cousins in the media business as well. In other words, lots of family in the media business, so my dad and I have always liked to tell people, "Yeah, it's in my blood. I do it for a living."

I was fortunate enough that when I graduated from school, my dad jumped off the cliff, so to speak, and left the best job in the region to start his own PR firm. He was very good at what he did, and this was evident as his previous employers ended up breaking his responsibilities into different departments; it took four or five people to replace him. Nonetheless, he was more than happy to let me get involved with his new firm. I can tell you now, as he and I have told countless others: I do have this in my blood. I learned from the best, from the ground up, how to serve clients and how to provide that service both ethically and responsibly.

Public Relations, Reputation & Recognition

I like to say that PR really stands for Public Reputation, and that your relationships are strengthened or weakened because of your reputation. Something that my dad taught me was the need for having the P and the R for good PR (that's Performance + Recognition.) At our firm, that's exactly what we've helped people do: establish their reputation through their good work, and receive the recognition they deserve for it.

I find it interesting that so many people feel like they know what PR is—and the same can be said for marketing. Everyone becomes an "expert," even more so in today's age. They watch or consume the news, or they find a webinar and somehow they know exactly what this is all about. Well, there's more to it than what it seems to be on the surface. In order to have really good PR, you need to define your messages and package everything into a good platform as to make the job easier for the media outlet. By "media outlet," I mean anybody, whether that's traditional media or a social influencer.

In terms of developing the package, it's crucial to understand what your audience is interested in. Right? You wouldn't want to pitch your story about luggage to an automobile reporter or influencer who specifically focuses on car dealers. Unless you can make a tie-in to the automobile reporter, they will say, "Why are you wasting my time?" So, you need to know two things:

A. Who you're sending your information to

B. How you're packaging that information (so P is for packaging, too)

You need to have it packaged so it's easy for the media outlet to say, "Sweet, you've got it all together and I can just add my two cents…" or "I can just forward this on to my people as is." They're looking for content to stay relevant with their audiences. You provide them good content, they will utilize it, and that helps get your message out. Simultaneously, the result adds credibility to you because they already have an established credible relationship with their audience. You now become an extension to their audience. As people start sharing more info (be it electronic, radio, TV, social, etc.) you can then utilize that content to get further exposure. You know, success likes success. Once you've been in any kind of newsletter (or anywhere) then you can tell the next media outlet, "Hey look, here's where I've been featured recently," so they know that you are validated.

As you generate more content, you really don't want to just regurgitate the same thing and have the exact same article for 20 different outlets. You need to make it fresh and different. You can still hit on the same points, and you should hit a lot of the same points so your message is consistent; however, it's important to vary it across the board. For example, for one outlet, you're sharing more on the WHAT, and for another, you're sharing more as to the HOW. So, when you create your content and messaging (and you really should create your messaging), you can do it significantly—as in a yearlong campaign. You can develop all of this content relatively easy.

For example, we were working with a health insurance company. Their overall message was, "We help people become healthier and take advantage of healthy situations." From that we were able to then direct a whole array of quarterly health messages in various forms to various target audiences. This included newsletters, e-letters, mailings, news shows, interviews, and advertising. I think we came up with 10 or 12 areas or main sub points in each quarter and then we developed each of those points into specific messaging depending on the target audience. Some examples:

- If you are a smoker, it doesn't matter if you've smoked for one day or 20 years, here are the reasons why you should quit...
- If you're a smoker, here's how you quit...
- If you're not a smoker don't start...
- Top 10 reasons why you shouldn't start smoking...
- Why second-hand smoke is bad...
- Here are the signs of cancer...
- Here are the things you can do to avoid cancer...
- Top 10 foods with anti-cancer fighting properties...
- Easy anti-cancer recipes...
- How to incorporate healthy food into your day...
- How to get in shape...
- How to get your kids to exercise...

Giving yourself an array of fresh content is a great way to establish yourself or your client as the expert. The goal is developing meaningful content that people can readily digest and share. Leading up to the next quarter, you'll have another three months to get your message out with even more content. As you continue doing this, you become or your client becomes the go-to for ideas and concepts pertaining to the topic and/or industry. Part of keeping everything digestible comes down to creating anticipation. The target audience will then look forward to the next quarter and the next round of information however they receive it. If it's not digestible, then they will likely keep their attention elsewhere.

Once we had everything arranged for the health insurance client, they were able to take their media to potential consumers and individual companies. This enabled them to have credibility as they communicated, "We're a good company looking after the health of citizens," because they could back this up with, "Take a look at what we're doing." This also created a space in which they could approach media outlets and tell them, "Here's our doctor, who you can interview on the topic," and so on, and so forth. So, good messaging naturally leads to getting assets out to the consumer.

Now, something to keep in mind is that while our client was a health insurance company, they weren't selling health insurance in their messaging. The focus was not making sales. Sometimes people forget this aspect and they continue developing everything with the thought, "I've got to sell this thing," when they should really be selling the overall benefits. For our client, did we ever do articles on health premiums? Sure! But because our strategy was about the overall message, with the focus on increasing health awareness for everyone. This approach was beneficial to existing and potential consumers regardless of whether or not they had or would have insurance through this company. This approach everyone wins with the information. [need a verb (like guarantees) or some other word before the rest of the highlighted sentence.]

PR in a Time of Social Media

The social media revolution has definitely changed things over my career of 30 years. In some respects, it's made it more challenging, and in others, it's made it easier. There are so many more outlets available for you to get your message out: your own Facebook page, Instagram, YouTube channel, and new platforms being added all the time. While there are many options, this enables you to create specific content, which means you're creating, and creating, and creating. Today there are so many outlets and assets that you can utilize; the key is to provide content that's packaged well and targeted to the right people. Once you fulfill the many opportunities available, other outlets and influencers will then share your information, further promoting you (and your product, service, program, book, etc.) in the process.

When it comes to getting that promotion, be smart about it. Don't go to a direct competition and say, "Hey competitor! Please promote my business." No. Just no. That won't work. For someone within the umbrella of what you do - now that's a situation in which it would make sense to promote you. If you're a chiropractor focused on injury recovery then yes, absolutely, you can establish relationships with some lawyers and doctors who represent clients in accident cases. To establish a relationship with them, you just need to approach them and showcase what you do. Don't enter into this thinking you're the only one who will approach them; you aren't. And once your relationships are in place, and they're third-party endorsing you, be sure to scratch their back—the more you do, the more they'll continue scratching yours.

At that, don't be afraid to demonstrate your resources! In the case of a chiropractor, you should offer something like free adjustments. Share your capabilities and why others should recommend and work with you versus somebody else. All good PR involves how you standout. As you have more content to validate the status of your expertise, you can officially start taking advantage of standing out.

For chiropractors who help athletes recover faster from injuries, or even help with injury prevention, you should try going to a sporting event. Get a booth at one of the big races. Sport a banner over your table and provide some service. This will generate awareness. Later, people might see your practice and remember, "Oh yeah, I saw that guy at the race. I should go see him." This extra mile is all about making more connections. Don't assume that just because you have a business anyone will come without any effort on your part. Sure, you can get family and friends but how long will that last? You need to be smart about your marketing and promoting.

Obviously, before you can use events to your advantage, your content needs to be in place. Something that needs to be done is ensuring you have media readily available on your website. People often forget that they need to create awareness and buzz on a continual basis. Keep in mind that babies don't start walking right away; they crawl first. You need to start somewhere, right? Today, everybody has a camera or at least a video recorder on their phone. You can make your own quick video. And you should be human. Let them know, "Hey, this is the first video I've ever done. I just want you to know, I specialize in _____, and this week, if you mention my video then I'll give you 20% off _____." Once you have this online, then you'll see whether or not you can generate the necessary buzz.

Overall, I encourage you to take advantage of the social media platforms as you set everything up. Of course, if traditional media would make more sense for your product, you should go after it on your own. One of my clients owns a fashion boutique. Her industry is already segmented into quarters of seasonal trends for clothing. Boom! That surely helps her develop relevant content for local TV shows. And guess what else? Holidays! And no, I'm not just talking Christmas shopping season. There are other holidays as well, such as Easter, Mother's and Father's Day, Graduation, the Fourth of July, etc. Every year, when June rolls around, she can then tie into the end of the school year: "Hey, you want to look sharp at your child's graduation? We've got some great new line ups and here are some fashionable colors and new trends…" Being aware of the calendar will most certainly support you and any of your media outlets in staying relevant and fresh to the audience. It will pay off!

The R Stands for What? (Reputation)

Never forget that you need to tell the truth, trust your gut, and stand by your values. Your reputation is always on the line, and it affects your relationships. If you're in the business of promoting other businesses, this is an area where you can still ruin your public reputation. It's your reputation that helps bridge the gap between the media outlet and your client. You don't want to jeopardize that just because you didn't tell the truth, or you didn't stay aligned with whatever you stand by.

Case in point, I was approached by one of those paycheck loan companies. In my opinion, this industry takes advantage of disenfranchised people. Nonetheless, they called me and it was clear that they would benefit from my services. In the quick few minutes of their unsolicited phone call, I thought, *You know, I never thought of them as a potential client...* Still, there was no denying that I immediately started thinking of how I could start positioning things to showcase the benefits of their service/company.

The more I thought about it, there were quite a few things where I knew they could benefit from our expertise. I'd be lying that a part of me wasn't excited about the challenge. On the other hand, my gut continued telling me, *I don't agree with their product. I don't agree with what they do. I can't get behind them. I can't and won't jeopardize my reputation trying to help them increase their reputation.* And so, I just politely declined and said, "No." I even went as far as to say, "I know we could help you but I just don't feel like we're a good match. Unfortunately, I don't think that we can serve you."

As you can probably guess, that was not the answer they wanted. We were the go-to PR firm, and at the time the only one in the state to win a Silver Anvil (the highest award in the industry). On top of that, we actually had one fellow and three APR on staff. So yes, we could have served the company in question. When I declined, the representative immediately offered more money—as if that would sway me. Now, it might sway somebody; but I'm happy to say that it only strengthened my resolve. I declined again, to which the comeback was, "Well, I know your father, the president of the company, and since you're only the vice president, we'll wait and speak to him when he's back in town next week."

Remaining polite, I replied, "Okay, sure, go for it. The answer's still going to be no...but okay." And no, we never did work for them. This experience very much solidified the fact that I needed to trust my gut, and know my morals, standards, and what I stand for. If you follow suit, then you'll be in a better position to take care of your business.

Regardless of whether you're promoting anybody else's or not, it's still a good standard to live by.

Own up!

Whenever there's misinformation and you discover it, you need to own up to it ASAP. It's not one of those things where you go, "Oh, I hope they don't find out," or, "Oh, it's not that big a deal." It's a huge deal because it's your reputation. Do you want to be the one who believes themselves to be above and beyond accurate truth? I hope not. Always be better.

We worked with a real estate developer and during a property tour with a reporter, we were asked about the square footage of some obscure price on some materials. Honestly, it wasn't even in the top 20 important things of this new development, so we didn't have the information, but a quick estimate was provided, by the builder. As soon as we found out the correct information we notified the reporter, "Hey, here's the specific information, the estimate was incorrect." His reply was basically, "Oh yeah, okay, no big deal." Nope. It really was, and had we not corrected it, our credibility would be out the window. As it stood, our trust, reputation and relationship with that reporter was mutually beneficial for years.

You should aim for following through on the reputation of, "I will always provide you the correct information. And I will bend over backwards to ensure this will always be the case, or that I will correct anything that needs correcting." By doing so, you're protecting your reputation.

Great PR takes these guidelines into play:

P stands for: Provide value, Performance, Packaging, and Promotion

R stands for: Relationships, Recognition, Relevant, and Reputation

In closing, beyond the age of 10, I still want to help companies promote their product, their service, and their value. In this day and age, it's easier than ever for a lot of people to have their side hustle so they aren't necessarily hiring a PR firm—or they don't have a big budget to spend on promotion and marketing, and that's understandable. For such cases, we have many free resources on our website. We also offer products there; everything from basic news release structure to media relations, crisis management, and branding—you name it.

For anyone who wants to work with us directly, we're currently doing things on a first come first basis. Feel free to reach out, and most certainly, take a look at our online content. I wish you well as you promote yourself, your brand, product, service, and most importantly, your reputation.

Michele Zabriskie:

Michele is a national and local multi PR award winner, working for top-tier clients from Delta Airlines to Pepsi. She has served in a variety of PRSA roles, and additionally earned her APR status.

Giving back through serving on a variety of community boards is a big part of happiness. Work-life balance has always been a priority. "Work hard, play hard," is a motto Michele lives by.

Hiking, snowshoeing, backpacking and canyoneering since she was a teenager, she can be found hiking most everyday and says hiking in flippies is the ultimate! Michele celebrates all possible Holidays. Her favorites are Groundhog Day, Summer/Winter Solstice, Spring/Fall Equinox, and last, but not least Pi Day!

She's fond of writing Hikus and is inspired by all occasions. Michele once painted 200 snowman paintings as Christmas gifts for friends and neighbors. Her latest creative outlet is making one-of-a-kind necklace pendants, crafted from unique rocks she finds on her outdoor adventures.

3

THE AMERICAN DREAM

A New Movement for Homeowners Across the Nation

By
Peter Magana

I'm a broker, an entrepreneur, author, and founder of the 7-day path program as well as The American Dream, Yes We Can Movement. In this chapter, I'm sharing a positive message about home ownership that's given hope to the people. As I'll explain later, this all began with my second chance at life. My daughter and I developed an approach to real estate that simplifies the process for everyday people. Most often, it's easy to assume that bad credit and no money, makes this path impossible; but our program was specifically designed to support people in fixing their credit and first-time loan programs from lenders in the interest of bringing the American Dream to their lives. Through transparency and accountability, we establish trust, and this enables them

to achieve the confidence necessary to take action. Today, we've now helped thousands of people become homeowners.

Over time, our program and service transformed into live events. Where we were once working on a case by case basis, our events enable us to help hundreds, if not more, all at once. We work with contributing accountability real estate agents, credit repair representatives, and loan companies to ensure we have professionals on hand and ready to get started with anyone prepared to move forward in the program. With food and entertainment provided, we share stories of successful clients as well as our own personal experiences, all to motivate and inspire the consumer into taking action.

Never Give Up

A major theme of our live events is the importance of never giving up. Just as I share my own experience onstage with working towards something that felt impossible at the time, I will share it with you here and now. Back in 2004, I needed to pass the broker's exam. My vision was to serve my future clients at the highest level but I needed to take care of this step first. When I started the process, I was highly educated in the industry and I knew my stuff; but I could not pass the test for whatever reason.

Over the course of my first five attempts, I convinced myself I was lousy at testing. By that fifth time, flat out, I did not feel smart. I told myself, "I just don't get it. Something's not right." My emotions were kicking in and it felt like the future I wanted was only getting farther away from me. Most people would normally give up at this point because of all the failures leading up to it; but I knew it must be done. I had my dream of making homeownership possible to hundreds of families, and it would be worth the trials and tribulations ahead. I stayed at it. I went at it again. And what happened? I took it one more time. Three more times. Five more times. Ten more times in total and I still wasn't passing! But I was getting so much closer. I needed a 75 score to pass, and I was averaging 73 and 74.

During my last few attempts, it started feeling like a conspiracy against me. I thought, "That's it. The government doesn't want me to pass my test." If I wasn't feeling smart already, by this point I was definitely feeling stupid. But I knew I needed to keep trying. I was convinced, "Well, if I'm to do what I need to do, I gotta pass this exam." I kept reminding myself that I needed to continue moving forward and I did, for three more attempts. I still couldn't reach 75. Now, some of my family members were saying, "Hey, Peter, maybe this just isn't meant for you. Maybe just let it go."

It didn't matter that I knew what I needed to know. It didn't matter that I had the passion to get this done. I could not escape the sinking feeling that I was stupid; that the world itself was working against my goals. But I kept on trying. And on my twenty-seventh attempt, I finally passed the test.

When I share this story at my events, I literally tell the audience that there's nothing that they cannot do if they keep on trying. It's important to never give up on ourselves in order to succeed in whatever we want. The emotional roller coaster rides of life are overwhelming; but if you focus on your vision and never lose sight of it, you'll definitely never lose.

Today, I've earned my confidence level because I've set my mind to it. I know that anything I do will create what I'm asking for. That same roller coaster of emotion towards success is pure excitement. As I work towards my goals, I feel good and I believe that anything is doable and possible.

I will always believe that the universe is open with many possibilities; it offers another door when another one closes. I always tell people that the only time we truly fail is when we close the door on ourselves and leave it at that. In my journey, I tried one door and it didn't work, so I worked on opening the next. I repeated this until I found the passage that I wanted; that worked for me. The universe is open. Never give up. Don't close those doors. I'm a high school dropout. I got married very young. I made myself who I am today through hard work and persistence. If I can accomplish my goals, so can you.

The Path to Homeownership Program
(And my second chance at life...)

What happens when you have a shot at a new life? You literally notice everything that's going on with society. You have an opportunity to embrace a positive outlook, and that's never giving up. It's beautiful. We can do things and we can become stronger together.

My passion has remained in the real estate sector for over 27 years now. When I tell people that anything is possible, part of my confidence in saying so is found in the fact that I survived a near death situation. This really inspired me to step up my game because the experience left me with so much gratitude. I have love in my life, and I want to give back as much as I can.

In 1999, I was having some issues with my liver. I want it to be abundantly clear that this was not caused by drinking; I had cirrhosis of the liver from a previous employment, which was in the paint industry. Due to toxins absorbing into my body through pores, my fate was sealed in 2008, 15 years later. My health started going downhill and it became a very tough time. It was insanity. I needed a liver. Of course, there was something called a living donor program where a live donor could provide a portion of their liver for me if they had the same blood type and good health. After that option came into the picture, in 2014, my daughter stepped up to the plate. She was in great health, had the right blood type, and was able to provide 65% of her liver so that I might have a chance at a new life—no more pain or suffering. Immediately after my recovery, I knew it was my time to spread positivity, joy, and gratitude by giving back however I could. For the last five years, I've continued visiting patients at the USC tech medical center through a liver transplant support group, and visiting on request from friends and doctors who needed hope and I plan on doing so for the remainder of my life.

For me, it's all love, life, and gratitude. I realized that in life we must take action to keep momentum. I incorporated my new outlook into my real estate company when my daughter and I developed a simplified 7 Day Path to Homeownership. We developed an action driven, accountability program that gets people motivated to take action towards homeownership the same day they have contact with us. Here is a general overview of what this looks like:

Day 1 – Your presence or phone call, social media etc. lets us know you are interested in buying a home. On Day 1 I help you craft your Credit Cleanup Plan or identify a pre-qualification plan.

Day 2– We simplify the process by offering Real Estate Agent and Consumer Choice Lender pairings. This is the critical piece to our program where we become one in working together towards helping you buy your home.

Day 3-6 –We are the their[not sure if this should be the word "the" or "their" but you don't need both words] Voice!! Ensuring that our clients have a communication plan and are satisfied with their team involved in this process.

Day 7 – In one week, our clients have personally determined if they are ready for a homeownership and/or structured plan.

People often assume the American Dream of home ownership is impossible. I found myself capable of pulling people out of their negative mindset to look at the positive. The more I help out, give back and make people see things a little differently, the more I'm inspired to continue forward. As we developed the 7 Day Path to Homeownership, I decided to do the math, get it all out of the way, and make the process much simpler for the modern consumer. Honestly, beyond assuming that it's impossible, the main setback for most people is procrastination. If they never take action, they can never achieve the dream. On day 7, our clients have personally determined if they will be on track towards homeownership.

In the interest of making it easier to actually take action, we mapped everything out so that they can just engage and follow the process in seven days. Everything about buying a home is difficult; there is too much information to understand and funds are not so readily available.

The majority of consumers believe the following four things, and I believe this is why they assume they'll never own their own home:

- You need 20% down
- You need perfect credit
- Thinking it is complicated or
- Overwhelmed

Little to no money down. Today, there are programs available for little or even no money down. For any consumer held back by this fear, we can easily get them setup with the right fit for them. For consumers with bad credit, they usually have some bankruptcies, foreclosures, charge offs, or some old issues, and they won't try moving forward because they assume they'll be completely ignored. Honestly, it's just a slow process, but they are unaware of what they can do. Well, we know what they can do, and we are prepared to walk them through it.

When it comes to lack of understanding, we simplify the process to make it so easy by showing testimonials of those who achieved the American Dream by following simple steps and taking action towards becoming homeowners. It all begins with a quick pre-qualification which can establish whether they can be approved within 24 hours. After that, we begin the 7 Day Plan.

Before, this process would be handled at our headquarters office in LA county. Today, we also get consumers started at our live events and by word of mouth via telephone, all social media, podcasts, Facebook, Instagram, YouTube, LinkedIn, TV, radio, etc.

Once we know the current status of their credit and income, we have them bring the necessary documents: bank statements, paycheck stubs (unless they're self-employed), and two years of taxes. If credit is in good standing, they'll move forward once they're approved. If their credit needs some work, then we help them put a Credit Clean Up Plan in action towards credit repair. We even pair them with companies that will help them do this as fast as possible.

Once everything is moving, we simplify the process to educate them so they know what they need to do. With documentation in hand, we get them fully approved for a loan. This is a very exciting step because the consumer knows not only that it's possible but that they can start planning for the home they'll be able to purchase. The next step is getting a realtor.

Today we pair the actual realtor partner directly to the consumer in the venue of our live events. While they're waiting on the quick pre-qualification, they are already moving forward. Our partners know how our process works and how we engage the consumer. During this event, we also pair them with a consumer choice lender so they can keep momentum. Once they find a house and they make an offer, if it's accepted, escrow opens. Usually, between 15 and 60 days depending on the lender, escrow then closes and then it's time for them to move into their new home! Part of our program includes support through transitioning into their new residence (change of address for utilities, arrangements for movers, etc.).

The Yes We Can Movement

In February of 2019, we hosted our first live event. Leading up to it, we weren't too sure how we would be able to get people involved. We worked with a promoter who told us that we should bring some entertainment and that should draw in the crowd. Soon after, we were very fortunate to get into television and we were able to meet and work with a Latino influencer and musician. We found four other musicians as well as a DJ. We made arrangements for food to be provided so that the consumer could simply arrive, be entertained, and listen to our message.

On the day of our event on February 2nd, it should not be superscript it was the worst weather ever. There was a massive storm that day and we had no clue if we would be able to host everyone arriving or if anyone would actually show up. But they did come. In fact, we were packed. Over 300 seats were filled; we were beyond capacity with a crowd ready to seize their dream. We were overwhelmed but we got through it.

We helped as many of them as possible and had the pleasure of hearing their stories. Everyone had experiences with getting burned in the past and many of them were having issues with a lack of trust towards the industry.

When it was all over, we weathered the storm, and we saw a new way to provide even more services for the modern consumer. We then began expanding our horizons, looking to try another event in Las Vegas. As we had no realtor, lender, or credit repair partners in Nevada, this required some work on our part. At the end of the chapter, I'll tell you how it turned out. But first...

Calling All Partners!

I'm now calling all realtors, lenders, credit repair vendors, promoters, entertainers, hospitality vendors, and sponsors to become our accountability partners because we're actually bringing in value and business, building trust, and becoming the voice of the consumer. This is a win for them in every level because they start the process with new clients on the spot. It's not cold calling; it's a direct approach to the consumer to start the 7 Day Path to Homeownership process immediately.

I think my daughter and I have created something truly beautiful. Everyone involved becomes one as we serve the consumer. Together, we can put our skills to use towards helping them accomplish the American Dream. Yes we can!

Overall, we're looking to host more events in as many places as possible. This means that we need new partners to join the cause so that we can bring more business to them and more homes to the locals in their area. We already have our system in place, and setting Virtual Events, Bootcamp, and mastermind due to COVID-19 epidemic. All we need from people joining the cause is their physical presence at a booth (or virtually) where they'll meet new clients and start working with them right away.

Primarily, we want to work with realtors working for themselves who mentally have positive mindsets as entrepreneurs, as opposed to representing big brand companies . We are not expecting them to make any speeches onstage. Instead, we just need them to be ready to receive people with the highest level of integrity and customer service (after we've gotten them through their approval process and after we've received necessary documents.) We literally pair our partners with business on the spot, and all they need to do is understand our process and help the consumer accordingly. Same goes for lenders.

For credit repair companies, we seek for these partners to be prepared to keep clients in line. It's a 2-6 month process towards credit repair, and sometimes it's a little longer. Many consumers hope for an immediate result, so they'll need some encouragement from our organization to inspire and keep them motivated to stay on course. Nonetheless, within 7 days, we will know where they're at, whether they'll be fully approved or have a structured plan to achieve the American Dream.

In terms of entertainment, we're looking for promoters who are well connected and are aligned with the cause. We're also looking for entertainers with quality music and local connections. If they know more performers who would be interested in participating, the more the merrier! Our events are free and we want entertainment in place to keep the environment positive and hopeful. Entertainers help attract the crowd, even for virtual events, because they keep spirits up, and then we take care of the rest. Overall, this makes for the best experience, because we're celebrating the consumer as they're taking action towards the American Dream. Yes We Can Movement!

At that, for all hospitality vendors, we're looking to partner with people who can provide good food so that our clients are nourished and feeling well as they think about their future. For any vendors who have access to large venues, they are most certainly welcome; we're always eager to ensure we have great surroundings. We want to provide the highest value possible, and these details certainly bring peace of mind as well as excitement. Not only will they live the dream, they can be in the dream as they get started.

Again, we provide a free event for the consumer to be a part of the American Dream Yes We Can Movement by starting the 7 Day Path to

Homeownership. We want to work with partners who believe in our vision. That is number one. We definitely need people that are energetic and positive, because this is a movement, and is 100% based in the philosophy that anything is possible—this is the Yes We Can Movement! As the process still takes the time it takes, we keep the following values close to heart: transparency, accountability, and trust. Modern consumers are very worried about real estate and home ownership, so we want to ensure our partners are prepared to be honest and to share what they know in simple terms. Likewise, we need them to be trustworthy as they help clients move forward, and to be patient. If anything is not going well, we will intervene and become their voice and correct the issue to get everything back on track.

We want to ensure the consumer is well taken care of and we'll do whatever it takes to make that happen. We will provide service at the highest level. Everything is possible in this cause. The movement is real and it's already happening and gaining momentum. Over the course of 2019, we've been winning prompts and awards for our efforts. For now, it's all self-funded. I invested in this movement myself because I needed to prove to myself that everything is possible. I believe in my vision of uniting everyone to create a massive, consumer oriented, action driven experience. I know what makes them tick and act, and I know what it takes to help them achieve the dream of homeownership. With our partners and our clients, we work together as one.

Vegas 2019
The Next Territory

After our event in LA in February 2019, we ended up meeting a promoter who works for the Las Vegas library. After a fruitful discussion about potentially hosting a live event out of state, we decided to give it a shot. As it was offered, we chose the library as a venue. We found partners by way of realtors, lenders, credit repair companies, and we also found entertainment and hospitality, and even some amazing authors.

We were even able to arrange for prizes. Overall, our setup was a repeat of the February event; but we learned some lessons during that storm and we were ready to switch it up a little bit.

The first step for the consumer was to provide proper documentation. We made sure to communicate this well because we didn't want to be demanding and scare anyone off. We understand how unsettling all of this is, and we focused on establishing trust off-the-bat. As people came to the event, we got everything moving right away and continued building momentum, ensuring trust factors were in place to move forward. For some of the consumers that attended, at the time of this writing, they're already becoming homeowners. For those that needed it, we got them started on cleaning up their credit, and things are well underway to achieving their American Dream.

Our realtor partners really loved what we created and have even requested that we host other events soon—the same goes for the consumers in the area. Our movement is gaining traction to the point that we are now becoming the hunted (as Rob Kosberg likes to say!) The people who attended felt comfortable and engaged, and they felt that we can help. I could really sense the difference between the events as I learned to engage with the consumer even more than before. Honestly, my confidence level has increased tremendously in public speaking as I reached out to their hearts, attracting their emotions and creating action.

I really loved how Vegas turned out. We shared life stories, and boy, it was a really eye opening, tear jerking experience. The longer I live, the more it's clear to me that life is short. It's so important to take action, and providing encouragement to the masses is bringing so much passion and fulfillment to my life. I'm so proud of the work we did and continue to do. We're keeping it alive and ensuring that the consumer immediately understands that we know what we're doing and we can make the American Dream come true for them. It's an honor celebrating their first steps, and it's our privilege to help them find their new home. Anything is possible.

Yes We Can
How to join the movement

I am loving life. There are so many doors opening around me. As I continue overcoming any negativity that comes along, I focus on the light, the positivity of the future. Knowing that the vision I had after my daughter saved my life can be achieved, I've now thrown it out to the universe. There are so many possibilities awaiting us.

We weathered the storm in February, and we're pressing forward no matter what happens. The dream is real. And it's never been more real than it is today, right now. For anyone looking to begin their homeownership journey, you can find more information about the American Dream Yes We Can Movement at info@yeswecanmovement. com and begin your 7 Day Path to Homeownership. We have plenty of social media, videos, radio, TV, and more as we continue growing. We are gaining a big traction of followers. We have more events coming your way, mainly in California, but hopefully soon in other states as well.

If you're interested in partnering with us, please visit Info@ yeswecanmovment.com. You'll find our contact information as well as other resources regarding the work being done at the moment. If you want to get involved, we welcome you!

In closing, I hope you feel that anything is possible. I'm filled with so much hope as the movement grows. May all the doors in the universe open to positivity and faith. Never give up on your dreams. The future is good. Yes We Can!

Peter Magana:

Peter Magana is a real estate broker. In 2018, he started his 7-Day Path to Homeownership Program under the American Dream Yes We Can Movement which is currently changing the homebuying landscape. It's a take action approach, and it simplifies the process by being transparent and accountable, and building trust. Often, he finds that people procrastinate and think too much. Through his approach, his company is minimizing the work and showing everything can get moving in a matter of days. Due to the speed they've accomplished, clients are actually engaging with his business and solving the root of their problems to homeownership.

Within 24 hours, they'll find the proper direction for the consumer. They'll learn about their credit, income, and then they start looking for homes before getting a full approval. If the client has credit issues, they establish a path to credit repair immediately and actually reimburse the buyer to get them started. Beyond the approach itself, Peter has started a movement, which is the focus of his chapter.

He dedicates the following to all:

> *"I am committed to making the American Dream of homeownership a reality for thousands of people. This dream and vision was created from the combined passion of my daughter and myself after she saved my life. My daughter showed me how powerful, caring, intelligent and loving women are. Together, men and women can create success with my approach. I unite the industry experts as one, and establish accountability to create trust and then welcome families into their new homes."*

4

THE CHIEF HUMAN OFFICER:

Combining Neuropsychology and Organizational Framework for Sustainable Results and Meaningful Impact

By
Dr. Aimée V. Sanchez, Ph.D.

When I first began working in the field of psychology nearly thirty years ago, many of the obstacles that I had to overcome specifically were in regards to mindset. I needed to believe that I had the ability to help people guide themselves towards a pathway to healing, while also achieving sustainable success and growth in the individual areas that they identified. As I gained more experience in being able to help these different populations, along with confidence in my skills, I found that there were some recurrent themes present with the population in regards to how people go about achieving success. Some of those themes

primarily had to do with people feeling as though they were making a meaningful contribution in their areas of expertise, but also feeling as though they had values that were in alignment and consistent with what they believe their natural skills, abilities, and talents to be.

For myself individually, one of the obstacles that I've needed to overcome is being able to take that approach to leadership as far as making sure that my values are in alignment and consistent with my God-given talents, skills, and abilities. Another obstacle was being able to utilize that in an organizational sense on a consistent level with systems that are more rigid and less amenable to change. I've consistently been able to push the envelope and raise the standard by helping individuals, teams, and organizations shift their mindset a few degrees in regards to how they perceive their impact within their organizations, as well as the impact they have with the individuals they influence, by considering the necessity to become more innovative and more agile in their thinking when it comes to leading.

Performance, Demand & Results

One of the major problems today is that urban organizations are going through turbulent times due to market trends and external conditions. In fact, right now, we have all experienced unprecedented changes due to the worldwide pandemic that for many companies, individuals, and leaders has resulted in setbacks that will have impact for years to come. What these critical times of transition have revealed about leadership is that leaders are often lacking the fundamental skills required to manage within a constant climate of turbulence. This can add additional stress to leaders who are in positions where they're high performance, high demand, and they're expected to produce great results. So, how do you go about solving this? One of the things that we need to do is we need to take an approach that considers having a fresh perspective.

It's important to understand what some of the challenges are to be able to effectively impact innovation, while remaining open to being insightful and being able to implement interventions that are action-based, sustainable, and provide growth for the organization. CEOs and leaders throughout organizations know that they need to change the way that they work. And with the underlying pressure to adapt as individuals and organizations, they understand that there is a need to remain innovative.

But how do you do this? Many of the problems and the circumstances become more complex and there isn't a one-size-fits-all approach to doing this. Sometimes we won't even recognize what the situation is, but we must be willing to seek out opportunities to gain additional insight as to how we can improve as an organization, as a team, an executive, or as an individual—much of this comes with collaboration. There is a two-tiered approach to innovation when you're looking at it from the vantage point of an individual, team, or organization. And one of those tiers regards being able to develop an insight-based approach to innovation. The other tier is about culture creation. I'll share further on these points later in the chapter.

The Four Skills of Innovative Leadership

From a leadership standpoint, remaining innovative encompasses being open to the fact that we may have blind spots. We need to be willing to identify what those blind spots are, and identify a way to remediate those issues for ourselves. Some of our assumptions as to how we lead expectations about leading, and how we produce oftentimes must be challenged. And therefore, we need to put ourselves in a position to explore the best methods that will allow for creative, intuitive, and innovative input; as well as, those that will provide the best ideas and approaches for our solutions.

Industry leaders typically are lacking crucial leadership skills that are needed to remain innovative and competitive in a turbulent economy. All the research says that this leadership gap often has many different causes but some of the causes can be related to two factors primarily: 1 lack of mastery of the required competencies of what's necessary in that particular position or industry, or (2) a lack of focus on necessary skills. Either can be a problem in both the short and the long term.

For organizations and individual leaders, we must be able to avoid that discrepancy that exists between strengths and the areas of need. So basically, there's four critical skills that are important for any leader to remain innovative and lead with a certain level of competency:

- Inspiring commitment
- Leading employees
- Strategic planning
- Embracing the process of change

For those who are not thriving in embracing the process of change, and have the weakest competencies in the other three areas, they will find that they encounter the greatest challenges when it comes to being able to remain innovative. The gap in leadership skills is most prevalent, oftentimes, in high priority, high performance, and high stake areas. Other areas where there is a significant gap between the needed and existing skills are also areas related to employee development and self-awareness.

Leaders need to adapt quickly, but they also need to be able to leverage the relationships that they have across disciplines with those downward, of which they have oversight and an influence over. They also need the ability to do that in a quick manner so that they can impact change in a positive way. Part of what's lacking in regards to the approach in which a leader can be transformational is that they may struggle with having a strategic mindset when it comes to their management approach. They may also have difficulty being efficient when it comes to considering the process of change.

How do you go about being innovative? How do you go about creating an insight-based culture, having to do with innovation in an existing environment? You need to bring new thinking and different actions to how you lead, how you manage, and how you go about your work. That means that you also need to consider perspectives from others, but those people may often times not be your counterparts—they may actually be people that you have influence over. So, it's very important to remain open to the idea of leading differently, acting differently, and managing differently. This all comes down to shattering the ceiling when it comes to entrenched and intractable values, problems, or challenges that are keeping your organization stalled.

When you bring an innovative approach to leadership, the idea of remaining agile in your thought process and quick in your response also helps with being able to move the current along for your organization. When you talk about the process of remaining innovative, bringing a culture of leadership where you're creating an organizational climate where others apply innovative thinking to solve problems and develop new products, services, or ideas, helps the organization overall. And it really changes the climate in regards to the idea of change and how change is implemented. And so, it becomes about growing a culture of innovation, and not just hiring people who will follow the leader, or hiring people who need to be directed in every area.

Eventually, being strategic in your leadership means having an overall idea or a landscape as to how the processes that you do on a daily basis adds to the big picture. As you're leading from an insight-based approached and you're creating a culture that is cultivating innovation and creativity, this strategic approach to leadership will ultimately lead to exceptional performers. To improve upon these gaps in leadership and to remain innovative in the process, organizations must be willing to go to the area that is uncomfortable. Sometimes leaders, people in positions of influence, and high achievers need to be comfortable with being uncomfortable. And when we're talking about it in regards to culture change or transformation, organizations need to be willing to have a credible diagnosis of what's going on with their leaders in order to be able to implement change effectively.

Organizations also need to get a sober understanding of what's going on with their leadership and what their individual needs are in regards to development of training. They should ensure that when leaders are leading, they're not only managing from a standpoint of being skill-oriented, but they also are relational in regards to their leadership approach—they're clear in regards to the objective for their team, and that it's in alignment with the organizational goals and mission. That may even include having an idea as to how the company culture envisions daily execution of tasks, or what messages are being communicated from a top to down perspective in regards to from leadership to those that are direct service.

The ability to communicate an organization's culture is vital to this process—having regular dialogues around what the values of the organization are and how these are reinforced in every action and production of what is considered the daily business is needed. By inviting open communication and outlining clear expectations, people are inspired and able to articulate and move forward those goals and missions in a meaningful way. And then lastly, continuing to maintain credibility in regards to leadership is important, because everything rises and falls with leadership. The leaders set the culture. For an organization that's willing to consider changing their approach to overall leadership and maybe what their leadership imprint is in the real world, a hands-on approach is ideal.

Combining Frameworks

One of the things that I do when I work with organizations, teams, and leaders, is I utilize an assessment-based approach. From the results, I'll get an idea as to what is the current skill set of those in leadership, identify who the key stakeholders are, and then get a temperature on their values as well as the values of the organization. If we find that we're looking to embark on a journey of change, we'll need feedback and open lines of communication. Beyond those involved with the organization itself, we reach out to our customer base or, key stakeholders, gauge their involvement, and get feedback with regards to how our services might be translating in the real market. During this process, we consider whether or not we're continuing to perform duties that are meaningful to the organization.

The research shows that a customer-base's credibility with your product is heightened by the fact that they find your mission both meaningful and relatable. Customers like knowing what the message of your organization is. Clear messages will continue solidifying your brand and improving credibility. If you find that either of those things are being challenged or are in danger that's something that needs to be zero and down[doesn't make sense to me. Does the author mean. It's just part of taking a hands-on approach to assessing the status of the organization and leadership, and identifying what's needed in order to implement effective change.

During my 20+ years of experience working as a Neuropsychologist, I have specialized in assessment, and emphasize data driven, results-oriented processes to identify strengths and challenges. My approach to organizational consulting, leadership development and executive coaching utilizes my unique background in neuroscience to help improve performance and business outcomes. Together we work on developing leadership and personality, blending organizational and neuroscience frameworks to effectively improve performance, provide additional clarity, and assist with values alignment. I also utilize evidence-based approaches to coaching and assessment based upon my many years of expertise.

I provide services such as the executive and high performance coaching on a one-to-one basis for individuals, teams, and organizations. My individual and group coaching programs are designed for early, mid, and career transitioning professionals, CEOs, and business owners to help them to gain an immediate return on investment (ROI) by cultivating their critical leadership abilities which directly impact the bottom line. My work with organizations and teams is focused upon helping to optimize peak performance; and to bring strategic alignment with missions, values, and goals.

Statistics say that unhappy employees cost companies in the US economy approximately $550 billion a year. Fortune 500 companies that have done research in this area find that this overall impact to the US economy impacts the bottom lines for organizations; but also the quality of leadership can impact the bottom line of organizations. When they ranked poor leaders, good leaders, and extraordinary leaders, oftentimes they found that the quality of leadership either cost the company/organization money or it gained profits for them.

Poor leaders typically cost their organizations $1.2 million per year based upon this study, while good leaders were able to acquire a profit of $2.4 million. But extraordinary leaders more than double the profits in comparison to the other two groups—up to $4.5 million. If we take a hyper- focused approach in regards to systems, and we understand what's going on with the bottom line, we can almost work backwards in being able to identify an effective strategy that will impact the development and landscape of that organization or company in a positive way.

As previously said, we need to focus upon continuing to develop our leaders in regards to enhancing their individual skillsets and expanding their leadership capacities. This investment will benefit the organization, individual leaders, and improve relationships and credibility with key stakeholders. This approach to leadership development will allow for the opportunity to achieve sustainable results even in the midst of dealing with a fluctuating economy.

Resolving Dissonance

I have written multiple bestselling books, one of which is, *Disrupt the Status Quo: Living and Leading from Your Success Zone.* I also coauthored a book with Jack Canfield, the number one success coach in America, called *Success Starts Today,* and that book was also a bestseller. Both of those works speak to the idea of challenging the thought process of leaders, high achievers, and influencers. When considering that you are a cut above, you might not be the majority, but you could be the minority in regards to your perspective when you decide to start looking outside the box, and choose to remain agile in your thought processes. Thereby, making a conscious decision to disrupt the status quo allows the process of evolution to begin in regards to an individual's capacity to resolve dissonance. To fight against the desire to maintain "sameness" takes a concentrated and intentional effort.

Based upon my own individual and personal experience, I have been able to translate these experiences into my writings because I too was in that position. I worked in a corporate industry. I worked 60 plus hour weeks and I faced chronic fatigue and exhaustion. On a daily basis, there was a misalignment with my individual values and daily procedures. I found that this continued to push me into an area of malaise and feeling as though there was a rudimentary approach to leadership—even though everything was constantly evolving and changing. And so, this ultimately resulted in frustration.

I knew within my DNA and makeup that I could not be subscribed to living a life of mediocrity, and from that standpoint, I desired to become inspirational for myself, my colleagues, and my peers. My desire to ascend in my leadership presence became meaningful, it was about a pursuit of finding incredible solutions to these problems which are on a much larger level than I had been operating before. It required that I grow and stretch as a leader, and as a result, I had to seek to resolve these issues of dissonance for myself. Then and only then was I able to take these processes that I found to be effective in my work with teams, and apply it on an organizational level.

My professional pursuit really resonated with my own personal and individual purpose as far as how I'm uniquely gifted, skilled, and talented. In addition to that, it helped me remain strategic in the execution of what I believe to be important—as far as values, the values and agendas that I wanted to promote in my business and daily work. And so, that part of my life has been a springboard to the rest of the work that I have been doing since then, which is what I have termed my professional and leadership legacy.

I've now been consulting for the last 15 years in the corporate arena. I also work with nonprofits, churches, and entrepreneurs. I help my customer-base bring the largest impact to their industries, while helping them adjust to any systems requiring culture change or transformation.

But also, I work with individuals within those different entities on an individual level to help improve their performance, provide additional clarity, and bring meaningfulness to their daily work.

The biggest impact that I've had in the corporate industry has often times been dealing with those who are part of government systems. In comparison to for-profit sectors, they too have mirrored the same type of experience in terms of feeling cajoled by a regimented way of practice. This results in an impression that things within the system were not amenable to change, and therefore it became a forced choice for anyone to either transition out of the organization or to stay and try to evoke change at their level. Over the course of working with individual leaders, it's become important for me to replicate leadership, not just with force multipliers, but also with those who have an ability to influence others at a much larger and impactful level.

Your individual values and attitudes impact your life, your credibility, as well as your leadership legacy; but it might not change the overarching culture if you're dealing with an organizational system. It's important to remember what your why is; why you're doing this, why it's important to you, and what the purpose is for you; keeping this in mind enables you to work through frustration and dissonance. The noticeable impact of resolving these issues for myself, my colleagues, and my clients is why I continue doing what I do.

If you're a leader who's considering changing the way you lead because you want to be more innovative and you want to evoke sustainable cultural change, you might have some fears. You might even have some paranoia as you develop your staff, that you might be training someone who is your replacement. As you consider the impact you have as a leader, you must understand that an extension of your leadership goes far beyond you. That part of your responsibility is the ability to take ownership over your leadership, as well as having a hands-on approach to the implementation of that practice. Another part of your responsibility is accepting the outcome of your efforts, and realizing that that you could arrive at a different point than where you started. Change is inevitable, and therefore, it should not be feared.

If you're concerned that your organization will be stalled in an innovative economy because they fail to grow, you could also be talking about your own livelihood being impacted as well. So, it's very important to consider what type of outcome you want out of this. If you stay growth-minded in your mindset, I believe you'll find that the outcome that becomes purposeful and meaningful in everything that you're doing is the most powerful.

You might also be dealing with a workforce that is used to having some level of rudimentary tasks, and therefore, they require a need for inspiration to even get to the point of considering innovation. This is where your credibility and your effectiveness as a leader starts to shine through because it then become your responsibility to inspire others. But your ability to both influence and impact is best revealed in your capacity to leverage established relationships. And so, if you're not a relational leader, then you will probably struggle with becoming a transformational leader. Remember, relationships are currency.

The Life of a CHO

Currently, I live in the Central Valley area. Over my twenty years here, I have seen the culture shift dramatically. It's a growing community, and it's gone from being rural to being somewhat metropolitan, which has resulted in a shift of the climate of local business. As a result, my professional mission has also evolved into educating those in my local area about the benefits of organizational consulting and executive coaching.

For over 15 years, I also have had a very successful private clinical neuropsychology practice, which is primarily assessment-based. I see individuals from different referral sources that might be dealing with some form of psychiatric impairment, work/functioning issue, or they might be in need of a neuropsychological assessment.

I continue to utilize my clinical training and expertise in the area of organizational consulting in leadership development because I've seen it work with hundreds of thousands of patients as well as the thousands of employees that I've worked with in my practice of organizational consulting. Not only do I strongly believe in the benefits of neuroscience-based strategies, I also have great belief in the commitment to coaching.

I've been told time and time again that I have a remarkably intuitive way about getting to the heart of any challenge my clients are facing. Utilizing my over 20 plus years of psychology and neuroscience experience, I'm able to assist my clients with pushing forward in order to elicit meaningful change. I'm on a mission to share and use the most effective performance coaching strategies to assist individuals, teams, and organizations to achieve ultimate success and maximum results.

My proven strategies have been effective also with individuals and groups of high achievers to help them soar personally, professionally, and financially. Part of what I'm doing now is about taking the years of expertise and knowledge that I have and making it available to people in an online venue. I want to help as many people as I can so they too can get the help they need to be able to generate successful performance, reach their maximum potential, and grow their businesses.

On an individual level, I typically work with the individuals who are free thinkers, game changers, force multipliers, and mass action takers. All of them are professionals with a strong commitment to personal growth, who desire freedom and sustainable transformational results.

They usually fall into one of three groups I find consistently:

- High flyers (corporate management, professionals, leaders)
- Practitioners (doctors, lawyers, accountants, etc.)
- Entrepreneurs (business owners, speakers, coaches, authors, etc.)

High flyers usually need help creating their own pathway to success, either by leveling up in their performance, transitioning into other business ventures, or they require assistance as they work through a professional-personal transition. Practitioners intend to invest in themselves and pursue the blocks that are limiting their individual wealth and performance. And entrepreneurs often need help overcoming mindset challenges that are keeping their businesses from growing and thriving.

Each of my programs is individually designed, and my approach is personal and practical. I provide the most relevant mindset in neuroscience strategies, which have been proven to bring the quickest sustainable results. Working with me provides accountability, clarity, and a high energy approach to transformation. I have a specialized online program called Rewired For Success. I also provide an Executive Coaching program designed for Women Leaders to address the unique challenges women face. This program serves clients through the US and internationally. It also supports them in identifying core competencies, increasing their leadership presence, and gaining the competitive advantage by helping them to outline strategic next level outcomes that allow them to achieve breakthrough success by making the biggest impact in their industries and communities.

I think of myself not only as the CEO of my business, but the Chief Human Officer (CHO). I look at the human side of leadership, and I talk about the things that people struggle with when they're trying to lead and manage at an extremely high level. Essentially, I've made it my mission to teach leaders and organizations innovative ways to disrupt business trends by shifting from IQ to EQ in a transformational and meaningful way.

In the future, I hope to gain more visibility and a larger audience internationally as well. I want to inspire an open forum regarding leadership topics that are cutting edge, current and ongoing, and are commonly faced by people in the corporate and private arena.

If you're interested in learning more about me, what I do, how to work with me, or if you'd like to obtain a free copy of my latest eBook, I encourage you to visit my website: www.dravsanchez.com.

Dr. Aimée V. Sanchez:

Dr. Sanchez is exceptionally passionate about Organizational Consulting and Leadership Development. Her 20+ years of expertise in Neuropsychology, Executive Coaching, and Organizational Consulting, helps individuals develop and implement strategies that will enhance their personal and professional effectiveness. As an author, speaker, and certified executive coach, she utilizes her expertise to bring a unique approach to business innovation.

Her work has been featured on CBS, NBC, ABC, FOX, A/E, and more. Dr. Sanchez works with high achievers, leaders, organizations, and teams to achieve success by guiding them toward methods which provide clarity and strategic alignment with missions, values, and goals. She is also the creator of the Rewired For Success Program For Women Leaders geared toward early, mid- and senior-level leaders to help them expand their leadership capabilities and position powerfully for promotion, speak with more confidence, and negotiate for more pay so that they can make the biggest impact.

5

MONETIZING MY DEGREE

From Full-Time Physician to Medical Mogul

By
Dr. Draion Burch

I was the youngest of 8 children in a family that grew up in Southern Mississippi. As a child, I would go along with my grandmother when she cleaned the houses of doctors in our area. I played with their kids because they had better toys than I did. I discovered that I wanted to be a doctor when I was just 6 years old, when one of those doctors let me listen to my own heart with his stethoscope. I heard the "lub-dub-lub-dub-lub-dub-lub-dub" of my heart beat and fell in love. I knew from that moment on, I was destined to be a healer.

I started studying the human body. I graduated at the top of my class in high school and went to study at Xavier University of Louisiana. I got my Doctor of Osteopathic Medicine degree from Ohio University and went on to my Obstetrics and Gynecology residency at Michigan State University. I ended up graduating at the top of my class at all 3 institutions. After school, I landed my first job working for a non-profit organization. I worked at a total of, and managed, 10 offices in a hospital system that had an operating budget of $12 billion. I served on a major medical board that represented over 100,000 physicians.

As a doctor, I have delivered over 5,000 babies and performed over 3,000 surgeries. So far, it's a record I am very proud of. Yet, with all this success, I had an embarrassing secret…I was unhappy.

I hated what I was doing every day. It reached the point when I would drive up to a hospital or clinic and I needed to force myself to get out of the car and walk through the doors to do my job. Physician burnout is REAL! I was mentally, physically and spiritually exhausted. I would work extended shifts, chart until midnight, sleep for a few hours—and then get up and do it all again. The stress of being overworked and underpaid was taking its toll.

But I didn't want to admit to my misery. I mean, I was living the dream, right? I was a doctor, working in my chosen field, caring for patients every day, bringing babies into the world and supporting women in their ability to make the best health care choices for themselves. Nonetheless, the stress of working daily within the constraints of the American healthcare system was just too much. I found myself overwhelmed on a regular basis.

How could I heal others when I was not able to heal myself? I needed to breathe and destress. Unfortunately, the 24-7 demands of a doctor did not allow for that. Until the night it happened…

I fell asleep while driving home after working a 36-hour shift (not uncommon work hours for me). A police officer woke me on the side of the interstate, just 2 hours before I had to go back into work. I realized that God was sending me a very direct message and I needed to listen! I could have died, right there on the side of the road!

I wasn't living my true purpose. My passion for my chosen profession was gone. My gifts and knowledge were being wasted. I was holding myself prisoner to the income, patients and perceived fame I had as a doctor. From that day forward, instead of charting for my patients until midnight, I started charting my own EXIT PLAN.

During all of this, I started blogging, because it gave me a creative outlet. Other doctors, clinics and hospitals found out about this, and asked me to do it for them. I started writing email autoresponders, blog posts, and social media posts. I spoke at local events, international conferences and on national TV and radio.

I took my knowledge and experience as a doctor, and channeled it into these efforts, instead of into practicing traditional medicine. I learned more about all of these platforms and turned them into ways to monetize my medical degree and live my true purpose—which is still to help and heal people, but on a very different scale.

It took me 3 years, 15 coaches in different areas and methods, and a whole lot of hard work. Today, from all of that…

- I have an award-winning healthcare blog
- I'm an 8X best-selling author
- I get paid more than six figures to speak to audiences all over the U.S.
- I'm seen regularly on TV in the top 10 media markets, where I promote medicine to millions of viewers, instead of helping just thousands of patients.
- I've served as a brand ambassador to Fortune 500 companies
- I have served as a medical consultant for TV shows
- I am an award-winning business coach
- I take care of celebrity patients
- I have over 50,000 followers on social media

Finding and living my purpose has allowed me to coach other burned out doctors, like my past self. I help them use their medical expertise to make money through other channels and in other industries. On that note, to the doctors reading this book! If my story resonates with you, because you see yourself in the same state I was, I have good news for you! You can change your life! You can find the freedom and joy you believed you would achieve in medical school. You too can live your purpose, monetize your medical degree, affect the lives of more people than you would in a hospital or clinic, and be HAPPY!

You are far more than just another doctor in the halls of your hospital or clinic. Your knowledge has value and you have every right and every reason to take that knowledge and use it to improve your own life, and the lives of others. You too can be a #MedicalMogul.

The rest of this chapter is dedicated to showing you exactly how you can push beyond the hospital or clinic walls and become a better, more productive, happier you. I'll show you how you can achieve everything you really want in life by using the skills and knowledge you already have. I am over the moon that you are raising your hand and saying, "Yes! I want this change!" It's time for me to take you on your new journey, "From Medicine to Mogul." Get out your pen and paper and prepare to answer these 4 actionable questions:

1. What is your purpose in life?
2. What audience do you want to serve?
3. What problems are you solving?
4. How are you making profits?

What is Your Purpose in Life?

"To have passion, to have a dream, to have a purpose in life; there are three components to that purpose. One is to find out who you really are, to discover God. The second is to serve human beings, because we are here to do that and the third is to express your unique talents and when you are expressing your unique talents you lose track of time."

– DEEPAK CHOPRA

To sum up what Deepak Chopra said above:

- Find out who you are.
- Serve humanity.
- Use your gifts.

This is how you live your purpose in life.

Have you ever had the same reaction as myself to walking in the doors of your clinic? You know, the one where you have to force yourself through the doors so you can start your shift? Where you felt completely overwhelmed before you even reached the door?

Yeah, that feeling. If you've ever felt like that, you're not living your true purpose. This is The Universe, God, and your own brain and heart telling you that you need to find your true purpose. This is bigger, more important, and more necessary to the world and solves a bigger problem than what you're doing right now.

Let's talk about your gifts, passion and purpose. These are all different, but important parts of what you do. Your gifts are natural. They are things you are innately good at or have an immediate talent for. They are the skills people want to hire you for and that friends and family will tell you that you succeed in. For example, my gifts are strategic planning, seeing a vision in people they can't imagine themselves, coaching them to the next step, and showing them all the different ways they can make money with their current skills and knowledge.

Passions are what you love to do, even if you're not being paid to do them. Again, to use myself as an example, my passions are helping people who are stuck, teaching, and healing, or being a doctor. When you combine your gifts and passion, you find your purpose. My purpose is to help doctors who are stuck in the rut of practicing medicine—in hospitals, clinics, or other "traditional" settings—overcome their overwhelm. My purpose is helping them find ways to make money using their medical degrees so they can have the time, freedom, and joy they signed up for in medical school.

The easy way to clarify your purpose is to look at your own pain points. What is your TRUE story? I mean the hard one you know to be true; not the one you tell your colleagues when you're trying to impress them. If you can get clear on your own purpose, you'll be able to cut through the indecision and overwhelm that is clouding your mind right now.

Think about it. Why are you here? If I could remove all your fears, doubts and self-sabotaging behavior, what would you be doing with your life? You are here to serve humanity. You have the power, skills and knowledge to make a difference right now. You have the ability to share your gifts with the world. All you need to do to make that happen is to show up.

Find your purpose and transform your own life, as well as the lives of those you serve. It's time to make that shift, from being a "regular" doctor, employed by a hospital or clinic, and step into your greatness. It's time to see how many people you can touch with your gifts. It's time to build your dream.

If you don't build your own dream, someone will hire you to build their dream. Then they'll be the ones reaping the reward and getting all the benefits. You'll be stuck in the same place you are now: overwhelmed, over-worked, under-paid, and miserable. Starting your dream company and basing its mission on your gifts, passion and purpose will always be profitable, because you believe in what you're doing so strongly.

Discover your purpose, NOW.

What Audience Do You Want to Serve?

"A customer is the most important visitor on our premises, he is not dependent on us. We are dependent on him. He is not an interruption in our work. He is the purpose of it. He is not an outsider in our business. He is part of it. We are not doing him a favor by serving him. He is doing us a favor by giving us an opportunity to do so."

– Mahatma Gandhi

The first thing you must determine before you build your dream company is who you will serve. Who are the people who will benefit from your knowledge? In short, who is your ideal customer?

There are two ways to find your ideal customer, and you need to do both of them:

1. Create your Customer Avatar
2. Research

An avatar, in this case, is a fictional character embodying the description of your ideal customer. It is a conglomeration of the ideal characteristics of several of your audience members. It's also a good way to describe the audience you're targeting for your business. To create your Customer Avatar, write down the following information:

• •

Note: Yes, you can make some of this stuff up if you don't know specifics; but you should know the general range for each point.

• •

Demographics:
1. Name
(Yes, make up a name for your ideal customer! It helps you speak directly to them.)
2. Age
3. Gender
4. Race/ ethnicity
5. Marital status
6. Total and age of children
7. Location
8. Occupation
9. Job title
10. Annual income

Psychographics:

1. Hobbies and activities
2. Favorite books or magazines
3. Favorite TV shows
4. Political leanings
5. Religious/spiritual faith
6. Problem they have that you are solving

Knowing your Customer Avatar will allow you to:

- Know where, when and who to advertise to, so you're maximizing your exposure and not wasting your marketing dollars.
- Better connect with your ideal client by speaking their language and understand their pains, pleasures, desires and wants.
- Over-deliver superior products and services that your customers will actually consume because you understand their needs, behaviors and concerns.

To answer some of the questions above, you'll need to do some research. This is the second component to discovering who you're serving.

You can do this by:

- Finding the places your customers hang out on social media.
- Reading the same magazines and newspapers.
- Joining the forums they are involved in and looking at (and answering) the questions they ask, as well as the answers others in the group give.
- Interviewing anyone you know personally who you think matches your Customer Avatar closely.

Once you have everything on hand, and you've researched the details above, you'll be able to target the right audience. This will enable you to draw them in with the information you'll create in the next step.

What Problems Are You Solving?

"Innovation distinguishes between a leader and a follower. Sometimes when you innovate, you make mistakes. It is best to admit them quickly and get on with improving your other innovations. Things don't have to change the world to be important. Get closer than ever to your customers. So close that you tell them what they need well before they realize it themselves."

- STEVE JOBS

Every human potential analytics expert will tell you that a mere 15% of your success is based on these four factors:

- Your skill
- Your knowledge
- Your talent
- Your education

The other 85% is based on who you are. This includes how you contribute to your customers, as well as how you share yourself with them and the people you surround yourself with. It's your willingness to be brave and fearless. To amplify your voice and give of yourself fully, while moving forward with imperfect action.

As a doctor, you already have a marketable product, the knowledge and skills you've accumulated over your medical career. To create a solid, saleable product or service, you must solve the problems that your ideal customer faces every day. To do this, you must define your ideal customer's pain and pleasure points. People buy the result you offer; the idea that whatever you have will solve their problem and make them happy.

Here are some of the ways you can get the word out about your solution, and develop new ideas to offer your customers:

- Blogging and vlogging.
  (Companies will pay you to write sponsored posts for them.)
- Being active on social media, in your own community and in the communities where your customers hang out.
- Writing a book.
  (You can develop an audio course from your book.)
- Becoming a public speaker.
  (You can get paid to do this.)
- Consulting for other companies.
- Producing live seminars, workshops or masterclasses.
  (These can be online or in person.)
- Creating live or pre-recorded webinars.
- Hosting a live conference.
- Being a medical expert in the media.

The possibilities are endless; but you need to plan this out for the full year, so you know what you're doing, day-to-day. As you're doing this, always remember that your ideal customers want to gain pleasure and avoid pain. They're looking for the perfect solution to their problems. What do your products and services do to solve these problems?

Solve your ideal customers' pain and you'll always profit from it. Most importantly, focus on the goal, not the journey to get there. Show them their ideal picture of their lives after they've used your product or service. We're doctors. We're used to fixing people's pain. In this case, you're just doing it in a slightly different way.

How Are You Making Profits?

"The reason I've been able to be so financially successful is my focus has never, ever for one minute been money. The big secret in life is that there is no big secret. Whatever your goal, you can get there if you're willing to work."

- Oprah Winfrey

You can't make a profit without having a formula in place. Part of that formula is determining how many people you need to buy your product or service, to make it profitable every year. For instance, if you sell a $200 product to 5,000 people, that will make you $1 million. If you have 1,000 people paying you $85 a month for 12 months, that will make you just over $1 million. And if you offer 4 masterclasses (1 per quarter) at $250 for each class, and you sell it to 1,000 people, that will make you $1 million.

You can combine dozens of these numbers to come up with whatever figure you want. And if you make it your goal to follow the power of 1,000, you'll be incredibly successful—monetarily and in terms of the number of people you're helping regularly. Will you be able to do this right away? Probably not. So start with the power of 100. Make it your goal to sell your product or service to 100 people, and then work your way up from there. Overall, this gives you the chance to get your name out there, see how your products and services do in the market, and fail. Yes, fail—if that's what needs to happen—so you can figure out what does and doesn't work, and try again.

Next, you'll need people to sell to. The way to do that is to build an email list, so you can contact your potential customers directly. To do this, you'll want to set up an opt-in funnel, which consists of:

- A landing page
  (this is literally the page people land on to opt into your email list)

- A lead magnet
(also known as an opt-in bribe, which is a useful piece of information you'll give people in exchange for their email addresses)
- A thank you page
(it's polite to say thank you and let your new subscribers know what happens next)
- A follow-up email sequence of 3-5 messages that show your customer the benefits of your product or service and offer them the chance to learn more, or to buy (depending on what you're selling and where you are in the process)

As you build your email list, you'll start converting your subscribers into customers. Once that happens, it's time to deliver on the promises you made. I always recommend over-delivering on those promises. Your customers will be so delighted, impressed and satisfied, they'll become loyal customers and evangelists who will spread the word far and wide about your products and services, bringing in *even more* customers.

It's Time to Change Your Life

Yes, this is a radical idea. It's a major life change. But as someone who has done it, and who has helped hundreds of other doctors change their lives, it's worth it. A year from now, you'll look back and be astonished at how far you've come. And how much your life has changed, for the better. You'll be able to thank the coaches, mentors, investors, family, and friends who have supported you in your endeavors—just like I have.

In order to do that, you need to act now! Make the change. Identify your purpose, find your audience, and solve their problems with your products and services. And remember, making money, building your business, and having a legacy to pass on is FUN!

Let's stay connected so I can keep you updated on my activities. Here's how! Simply click on the link: MedicalMogulsLab.com.

About the Author

Dr. Draion Burch

(Dr. Drai®) is the CEO and "Chief Medical Mogul" at Medical Moguls Inc., an educational company that teaches doctors how to monetize their medical degrees outside of the hospital and live their true purpose. He is a board-certified OB/GYN and has served on the Board of Trustees for the American Osteopathic Association and the American College of Osteopathic Obstetricians and Gynecologists. Dr. Drai owns and runs Amare Concierge, a boutique women's health service promoting a new, holistic standard of healthcare for women.

6

REALIGNING LIFE

A Record-Breaking Journey from Shopping Carts to Aspirations

By
Stuart Burrell

I'm 41 years old, and I'm from the United Kingdom. I have the unique privilege of being a twenty-time world record holder for escapology and stamina weightlifting. What I offer to clients is the opportunity for them to learn how to find the strength and power to escape or overcome whatever situation is restraining them, be it in life or in business.

Having established all of that, my true passion lies in business studies and counseling. I didn't know either of those things was possible when I was attending college; I was convinced I would graduate and then immediately become an Indy Car World Series champion, or win the Indy 500, or win the Formula One World Championship. As all students do, we dream and then time moves on, and we suddenly realize that our surname isn't Mansell, Unser, Petty, Hamilton, or Andretti, and we'll never be a racing driver. We fall into taking any job to pay the bills.

I became a shopping cart collector in a supermarket for three or four years, and I got quite despondent, but I had an unexpected interaction with someone I knew from school, and they were doing very well for themselves. They told me to snap out of it. Our chance encounter helped me realize that it's important for us all to motivate and encourage each other towards reaching our goals; reaching a point where we are doing what we want to do.

My old classmate's words are something I've carried with me as I've gone forward. I left being the trolley collector and off I went, back to college to earn a business studies degree with a focus in human resources. After I finished college, I went to a local advice center and community group, where I then went on to join the local government. I've now reached the point where I'm leading a team of eight or nine people, depending on the day of the week, and all of that came about because I wanted to give back. My classmate snapped me out of it, which helped me, so I wanted to help others. Now, that concept may seem odd; you might be thinking, *Stuart, how do you get to be a twenty-time world record holder, a world champion, by giving back to people?* Well, that came about purely by accident.

I set about trying to raise money for a charity. We planned their fundraising event, which was basically a coffee morning; those in attendance went along and sat down, and they had an opportunity to talk to a number of very famous people from the TV show, *Robot Wars;* the UK equivalent of *Battle Bots.* Unfortunately, the participants from *Robot Wars* were actually off in the US filming an episode of *Battle Bots,* so they couldn't attend. With six weeks to go, I had no event and no way of raising any money. I sat down and thought, *what else could we do?* I ended up thinking, *Well, I've just joined a local magic club to learn how to do magic tricks to entertain my nephews and nieces. Let's try and see if there's something magical I can do.*

I found out I was good at escapology, specifically lock picking. So, I wrote to Guinness World Records, asking, "Is there a world record for this?" I sent an online form, and somehow either I sent the wrong form in or they read the form incorrectly, and they said, "Okay, you're gonna set a world record," and it was like, *right...I hadn't planned to do that –* but I took advantage of the opportunity, and off I went.

I found myself in a six-week period, starting as a complete novice. I had to speak with world record holders and escapologists all over the world; in the US, Canada, France, Germany, the UK, and Scotland, and many more – throw a dart at the map and you'll find a country that I communicated with. They all said, "You're mad. You're not gonna do it." But I felt I had no choice; I'd promised this charity that I would raise money for them. So, my fear of failure and embarrassment drove me. I was in a situation where I needed to overcome my anxiety, where I had to believe in myself to the point that I could be positive and achieve this great outcome.

With a lot of effort and a lot of strength, I was actually able to escape from 301 handcuffs in one hour – and I say this now to anyone wanting to break that record: That number has gotten bigger. More talented people have come along and beaten me, it's going to hurt, so please don't enter into it lightly. Please do not go into it thinking it'll be easy; it's not. To this day, almost 15 years later, I still have moments where I move my fingers, and they click, and I move my hand, and I get a little twinge. So, I know what it takes to be a world record holder.

How does that actually help anyone in business? We all feel fear. We all have anxiety. We all have a thought that it's too much for us or it's too much to be done, be it in business, in the necessary motions of setting up your company, going for that promotion, or be it with the general goings on of life. We're convinced that our life is the way it is because we need to pay the bills (you need to keep the mortgage company at bay, you need to pay for everything), and as a result, we feel safe where we are. So, we don't take any opportunities that appear before us. Because an opportunity was thrust upon me, I learned how to take a chance; but, I also knew that it was important to help everyone else try and move beyond what's holding them back. That is why I try and why I do what I do, which is coaching.

Going the Distance

How can coaching help you take that next step? The reason I wanted to explain this in detail is that the biggest anxiety everyone I've ever spoken ever had comes from looking at where they want to end up. They look at where they want to be, and the distance they must travel, and they think, *I can't do that*. It's like convincing yourself that you need to walk from California to New York; while the simple distances are incredible, it can be done as long as you realize it'll take time, and you need to go from point A to point B all the way through the states before you get to New York.

From my experience with coaching, I have several examples of going the distance, and a particularly good one is a colleague of mine, who was desperately trying to become a manager. He was an environmental consultant. He was already managing his own workload, and he was managing colleagues. In all but the name, he already was a manager, but he was afraid that he couldn't just go off and become one. He couldn't see himself as such because nobody ever told him, "That's what you're doing already."

He was part of the local government's response to climate change. He was very passionate about the environmental side of things. He would talk at great lengths to people about the impact on a global level, and this was a great strength to him. However, he couldn't explain that impact to people locally (what it meant for their families, their husbands, their wives, their children, their parents), and that was always holding him back.

We ended up having to sit down for a couple of days. We went through why he couldn't see himself being a manager, as well as, why he was focused on the bigger picture. We reached a breakthrough when he recalled a story. He originally entered into environmental awareness and protection not because he wanted to change the world, he actually wanted to help relatives of his. One of his parents had a huge energy bill that was unaffordable, and this resulted in them getting disconnected in the middle of winter – which was something that should never have happened. But, mistakes were made and that fired him up. He thought to himself at that moment, *I'm going to not only deal with fuel crisis and energy efficiency problems, but I'm gonna try and make the world better so that we get cleaner energy, we get cheaper energy, and we get everything to stop this sort of thing from happening.*

Yet, he'd never told anyone that specific moment was the source of his passion. As soon as he started to explain it to people in his company, the managers of the organization suddenly realized why he was inspired to create a better world for the human element. It wasn't just polar bears, Amazon rainforests, or rare frogs in Papua New Guinea, it was his parents, and it could be your parents also.

As soon as he was able to bring that to life, to explain it to others, they started calling him into meetings to share his thoughts. Because senior management was able to meet with him, and hear his story, they were able to understand his truth. Of course, this helped him overcome his fear of never seeing himself as a manager. As soon as he was in those meetings with management and able to speak with them, to engage with them, he suddenly realized that he was as good as them. Also, management was able to see him work with his colleagues, being the go-to person that he was. The only difference was that this time he wasn't hiding it from them.

To be clear, he was not deliberately going out of his way, showing and saying, "Look at me. I'm doing this…" He had a confidence that wasn't apparent before, and it was gaining that confidence that enabled him to overcome a barrier, a blockage that prevented him from moving forward. The same thing happened to one of my brothers.

My brother was a service engineer. He went on to fix photocopiers and electric doors, but he genuinely wanted to be a paramedic. That's a bit of a change, a bit of a switch between fixing automatic doors and photocopiers to saving people's lives. He wanted to be a first responder. The problem was that he had never really understood or experienced the recruitment process. He'd always gone in as an engineer; he could turn up and talk to people about fixing things, and his reputation preceded him.

Suddenly, my brother was applying for a medical course, a medical qualification, and he encountered the recruitment application, the job description. Now, if it had been, "Can you fix this device or this device," he could say yes; but as soon as he started reading, "Able to work as a team player and work towards___ and achieve this goal," he panicked. It wasn't that he wasn't a team player; in his mind, he just wasn't sure how he would demonstrate that he could work collaboratively in a team, when he was always in a team of one on the job, isolated in the middle of nowhere fixing a photocopier.

So, his mindset was, *I'm never gonna make this change. I'm never gonna make this transition to be what I want to be.* It was the first real example I can draw on where I had to sit down with my brother and go through it together. I asked, "Well, have you worked with other people?"

"Well, yes. Yeah, I've worked with other people," was his reply. "Then you've worked in a team."

It took two or four back-and-forth's on that topic before he started to realize that just because he worked on his own, he was still part of a service engineering team. He'd gone off to do the task by himself, but he'd worked in a team. He made reports to his team, and also made suggestions and attended meetings. His misunderstanding of "team" was rooted in an association with school, like a team on the sports field. But, you can be part of a team and be 50 miles away, or even 500 miles away. An example of that is the International Space Station. That's a team effort up there. The astronauts didn't put it up there themselves. They are part of one gigantic team, conducting the science and the research. But, more importantly, the people on the ground are there to keep them alive. It's a team effort.

Equally, and again, from my brother's point of view, it was breaking down the process into manageable, small, incremental steps. That's what I always find beneficial with regard to coaching; it's about finding out who you are as the person who has engaged me in this service. My approach is about finding out what you want to do.

Looking Beyond the Distance

I could fix a problem from my point of view, but my solution may not fix what you need; so, it's important for me to help you find your answer. The process is about me trying to help you work through the problem. You need to fix it, but it's about trying to find that answer. I could give you all the specifications for the brakes on your car. I could tell you the brake shoes, the brake disc manufacturers, the brake pads, the drums, every conceivable bit of information; but if you don't put your foot on the brake to stop, that's where you'll hit problems, or possibly even a wall. So, it's about me trying to help you become a better person and achieve what you want. The first step of that: <u>don't try and look at the last hundred yards of the journey.</u>

You need to figure out your destination, and then you need to work out that first step – it's a cliché, but it's true. After that first step, then it's time for the second, then the third step, etc. It's all about trying to help you achieve the seemingly impossible.

Now, that brings me back to the world records. When I was at school, I wasn't the biggest guy. I wasn't a jock; I was a bit of a nerd. When I watch The Big Bang Theory, I feel a great affinity for the guys on that show. But, now I'm a world record holder for bending frying pans like you might see Russian strongmen do. Now, I'm the guy who lifted eighteen tons in an hour doing a certain weightlifting exercise. It just goes to show that if you work out what you need to do and how you'll do it … you can achieve it.

That goes a long way towards breaking down how you can actually work out what you need to do. It's all about taking that first step; it's one foot after another. So, you need to break the task down into manageable steps. You need to break it down into specific point movements. If you want to set up your own business, you need to understand what it is that you need to do to get that organization, to get that business going.

At some point, we all think, *Oh, I've got a great idea for a company.* Fantastic. I had a great idea once. It was for the Tamagotchi – about the same time as they debuted. I have no idea if I could ever have made it myself because I have no software engineering experience, and I have no electronics experience. Having the idea is one thing, but, I would've needed to break down the process of manufacturing that product into its most simple, incremental steps. The same goes for any life problem you're facing. It's taking those individual small elements, those small steps, and working towards the eventual outcome.

Where I am, at this moment, is trying to help you work to your outcome, to work towards where you want to be, and that's what I offer with my coaching. It's very easy. We all go to seminars. I've gone to seminars, and they've been brilliant. These usually involve a venue with 40-100 different people, and we're all working towards a new goal. We've all been told, "Yes, this is the new product we're going to launch. This is the new way we're gonna manage the company. This is the new way we're going to overcome these obstacles," and it's great because there are 40-100 people, and everyone's really enthusiastic and motivated. The problem is that as soon as you finish that seminar, you're on your own again.

There aren't 99 other people around you to help you and shout, "Yay," for your accomplishments. You're on your own. That's why I prefer to do things alone and one-to-one. I can sit down with you and work out what steps you need to take. You don't need to know every step you'll make towards your final goal, because you can't see the whole journey. You won't be able to look at the proverbial map and know every street corner; you won't be able to know every obstacle along the way. Things will happen, but you need to be able to work out what you need to do to start on that journey. This is one of the things I am very pleased that I've been able to help people with in their lives: be it someone moving out of a house and re-engaging with their family for the first time in five years, or be it working with that colleague of mine who became a manager after having the opportunity to prove to himself that he could be one – because he was able to re-engage with everyone, not with a grand vision, but the smallest of incremental bits of information.

Equally, it's challenging to work out the smaller and smaller and smaller steps. I want to work with organizations, individuals, and help them take those first steps. It doesn't have to be towards setting up a business. It doesn't have to be towards developing a new product. It could be something as simple as moving forward from where they are in their life.

Moving Beyond Fear

Now, believe me. I've been there. There is nothing more depressing than being in a historic English town pushing shopping carts. There is nothing more debilitating than that. It's equally almost as debilitating as seeing someone you were at school with coming up to you and saying, "What are you doing? Why are you still doing this? You graduated two years ago. Why are you still doing this?" and not having an answer for them. Been there, felt the frustration, and felt the rage. I wanted to scream at the moon, to reach up into the heavens and rip the world apart. Then, I sat down, and I worked out what I needed to do and where I'd gone wrong; and after a lot of saving, I went back to college.

It's more about taking those goals, those targets that you have for yourself and making them achievable. As I said, I never set off on my journey in life to be a twenty-time world record holder. I love it! I love the fact that I can drop that in conversation. It's a great attention getter. It's brilliant. It stops people when they're talking, especially when I'm shopping or just walking around, and someone complains that they had a hard day at the gym. It's grand, but it's not all that I am in the same way as the roles we all play, aren't necessarily all we are in life.

I know some great people who are fantastic radio presenters, who are fantastic storytellers, who are fantastic caregivers, yet these are all things they do in addition to their day jobs. Yet they want to make that their career, but it's the economic fear that holds them back, and I genuinely, genuinely, genuinely want to help them. For the same reason, I want to help you. My own personal mission statement is helping people online.

If you are willing to come aboard with me, I will help you achieve what you want to achieve.

For me, I want to set three or four more world records. I want to set a few more personal goals, which include doing more work online, doing some podcasts, and maybe entering a local film festival. Now, bear in mind, I'm not a great actor, I'm not necessarily a great podcaster, but I can work at it. You can work at it. You have to do it. If you put yourself in the situation where it must be done, you will do it. You will achieve it. In closing, if you want guidance, if you want help, if you want to achieve, you don't necessarily need to come to someone like me for training. You can communicate, you can learn from what you read – reading this wonderful book is the first step. If you want to get in contact with me or any of the other authors here, please do. But you need to work out what that first step will be because you'll never reach your destination unless you start by taking that first step. I never knew when I was at school what my first step would be. I was convinced I would be a record-holding world champion racing driver, but I never got past learning to drive.

I love driving sports, but I'm not fast enough, nor am I talented enough and I accept that. I didn't allow that failure, that inability to define myself. I didn't allow not being good at something to hold me back in my life. While I know I can't cook, I do try – and I haven't poisoned the wife yet, which is good. It takes effort to achieve what you set out to achieve. There's one thing I learned right at the very beginning: <u>Fear can stop you from doing anything, no matter how good you are.</u>

I've seen people who are fantastically talented not try something because of their fear of failure. If you're afraid to even think about moving forward in your life, then fear has won. If those fears of moving forward make you look at everything very closely, examine every detail and work out what you need to do so that you can be better so that you do not fail. Then, fear is a good thing. The trouble is that we never know how much fear is too much. I never knew how much fear I would have in my life regarding moving forward, with regard to doing these projects, each time, it's a revelation.

Every time I step into a world record, I am petrified. My most recent world record was bending the frying pans, and I was up the night before, white as a sheet. I was scared to death because I didn't want to fail, but I knew there was every chance I would. I didn't want to get injured. I'd already bruised myself in training.

If you're reading this and you're scared, that's not a bad thing. If you're reading this and you refuse to do anything because of your fear – that is a bad thing. There was every chance I would fail, but I accepted the fear. I owned the fear, and that made me realize what I needed to do. If you have read the above and you would like to get in touch, with no obligation, and see if a consultation would be right for you, then please get in contact via stuart@burrell.life, and I will endeavor to help you further.

7

AGAINST MYSELF

From Mindsets to Self-Help Groups

By
Beth Underhill

I began experiencing unfamiliar changes in my body in February of 2015. I thought they were physical changes resulting from my preparations for a bodybuilding competition; but those changes were actually related to an endometrial type cancer, specifically in the uterus. I clearly remember the phone ringing. Having just finished a workout, I was driving home and didn't pick up the call. Then my phone rang again. When I had a chance, I glanced at my phone and saw a missed call from the nurse.

I pulled into the nearest parking lot and called the doctor's office back. She told me, "Beth, we need you to come in today." And I thought to myself, *that isn't a test result.* I asked her to tell me more over the phone, and eventually, I begged, and I pleaded. She couldn't tell me anything – deep down, I just knew. Tears were shed, but those would be the few that I would release throughout my journey. It was at that moment, in the parking lot before any of my future appointments, that I definitively set my mind in motion.

I'm gonna fight this thing. I'm gonna fight it with every single ounce of strength within me. I knew this would be a battle. I knew this would be a journey – and that it would be a journey about me against me, and nothing more. Yes, there was cancer. Yes, it was inside my body. And yes, it would do whatever it would do – physically. So, I needed to mentally prepare myself, ensuring I would be as strong as possible for my family, my husband, my daughter, and for my friends.

As a fitness professional, I wanted to show other women that, *Hey, I'm not gonna let this knock me down and nor should anybody else.* And so, I embarked on a seven-month journey to focus on each of these seven mindsets, which formed the basis of my Me vs. Me program:

1. Self-awareness
2. Self-esteem
3. Self-control
4. Self-motivation
5. Self-image
6. Self-discipline
7. Self-dimension

The first mindset was self-awareness. I would be open, take time to understand who I was, my character and my emotions, what I believed in, where I stood in life at that point in time, and how all of that connected with my diagnosis. I sought to be very vulnerable with my thoughts and feelings, to where I aspired to share those thoughts and feelings with others. You see, I had already experienced a "cancer" for 26 years: fighting an eating disorder in which the lack of vulnerability and the lack of openness on my part had destroyed so many relationships with friends, family members, boyfriends – you name it. So, in this journey, I aimed to be as open as possible. After all, it took me 26 years to learn the value of those relationships, and I was determined not to lose them again.

The second mindset was self-esteem. I was aware that my self-worth, my self-respect, and my self-confidence would be rocked, or at least that it could be rocked. I desired to own every single ounce of me, even when I had to give up ounces of me, and in the case of chemotherapy, that was my hair. *I will not choose to be afraid of baldness; I will choose to embrace it.* As a woman, it's not easy to lose something that you feel defines you or your confidence. But I thought to myself, *No. Chemotherapy can take my hair, but it cannot take my courage unless I allow it. I'm not gonna be afraid of what chemotherapy may or may not physically do to me. I will not let this defeat me.*

The third mindset was self-control. All of the choices that I would make on this journey would be 100% my responsibility. Thus, if there was something that resulted in not being the right decision – according to whomever – it would be the right decision for me, made by me, and each of those decisions was the right decision.

The fourth mindset was self-motivation. Fear was not welcome. The only thing constant in life is change, so cancer would not scare me because I could count on change. If I invited fear into this change, it would be destructive. My daughter would unknowingly help me ward off my fears because she needed to see I was unafraid. We were on this journey together, and I refused to let her sense fear, else it would grow within her. Together, we would grow mentally stronger.

The fifth mindset was self-image. Even though this is about "self," this mindset has much to do with how others perceived me. If I displayed optimism and positivity, it would return to me. It was important to me that people recognized I was fighting the battle, and that I was winning it. *I want to hear them cheer; I want to see them motivated.* I had one individual convey, "If you can do this and still work out while doing everything that you're doing, then you know what? I can do this. I have no excuse for not getting to the gym. I have no excuse for anything that I give myself an excuse for." As a coach, that was incredibly powerful to hear.

The sixth mindset was self-discipline. This came along naturally. I always made sure I had a plan. Being disciplined in how my days looked was essential as I still hoped to be able to work out four days a week. My goal after six chemotherapy treatments was to minimize every single side effect that could possibly occur after that sixth treatment. I wanted to make certain that when I got to that sixth treatment, I was stronger than when the first treatment occurred. So, I took steps to ensure it. There were things that I did, products that I took, and regimens that I developed after that sixth treatment. At that, I actually had the least amount of downtime with that treatment, so the discipline from this was very purposeful. I was seeking a goal, and that made all the difference in getting through this journey.

The seventh and final mindset was self-dimension. I wanted to ensure that I intimately knew who I was, understanding where my spirit and my heart were. God played a significant role in my journey, and I was able to share this especially with my immediate family – letting them know that I was in tune with what their needs were and that together we would get through this. I continued putting their needs before mine as I had before my diagnosis. Again, I wanted to show them that I was still that same person, and nothing had changed.

Throughout all seven mindsets, I shared so much of my journey, and it led me to create –and be very passionate about – everything beyond that. Personally, I love seeing women go through transformations. I love when they can reach the other side of their journey, be it cancer, eating disorders, weight loss, divorce, or being told that they can't have children. Whenever someone goes through something very significant in their life, there's a transformation process, and they come out on the other end stronger.

Me vs. Me

From my experience with those mindsets, as well as other journeys in my life, I developed Me vs. Me as a way in which people can get more in touch with who they are in order to reach their full potential. Richard Rohr has said, "transformation is often more about unlearning, then learning." Transformation is a positive thing; it's what makes you grow.

Today, Me vs. Me currently holds my heart, as does helping women through whatever their transformation might be. The goal is connecting the heart, mind, and body of each woman; specifically, women who are looking for change.

The biggest obstacle that I hear daily, and see women put in front of themselves, is that they don't believe enough in what they can and cannot do. I experience it often, even still within me – even after overcoming an eating disorder and cancer journey – there are still days when I question my abilities to go out there and make life happen. There are times when fear holds me back, and as always, I seek to uncover the root of what that fear is. Generally, it's about being afraid of what others will think; maybe something is still deep inside my head, in my mind, in my heart, buried from years past, negatively affirming that I'm not worthy of certain things. For me, I struggle with fear related to money; the asking for money; my value; my worth. *Where is it? Where should it be? How do I put a price on my services?* Sometimes, I often shortchange myself with that.

Me vs. Me focuses on spirituality. Of course, every client is unique in their levels and beliefs; everybody has different levels and different beliefs. Some believe in a higher power while others don't. Wherever a client's spirituality lies, however, it plays a role in their life, the significance of it is something that we hone in on and discuss.

Much like my seven mindsets, the overall focus is self-belief, self-worth, and self-confidence. It's about finding that value of who you are as an individual, what that's supposed to look like for you – not what that's supposed to look like for everybody else – and understanding that you are a unique individual. You are someone who represents something here on this earth, and you were designed for a purpose.

For the challenges involved with transformation – be that in mind or a physical transformation, and so forth – information alone will not suffice. Through the program, people will understand themselves through six key points:

1. Everyone wants to be a better version of themselves. I often ask clients, "What do you want out of this?" Typically, they tell me, "I want to be better than I was yesterday."

2. Everyone needs support. Me vs. Me is designed to offer a level of support in order for clients to do this in conjunction with others. Everyone can share in the challenges, the struggles, and the victories together. That kind of support is so important.

3. Everyone wants a return on their investment. They want to know that whatever they're putting into it, they'll get something back. I don't mean ROI monetarily, I mean the intrinsic value of, *If I'm putting time and effort into this, I want to walk away feeling better. I want to walk away feeling empowered. I want to walk away with tools and feel equipped to actually go out there to do more and be better.*

4. Everyone wants to feel important. They want to be important. Everyone likes to know they have value and worth.

5. Everyone wants to be a part of something. Community is such a big deal. You tend to stay in something longer if you're a part of something, and Me vs. Me is designed as a group; a group of women on a 6-week journey. For me, battling my cancer journey was easier to go through when I had support. It was a lot harder to go through my eating disorder journey when I was virtually by myself.

6. Then, of course, everyone needs accountability. That's exactly what the Me vs. Me program is designed to provide. It provides clients with that extra nudge and push. When someone feels like falling off that ledge, we can talk them down from it.

In 2015, I executed a beta test of Me vs. Me with 18 women, each of whom went through their own transformation. From this program, I've homed in on just exactly how it is that I can further help women. This is about diving into women on a level that is far greater than just the surface of losing weight, of being told how to eat for 30 days or repeating an exercise regimen.

One of my most active participants had this to say: "I never felt strong. I know the things I have been through in my life, family, health, and relationship-wise that I looked at and said, **'I made it,'** but I still didn't feel strong. Me vs. Me is where I discovered my love for strength and my love for myself."

And what did this participant share that ironically, as a personal fitness instructor, meant the most to me and her transformation?

"I don't even notice the physical change at times…most importantly to me is the mental change I feel in believing in myself and the feeling of being worthy."

Often times, women will measure transformation on a scale, and while they'll feel somewhat victorious, they measure their worth by then looking into a mirror where they think, *It's not enough*. This program is about giving women the permission and resources to look in the mirror every day – regardless of what measurements they're taking – and say, "I'm okay with who I am… I *like* who I am." That's the goal.

The Future of Me vs. Me

I launched a 6-week beta test of Me vs. Me, where the group met in-person once a week at a physical location in Cincinnati where they completed activities and assignments, and then they continued their engagement with me over email and/or in our Facebook group. From this, I plan to implement the program online after revising, and then I want to commence Facebook accountability groups with it.

Eventually, the goal is to license Me vs. Me and train other fitness facilities or fitness programs that have a desire to help women go beyond just a physical transformation. Honestly, I don't believe people can make or maintain a physical transformation unless they are ready with their mind and their heart – because a transformation requires both parts of your being. You need to be ready. You need to accept the journey. And you'll need to accept yourself at every single point in the journey – whether you're on a high, a low, or somewhere in between.

Summer of 2018, I hope to establish Me vs. Me in several different entities, with a goal of 10 licensed facilities or programs. I've commenced discussions with schools about implementing a smaller scale version for high school teenagers. For many of us, our development in our younger years can determine our mentality in our later years. Teenagers are bombarded with numerous messages on a daily basis – particularly young girls – as to how they should look or act. With the added lens of social media, comparison is rampant, and can truly make for a very challenging environment – one that many teenagers are not equipped to manage.

In raising my 14-year-old daughter, I watch, I listen, and I learn as she shares with me. I take the information, and I make notes, constantly analyzing what her development is all about; where she struggles; how I can help her. I look at the things that I do on a daily basis. *Do they make a difference?* I constantly keep myself in check. Sometimes, I'm a good mom; sometimes, I fail miserably. This has led to my desire to work with young women further and to be established in schools starting in 2018-2019. Several teachers – who are aware of my beta tests – have approached me, stating, "We are on board, and want this in our school ASAP. We want to help because we know we need it."

After several speaking engagements in both 2017 and 2018, I hope to continue down that path and speak to youth groups and in high schools; to be in front of as many people locally as I can to encourage, "You can get to the other side." I also plan to make them aware of Me vs. Me, and how this program can help if any of them are struggling. It isn't a replacement for therapy; this is for women who are looking to go beyond a normal transformation of clean eating or exercise. This is for women who really want to understand how beautiful they are inside and out, and how balanced they can keep their life while still achieving results.

With teenagers 13-18 years old, I want to help inspire them so that they can be those inspirational women of the future. My desire is to help them gain self-confidence, self-awareness, and self-empowerment.

I aspire to help them feel good about who they are at any stage, whether it's their acne or their bodies changing.

Recently, my daughter shared an app with me, and I about fell out of my chair. The app determines how pretty you are. You can upload a picture, and from that picture, it tells you, "You're 26% pretty," or "You're 66% pretty." My daughter tested it on three different occasions. One time it said she was 92% pretty, another time it said she was 66%, and a third time it said she was ~20% pretty. I thought to myself, *how incredibly damaging is something like that?* It was absolutely insane. What message does that give to children? Three pictures with three different results? Furthermore, who designed this app? What was the intent of users taking advantage of that app? We don't need to build apps like that. We need to build apps that empower our youth.

From my experience around teenagers, I hear **a lot** of negative self-talk:

- I want to start working out now.
- I want to enhance "X" because "X" will like that.
- I need to hop on the treadmill because I feel like I'm fat.
- I'm not gonna eat any French fries because they make my stomach look fat.

These words are exactly what we need to begin eliminating. We need to replace them with, "I **like** how I look. I **love** who I am. I want to look good **for myself**. I'm proud of my body, and this is the body that I was created to be in, and this is the body that I need to embrace." Instead of reducing ourselves to an app, we need to independently recognize our value. And if we can root this in our journeys earlier on, imagine what we can become.

It took me years to learn how to replace that self-talk, which is why I've created Me vs. Me. It's about the seven mindsets that got me through my cancer journey. Of course, I still need reminders; but my foundation is strong, and it's built on focus and consistency with self-awareness, being vulnerable, being open, and feeling my value.

I am worthy, and in being worthy, I am responsible for seeing the worthiness in others and empowering them with it. As I make choices, I focus on accepting that with all of my decisions; I am responsible. And so are you. We are in control.

And in replacing negative self-talk, my mantras become alive:

- *I am motivated: my vision and the steps to achieve it are visible. More visible than fear standing on the sidelines, and I feel them stronger than the pain of any up-hill battle.*

- *I am disciplined: I have a purpose. My motivation tells me where to go, and my discipline will keep me on that path.*

- *I am human: I intimately know who I am, what I stand for, what my beliefs are. I can empathize and base my actions on empathy.*

Me vs. Me (Mental Strength Training with Beth Underhill) is about syncing your physical "me" and your mental "me" in order to reach your full potential. You can find and follow me at bethunderhillfitlife.com to learn more. I share more of my stories and clients' stories on my social media. My Instagram handle is @bethunderhillfitlife, and you can follow me on Facebook at facebook. com/bethunderhillfitlife.

You've made it this far, so join me on this journey. You are not alone, and I'm here to grow your mental "me," and help you rediscover your value. We are born with grit. We are resilient, and when we take the initiative, we are powerful. Let's awaken your power together!

8

ON THE LIBERATION OF SOULS

The Seven Rays of Divine Unfolding Light

By
Sh'Ari Shemoth

My name is Sh'Ari Shemoth, and I am a Soul Liberation Coach. I am dedicated to assisting the evolution of the human race towards becoming conscious and self-aware Divine Sovereign Beings who truly and completely recognize themselves as Sons & Daughters of God who are deeply loved and destined for greatness in the Divine Plan of Creation. My heart's desire – and as a result, my "work" – is to assist in the establishment of the Kingdom of Heaven upon Earth. Consequently, how I have seen that I can be of most benefit in helping to establish this in our world is to assist others in deepening their understanding of Who They Are, Why They Are Here and helping them to discern What They Are to Be Doing. My chapter is about understanding who we are as Souls; who we are as Divine Sparks of our Creator, who we are as Children of God! My own soul has guided me, as a result of my mission and purpose, to help others understand this and the reality of their magnificence, of their beautiful thread in the Tapestry of Creation – which is why I am a "Soul Liberation Coach."

As a Soul Liberation Coach, I endeavor to work with my clients to free the body, heart, mind, and spirit from their lack of knowledge about who they truly are as beings with a soul, to expose them more deeply to the majesty of our Creator and Creation, and to help make them  aware of the scope of living within the limitations of this 3-D world. Our limitations prevent us from the full realization of this. I am one of many who have been called to this work because the time has come to know within the core of our being Who We Truly Are and Why We Are Here and to begin to move towards this destiny in an accelerated way.

While there are many ways, many paths, and many religions that have been given to us to help us accomplish this, they oftentimes fall short of assisting the individual to understand these important aspects, and they leave many important questions that go unanswered. I asked these questions, too, and was blessed to be able to pursue the answers through a multitude of sources which was totally orchestrated by my Divine Higher Self. My seemingly circuitous (and certainly unconscious) path included:

- Being indoctrinated in Christianity through the Lutheran, Catholic and Evangelical religions.
- The teachings of the Indigenous through studies of the Ojibwa, Q'uero, Mayan, and Toltec Indians.
- Engaging Judaism as a result of my direct lineage and studying Kabbalah, Gnosticism and the Essenes.
- Experiencing Mysticism and finding it in all Paths.
- And, finally, through the Masonic as a Rainbow Girl, first being exposed to the 7 Rays and their existence in Creation.

Consequently, over time I was able to pick up many of the threads of the Tapestry which I would never have found if I had adhered with one course; one path; one dogma; one belief structure. At some point, I learned that my life was structured and designed so that I would not be bound or tethered to a certain belief system or structure, familial boundaries, or lineage. It was designed in that way to inspire me and give me the opportunity to find a common thread that runs through every path.

My path has deeply involved seeking and understanding that common thread. As a result, I have been shown to think of creation as one big tapestry and that each of the threads within this tapestry is incredibly unique and important for the overall design – the design of Creation. I have been driven to understand this design and, consequently, the threads and the role that they play (or can play) in the overall structure of Creation and the Plan of the Divine.

Through my further experiences and learning, I came to the realization that the threads of the tapestry are the individual souls! It was then that I realized that I needed to focus on learning all that I could about the soul. Through this pursuit, I discovered the science of the soul which is found in all the ancient wisdom and hidden teachings of spiritual leaders throughout time. I learned that as a foundation, we need to understand that there is a science of the soul and that the more we understand about this reality, the quicker and more effectively we can consciously grow. It's very difficult for us to evolve unless we know who we are, why we are here, where we are, and what the divine design is for our soul incarnation – which according to my understanding is about learning about the purpose of life, the work of creation, and the whole evolutionary process towards unity with the divine.

All of us are part and parcel of our Creator. The intention of our Creator is for each of us to participate consciously in His/Her creative purpose and Divine Plan by manifesting our own personal, archetypal nature in this world. One approach that I take to assist those who are seeking this understanding of their soul's essence is to introduce them to the Science of the Rays, or the Science of the Rainbow as it relates to the soul.

The Science of the Rays teaches us that we are energy beings living in a world of energy. The Rays are described as vibrational frequencies/ energies of Divine Unfolding Light which emanate from the Cosmic Heart of the Creator. These energies have differing levels of vibration and frequency, and they are organized into 7 major bands known as the Rays. These Rays correlate to the 7 Rays/Colors of the Rainbow and is why the Rainbow is often referenced in religious teachings. Each Ray has its own distinct frequency, coloring, vibration, qualities, and attributes. In the esoteric teaching of the Rays we learn that not only do our souls consist of a certain Ray, but so do our physical bodies, personalities, mental attributes, and our emotional qualities.

The rays of our souls represent the energy of God's radiating light which refracts into 7 different rays like the rainbow. It is the same energy known as the Holy Spirit and is literally the spiral that moves within a certain geometric proportion found in the energy of every single thing on Earth – including stones, to the relationship found in water, and the atomic structure of life. All life and form are patterned by a divine imprint that is placed into life, esoterically known as God. The influences that bring those energies into the pattern also have a number of qualities to it that are the 7 Rays. When we reflect upon them, the energy of 7 goes all the way into our planetary existence. For example, we have seven continents, seven human races, and seven days of the week – sound even has a relationship to them as there are seven tones of the octave.

Now, I would like to give you a brief overview of the 7 Rays that can be found in our world as they relate to the soul. In addition, to help give a complete overview, I have listed each Ray's strengths and weaknesses as well as the humans who carry that Ray.

THE 1st RAY: "WILL & POWER"

A 1st Ray human will have an abundance of will, power, energy, and drive. Because this Ray is exciting to experience, 1st Ray people are generally exciting to be around. As born leaders, they are a very dynamic and direct force in the human milieu and are often responsible for the breaking down of the old and bringing in the new. It is an "intense" Ray and is often called the "Ray of the Destroyer" because of the dynamic intensity of this energy. 1st Ray people use their will to focus on the target and move swiftly through all resistance to accomplish their goal. Through their abundance of courage, which arises out of their sure knowledge and the ability to stay focused on their course without questioning when encountering difficulty or discomfort, they achieve formidable accomplishments.

Rainbow Thread: Red

Higher Expression: Will-power; synthesization; large-mindedness; strong sense of purpose; power of beneficial destruction; one-pointed focus; leadership; fearless; truthfulness; values-oriented; power to govern; power to initiate; detachment; wisdom to establish/enforce the law; independent; liberator; prioritization; principles oriented; large-mindedness; the power to centralize.

Lower Expression: Egotism; excessive pride; separateness & isolationism; arrogance; willfulness; power-hungry; domination; destructive; stubborn; tendency to anger & violence; unrelenting ambition; hardness & cruelty; control & suppression; inhibition; impatience; obstinacy.

Notable 1st Ray Figures: Donald Trump, Winston Churchill, General George Patton, Napoleon, Adolf Hitler, Alexander the Great, and sports players in general.

THE 2nd RAY: "LOVE/WISDOM"

The Second Ray is the energy of Loving Wisdom; the ray of unconditional divine universal love. It implies a relationship between understanding, compassion, healing, teaching and the ability to let go when warranted. 2nd Ray souls give greatly of themselves and possess an innate desire for the illumination of others. Consequently, they have a tremendous desire for pure knowledge and absolute truth. These souls have the ability to raise humankind out of the darkness through their power of illumination and are often the great teachers that are on the planet. This Ray is often found mitigating the power/harshness which may result in an overuse of the 1st Ray in the world. Their professions that they choose generally require higher conceptual abilities, such as teaching or architecture.

Rainbow Thread: Blue

Higher Expression: Loving wisdom; magnetic, attractive love; magnetism; healer; philanthropist; reformer; power to understand through love; empathic; sympathetic; compassionate; exquisite sensitivity; desire for absolute truth and knowledge; intuitive love; clear perception and intelligence; humanitarian; tact; foresight; generous; great initiative; inclusiveness; power to teach and illumine; patient; serene; faithful; tolerant; power to salvage and redeem; power to heal through love; impressionable; slow to act.

Lower Expression: Fearfulness; self-pity; oversensitivity; vulnerability; tendency towards an inferiority complex; difficulty in forgiving sins against the 2nd Ray code; over attachment; despondency; overprotective; keeps knowledge to self; too altruistic; obsessive about things out of their control; excess sentimentality; self-righteous; love of being loved; non-assertive; obsessed with study; over-inclusive; procrastination; coldness; indifference to others; contempt for other's mental limitations; brooding/nursing grievances; stifling of others through possessive love; cannot play at friendship.

Notable 2nd Ray Figures: Christ, Buddha, Albert Einstein, Florence Nightingale, Martin Luther King, John the Beloved Apostle, Edgar Cayce, Gandhi, and Kabir.

THE 3rd RAY: "ACTIVITY & ADAPTABILITY"

The 3rd Ray is also known as the Ray of Active Intelligence or, to reverse it, "Intelligent Activity." It is known as the ray of the intelligent use of form building or manifesting form in all aspects of the creative effort. A keyword for this particular Ray is "perseverance" because of their unique ability to hold on to something. They are the organizers of the race and are the ones who get it all done. They have an innate ability to take the ideas/visions of others and implement them. They accomplish this through their intelligence, intense focus, and perseverance.

Rainbow Thread: Yellow

Higher Expression: Clear intellect; clear views of the abstract; sincere purpose; patience; caution; philosopher; skillful communicator; adept at all languages; can-do approach; doesn't get lost in the details; imaginative; executive and business aptitude; ability to plan and strategize; sincerity of purpose; the ability to get others to see things their way.

Lower Expression: Coldness; individualism; selfish; indecisive; aloof; intrigue; cruelty; inaccuracy in details; amoral materialism; disorder and chaos; opportunism; critical; dishonest; preoccupation and "busyness"; failure to support a crisis; cunning/devious; insincere; more attention to form than spirit.

Notable 3rd Ray Figures: Thomas Edison, Jacque Cousteau, Eleanor Roosevelt, Andrew Carnegie, Sir Isaac Newton, Marie Curie, Euclid, and Antonio Vivaldi.

THE 4th RAY: "HARMONY THROUGH CONFLICT"

The 4th Ray is oftentimes identified as "the Ray of struggle." It is the ray of art, music, color, and creativity. This Ray's energy drives its possessor to elevate the consciousness of humanity into the realization of the beauty and splendor of Nature and God through the means of beauty. In its highest expression, the 4th Ray soul strives to reveal this Divine Beauty in every thought, word, and deed. Through the synthesis of beauty, this Ray teaches the fine art of living. Essentially, it is the refiner; the producer of perfection within the form so that the objective world becomes a true house of Light.

Rainbow Thread: Green

Higher Expression: Harmonization; creative ideation; capacity to grow spiritually and psychologically through constant struggle and crisis; refined artistic and aesthetic sensibilities; love of beauty and the capacity to create or express it; love of color, musicality and rhythm; capacity to reconcile; peace-maker; balance; sympathy; strong affections; strong imagination; fighting spirit; facility for compromise/meditation/bridging; strong sense of drama; spontaneity.

Lower Expression: Embroiled in constant conflict; overeager for compromise; self-centeredness; self-absorption in suffering; inaccuracy; worry and agitation; lack of moral courage; strong passions; confused combativeness; indolence; extravagance; instability; restlessness; exaggeration; unpredictability and unreliability; ambivalence; posing; self-indulgent.

Notable 4th Ray Figures: Picasso, Van Gogh, Beethoven, Chopin, Mozart, and Tchaikovsky, musicians, actors, and artists of all types.

THE 5th RAY: "CONCRETE KNOWLEDGE OR SCIENCE"

This Ray is also known as the Ray of Logic and Reason. The driving impulse of the 5th Ray Soul is to discover knowledge to reach truth. They are driven to penetrate and purify the lower mind in order to know the Mind of God. 5th Rays have an appreciation, if not absolute devotion, to the laws of nature. The energies of this Ray have produced science and led to humanity's comprehension of the natural world. Because those of this Ray operate on the plane of the higher and lower mind, and because "man" is literally "one who thinks," the 5th Ray has special significance to humanity as this person can analyze a situation, take it apart, put it back together, synthesize it, and know the best way to productively undertake a venture. The scientist, the lawyer, the detective, and the mathematician can often be found on this Ray.

Rainbow Thread: Orange

Higher Expression: Accurate; justice (without mercy); analytical; unswervingly patient; brilliant mind; witty; capacity to think and act scientifically; keen and focused intellect; power to define; power to create thought-forms; facility for math; highly developed powers of analysis and discrimination; detached objectivity; accuracy and precision in thought and action; positive mind; specialization; great grasp for detail; independent; practical inventiveness; mechanical ability; technical expertise; common-sense; lucid explanation.

Lower Expression: Harshness; coldness; destructively critical; narrow-minded; arrogance; unforgiving temper; unsympathetic; prejudice; social awkwardness; excessive mentalism; excessive objectivity; mental rigidity; set thought patterns; excessive doubt and skepticism; too linear; lack of emotional responsiveness and magnetism; overly analytical; bound by the senses; unduly accentuates faults in others.

Notable 5th Ray Figures: Stephen Hawking, Benjamin Franklin, Karl Marx, Hippocrates, and Marconi.

THE 6th RAY: "DEVOTION"

This Ray is also known as the Ray of "Idealism." This individual who carries this Ray has the capacity to see the ideal; the reality behind the form. The 6th Ray endows man with the urge to penetrate behind the veiled and hidden realms. The human whose soul Ray is the 6th conveys a living spark of idealism which is why this Ray is found to be devoted to idealism. This soul is born as a devoted receiver for the needs of others and oftentimes accepts duties that are not necessarily theirs to perform because of their need to be of service. This is the Ray of religion and is where the devoutly religious can often be found. It is the Ray of self-sacrifice, goodness, and peace. The idea of this ray is complete self-consecration and self-sacrifice for an ideal, a cause, or a leader...even unto death.

Rainbow Thread: Indigo

Higher Expression: Peaceful; sacrificial love; devotion; transcendental idealism; single-mindedness; love; tenderness; intuition; loyalty; reverence; receptivity to spiritual guidance; ability to achieve "ecstasy" and "rapture"; intense sympathy for the suffering of others (stigmata); burning enthusiasm for a cause; fiery ardor; adoration; reverence; purity/goodness/sainthood; profound humility; power to arouse/inspire/persuade; self-sacrificing; unshakeable faith; optimism; one-pointedness.

Lower Expression: Zealousness; selfish and jealous love; intense devotion; partiality; over-leaning on others; self-deception; sectarianism; superstition; prejudice; over-rigid conclusions; fiery anger; self-abasement; masochism; martyr complex; idealistic impracticality; glamour; intolerance; rigid idealism; gullible; lack of realism; ill-considered loyalty; blind faith; addictive; extremism; hyper-intensity; fanaticism; militarism; emotionalism.

Notable 6th Ray Figures: Jesus, Mother Mary, Meister Eckhart, Luke the Apostle, John Wesley (founder of the Methodists), St. Thomas Aquinas, Mother Theresa, and Teresa of Avila.

THE 7th RAY: "CEREMONIAL ORDER"

This Ray is also known as the Ray of "Transmutation" and is identified as being very ritualistic. People on this ray experience great joy in all things done decently and in order in accordance with the rules and precedents. They always do things wholeheartedly as they believe that nothing can be accomplished from half-measures. Oftentimes, this is the Ray that priests, the ideal soldier, and the perfect nurse can be found on. Due to their love of pomp and ceremony, the 7th Ray Soul flourishes under the influences of practice and ritual. This person, in their highest functioning and as the primary purpose of this Ray, is driven to blend spirit and matter in order to reveal Heaven on Earth. They accomplish this through their focus and an innate understanding of nature, cycles, and timing.

Rainbow Thread: Violet

Higher Expression: Ritualism and ceremonialism; nobility and chivalry of conduct; "magical" gifts; power to work with nature; ability to synthesize; perfection of form; strength; perseverance; courage; courtesy; freedom; forgiveness; justice; splendor of estate and person; grace; dignity; extreme care in details; tidy; methodical; self-reliance; keen sense of rhythm; keen sense of timing; power to build; power to renovate; the ability to transform.

Lower Expression: Formalism; bigotry; pride; narrowness; superficial judgments; overindulgence of self-opinion; superstitious; ostentatiousness; pretentiousness; unscrupulousness; love of power and office; ready to use people as tools; mechanical performance of a ceremony to the neglect of the spiritual significance; tendency to use abilities for negative purposes.

Notable 7th Ray Figures: St. Francis of Assisi, Max Planck, John Lennon, Leonardo da Vinci, Nicholas Roerich, and Henry Ford.

The Universal Life~Light Academy

To assist others in finding out what their Soul Ray is, I utilize a questionnaire that assesses the qualities that they are conscious of having. In addition, we engage in a verbal coaching session in order to draw out anything that relates to their Soul and its essence that the questionnaire may not have captured. Between these two we can arrive at a conclusion as to which Ray their soul is aligned with and begin exploring what that means to them and for them.

In addition to assisting my clients towards the critical understanding of their Soul's primary Ray, I also coach them to develop an understanding of their Spiritual Gifts. Our Spiritual Gifts are tools that we have been bestowed upon us by Spirit which are to be utilized to help us achieve our Soul's Mission and Purpose in the fulfillment of the Divine Plan. When these gifts are consciously known and developed in conjunction with the awareness of our Soul's Ray, our consciousness can expand exponentially. The knowledge of these gifts is an important component to incorporate when trying to function as a Sovereign Soul that is dedicated to accomplishing the dreams and desires of our Creator for us. The Spiritual Gifts are tools that can be utilized to help us achieve our Soul's Mission and Purpose when used with the knowledge and understanding of our Soul Ray.

To help facilitate an individual in the discovery of their Spiritual Gifts, I utilize a variety of approaches. First, I have another assessment questionnaire which I have them complete as an objective tool to assist them in determining their Spiritual Gifts. In addition, I have found it helpful for their understanding and faith in the gifts which are revealed through the questionnaire to employ a subjective determination through interviewing and energy work.

Some of the gifts that we identify through these exercises include: prophecy; teaching; wisdom; knowledge; exhortation; discernment; giving; helps; mercy; missionary; evangelism; hospitality; faith; leadership; administration; suffering; healings; prayer-praise language;

interpretation of languages; apostleship; singleness; intercessory prayer; martyrdom; service; spirit-music; craftsmanship; exorcism; battle; humor; miracles; voluntary poverty; pastoring.

Another tool I use to assist those who want to achieve maximum consciousness growth is through the use of biofeedback. The reason for this approach is that I have found this tool to be tremendously helpful in uncovering and addressing obstacles/blocks that exist for those upon the path of soul liberation. Through its utilization, I am able to help the client understand the stressors that they have that are holding them back, and I can lead them to the resolution of these blocks and obstacles through an individually tailored program to address them.

Lastly, in terms of the resources that I incorporate, I teach the Science and Evolution of the Soul through "The Universal Life-Light Academy"; an Esoteric Wisdom Mystery School that can be found at www.tulaesotericwisdom.com. Through this website, I provide introductory classes on the Ancient Wisdom Teachings which have been given to us as a guide to lead us towards understanding who we are as Sovereign Souls, the Design of Creation, and how we as Divine, Sovereign Beings evolve. In addition, I am writing a series of books which will begin to be released in 2019 called: *The Tapestry of the Soul & Its Evolution: A Guide to Mastering the Shift of the Ages* which will cover these topics as well.

In summary, I believe we've been given an opportunity to spread our wings and rise like the Phoenix as Divine Beings – and the time to begin taking flight is now! To accomplish this, we need to have a basic understanding of who we are as spiritual beings – which means connecting to our soul in the most powerful and effective ways that we can. As a Soul Liberation Coach, I am honored to assist my fellow brothers and sisters in their journey of accomplishing this. It is time for the liberation of each and every human soul. The course is through recognition of our Divine Sovereignty as well as the pursuit of the knowledge and understanding of this and the reality of the Divine Plan.

9

CONQUERING GLOBAL MARKETS

Taking Your Message International

By
Carmen Ring

6 AM. Amsterdam. My alarm goes off. *Cows, tractors, jail. Les vaches, les machines, le prison. Vaci, tractoare, închisoare.* These words fly through my eleven-year-old brain as I make the superhuman effort of getting out of bed to start another long day in a Dutch prison, where I would translate agricultural regulations for a delegation of prison directors from around Europe.

Fast forward 18 years.

6 AM. New York. As I wake up to make a bottle of formula for my newborn baby boy, I keep thinking about *Mr. Right,* and *Mr. Right Now.* These are not easy phrases for translation. While it sounds very funny and catchy in English when Cameron Diaz says it to Selma Blair in *The Sweetest Thing,* it doesn't make too much sense in Romanian.

Today, Hollywood productions are my second favorite projects to work on. And my absolute favorite clients are entrepreneurs who run international businesses, charities, or global causes. My name is Carmen Ring, and I'm the founder and owner of SpeaxAll Incorporated; the company I started to help entrepreneurs and other organizations in taking their message and business into international markets. If you own a business and you are good at what you do, I believe it's your duty to make your talent available worldwide. If your products or services can benefit people globally, then it's your duty to offer and deliver them to those who need them; it would be selfish not to. Besides, your business can only grow so much if you only serve the same people in the same community.

One of my friends and mentors, billionaire Marquis Jet founder, Jesse Itzler, often says, "You haven't come this far to only come this far." It makes so much sense: you've worked your tail off to grow this business to where you are today – why would you stop here? Just go global. Right now, all of your prospects are being emailed every week by at least three of your competitors. And in the meantime, there's a hot market out there, eager for your services; but they currently do not have access to you because of a language barrier.

US companies recognized this need and fully committed to engaging these consumers. Almost a quarter of the marketing budget of the most famous brands goes to Spanish or bilingual media. Five years ago, the number of companies approaching this strategy was less than 30, and now it's over 70. Do you notice the trend? Where do you stand? Now is the time for you to claim your share of the international market.

For as long as I can remember, I was fascinated by different languages and cultures. I was about five years old when I became fluent in Spanish only by watching South American soap operas. I'll give credit here to the Romanian entertainment industry, which back then kept all productions in their original languages and just added captioning. So, pretty much every time I turned on the TV, I was exposed to a foreign language. By age six, my mom hired a private French tutor for me, and a few years later it was obvious I had a thing for languages; it was very easy for me to learn them and I was enjoying it more than anything. Every two to three years I would add a new language to my brain portfolio. Over the years, I studied Italian, German, Japanese, Dutch, Mandarin, Cantonese, Portuguese, and Russian. Today I'm perfectly fluent in four languages, and I have a good understanding of many others.

When I was ten, I started joining my mother at meetings and conferences to translate for her because she never learned any other language. For over 13 years, my mother was head of the only prison for women in Romania and for a short period of time, she was in charge of all prisons in Romania. She was often invited to international conferences, or she would host international delegations herself. Needless to say, many people were impressed by my skills and level of maturity at such a young age.

One man in particular, who worked with the agriculture department of the Dutch government, became a friend and mentor of mine for years to come. When I went to college, he offered me an intern position in his company OGIN Biogas BV in the Netherlands. I was in his company for almost 10 years, taking care of pretty much all things international marketing; from websites, brochures, and presentations in different languages, to international sales, foreign market research, and global client connections.

It was the job of my dreams. I was constantly traveling, meeting new people, and networking in different languages; but I eventually decided that I wanted a family and children. The airport lifestyle just didn't match my idea of raising kids, so I officially resigned from OGIN Biogas in 2014. I decided to start my own translation company that I could run from home while also spending a lot of quality time with my newly started family.

Business built up pretty fast. I was already in touch with a large network of international companies; it didn't take me long to let them know of my new venture and gain them as clients. Aside from them, my two biggest resources for leads were LinkedIn and Craigslist. From custom protections to hospitals, luxurious resorts to financial institutions, my clients continued keeping me captivated with unique stories and situations. After a couple years of translating in every field you can imagine – law, health, education, weddings, adoption, and so many others – I found my sweet spot, my niche; a target audience that brings song to my heart: celebrities and celebrity-status entrepreneurs.

I remember one of the key moments that inspired me to choose this sphere. I was in San Diego, California at T. Harv Eker's 60th birthday party. In his office, he showed me a large shelf with his bestseller book, *Secrets of the Millionaire Mind*, translated into over 30 languages. I pulled out the Romanian version, and I asked him if he knew which language it was. A little amused and totally honest, he said, "No idea."

How great is that? How wonderful to be able to serve people beyond a language barrier. If by any chance you haven't read Eker's book yet, I obviously suggest you do. I actually read it for the first time in Romanian. There's so much value in it and thank God almost everyone in this world can have access to it. I've heard hundreds of stories on how the information in that book changed and even saved people's lives.

I decided to work primarily with celebrities and celebrity-status entrepreneurs because they have a large impact. They can touch millions of lives, and I want to help them accomplish even more by taking their message international. By celebrity-status entrepreneurs, I mean the entrepreneurs who are clear on their message and ideal client. They are committed to the growth of their business and have a vision of serving more and more people because they believe their product or service can make the world a better place. They are already serving clients on their local market and are now ready to replicate their success in new, foreign markets; the only obstacle they have now is how to do it.

This is where my simple, three-step system comes in. However, before we go into this, we need to ensure you have a product that can be taken internationally. So, keep in mind the big vision. Can we actually make your gifts available to everyone? That means your gift may have to be delivered by someone other than you. I know this might sound scary; especially so when I work with coaches. I hear this very often, "But Carmen, I am my business. My clients hire me because of me. I work with them one-on-one. I personalize my coaching based on their needs." That's very nice and flattering; but if you want to expand your impact, you must give up some of this handholding of your clients.

There are only 24 hours in a day, so when it comes to working one-on-one, there's only so many people you can talk to at that time. So, think big. Think leverage. Think franchise-style. You can hire and train people to be you. And some of them might turn out even better than you at certain aspects. It all comes down to creating a system; one that can be delivered without you. You can put your expertise into a product and then if the user needs additional support to use the product, you can hire one, a few, or even 20 assistants who speak any language you want.

As an example, my husband owns an outdoor adventure camp in New York (Ring Homestead Camp), where he hosts hundreds of team building and personal growth events. We also develop and create leadership programs around the world – working closely with T. Harv Eker and his company. While the original programs were designed in English, we have students who don't speak English. We use live interpreters. Any students who need translation will wear headphones, and the interpreters will communicate through these, but there are times during certain experiential activities when headphones are not an option; we might go out in the woods or on top of a mountain. Still, even when there's no technology involved, it can be done.

I'm giving this example because a lot of people say, "You don't know my business. My business cannot be done via an assistant to run without me in different languages." But to this, I can say, "Yes, it can." We've been creating this kind of programs for over 15 years, and I've been there live interpreting. Sometimes there's a small group of people (five or six participants), and they have a task to solve in a limited time. Not two people in that group speak the same language, but they can still make it happen because we put a system in place – one involving signs and nonverbal communication. Everything can be put in a system; it just might take more creativity based on the kind of business you are running.

Creating a Product

As my example has shown how a business can be put into a product, let's go to the step-by-step system to actually do that.

1. Choose your format
2. Choose a name
3. Create content
4. Create a call to action

Step 1 – Choosing your Format

Eventually, you will have many formats, many types of products, and you can always change the way you deliver or charge for them. I'll just give you a quick guide to get you started. During this step, keep it simple; you will improve and develop it later.

The first most basic format you can choose is a webinar; usually 30-45 minutes long. This is the main tool for promotion and generating leads for your business – the more energetic, colorful, and educational, the better. These are free for the prospect, and they end with a call to action to buy something.

Another format is a 60-90-page workbook. Don't get scared; I'll explain why it's so long. These won't take you forever to build. It's a paid product, and it's designed to offer support and accountability on a long-term basis. Ideally, the user must fill one page per day. The reason it's 60-90 days is that no real change can happen in a very short time. By staying on track for two to three months, the users can create a new habit, which encourages change.

Another product you can create is an audio. This should be 45 minutes to an hour long. Again, it's a paid product. You can have as many recordings as you want. You can get them by recording calls with existing clients, or you can record specifically training to sell them. They can be educational, coaching, training, etc. It's designed to be listened to while driving, flying or exercising. So, ideally the audience doesn't need a pen or paper, or any other object to go through this training. They have the workbook for when you have them doing homework.

Step 2 – Choose a Name

Using numbers in your title is a great idea because it tells people what to expect and how to measure their journey. Guides and how-to titles are very attractive because they are practical. Keep in mind; you want to solve a clear problem that your prospects have. Some examples:

- The five steps to attracting the love of your life
- The seven rules of social media success
- How to lose 20 pounds in 20 days
- The ultimate guide to closing sales.

Step 3 – Create Content

What will you record? What will you present in your webinar? What will you walk the reader through via workbook? The best content you can give is examples and exercises. Are you teaching parenting? If so, include examples of games or routines they can implement with their kids – and as an exercise, challenge them to try a new routine for a week, a month, or even three months.

For example, at one point, my goal was to create better communication and a better relationship with my daughter; she was eight or nine at the time. I told myself that I would start implementing a routine in which every day, at breakfast, I would tell her a funny story from my childhood or from my college years. She loves hearing funny stories about when I was a teenager and a child. I figured that if I told those stories over breakfast, it would start her day with a good, relaxing atmosphere; and my chances of having a better collaboration with her would increase that much higher.

If you create a workbook, you can only write two or three lines per page; your customers need to fill the rest – so it's not that much work for you. If you're a financial coach, you can ask them to write down every day what they spend money on and what percentage of that money will bring a good return on investment. As an expert, you know your stuff better than anyone. I'm confident you can design many exercises like this to create a product. Keep in mind that people learn best by doing. To see a change in their lives, they need to do the work, not you.

Very important to include in your content is an accountability tool. One option is a 30-day calendar so they can check in and update as they go through their days. Another one is a Facebook group where they are encouraged to post every day or every week. Accountability is key to making progress. This is how they can measure their results and see the change or see where they are failing – in which case they can't blame you. They can't say, "Well, the coach is not working." Because you can say, "Show me your accountability. Is it checked every day? Did you do the work every day? Well, if not, this is where you might be failing." This is also to protect yourself from potentially unsatisfied clients.

All you need in your product are some examples, exercises, and accountability. You don't need to create the ultimate, unheard of, incredible product. If you can give people one "a-ha moment" – one big thing, one lesson from your product – they will feel satisfied; they will feel it was worth their time. You don't need to revolutionize anything.

Step 4 – Create a Call to Action

The next step beyond the other three is your call to action. This is where a lot of entrepreneurs stop; they deliver, and then they don't make a further offer – and I personally believe this is so selfish. If the person watched you or worked with you until now it's because they see the value in you; chances are they want more of you. You managed to get in their head and in their heart, so it's not fair to let them down now. Give them a way to continue their journey. Make an offer for further work. You can now offer a group program, a monthly subscription, private coaching, or anything else you see fit.

For example, "If you like my guide on how to create a product from your coaching services, go to www.carmenring.com and schedule a call with me. I can help you create and finalize this product in more than one language and then place them on the market. Make your services available worldwide. Let people have access to your knowledge regardless of where they live or what language they speak. And, of course, get the monetary benefits that come in exchange for your generosity."

Three Steps Across the Globe

Once you have your product and your call to action, now you are truly ready to go international. Now it's time for my three-step system:

1. Translate your core branding materials
2. Create your visual that goes viral
3. Build partnerships with influencers in your market

The first step you want to do is translate your core branding materials. That means your titles and taglines, your bio, testimonials, and your downloadable free gifts; basically, this is your international landing page. And of course, you should translate your signature package, which would be all of the above with bio, testimonials, and the products that you have created. That's your signature package.

The second step is what I call "a visual that goes viral." People respond very well to visuals. So, it can be a short video about your business and how you can help people; share your results in a quick video that once people see, they can't stop thinking about it, and they keep replaying it. When I was working for OGIN Biogas, I designed a picture book which explained highly technical concepts, which are usually not so easy to understand. But because of the pretty format and short text, my book was actually read, and it got me booked as a speaker on several stages in the industry.

The book was completely handmade, with pictures by an artist I knew. Even though the information in it was not for kids – it was all technical, as OGIN Biogas was all about building renewable energy plants – it was put in a very attractive format where people didn't feel like, *Oh, I have to read this whole book?* It was also not a brochure they could just throw away; it was an actual book, and it helped build credibility amongst my clients and prospects.

The third step is building partnerships with influencers in those new markets. Partnering with international influencers will be much easier if you already have a strong position in your local market. You can, of course, connect internationally even if you're not so strong locally, but it can be that much faster and easier if you're already seen as an expert on your local market. As an example, Shanda Sumpter is one of my business mentors, and I personally use her system to quickly and effectively build an audience and position myself as an expert in my initial market.

Another thing you can do to enhance and leverage your effort is getting spiritually aligned with your purpose. There are many teachers and programs offering guidance in this direction. Personally, I recently discovered Metta through a client of mine, Kelly Blaser. I started studying her work for the sole purpose of translating it as she is ready to expand her impact internationally.

One Saturday morning, I was driving back from breakfast with a friend of mine, and I was listening to some audio that's part of Kelly's online program about how to activate Metta in our everyday lives in everything we do. Over the past years, I studied some spirituality and meditation, and I understood how it works; but I never had any big life-changing experience in this field until that morning. I was so overwhelmed by the energy of the audio that I lost control of the wheel and I almost flipped off the road completely. It's hard to explain that feeling. If this was a movie, they would probably show a flow of white fog passing through me.

Less than a week after that, my business grew exponentially. I had clients coming to me out of nowhere; people to whom I had never pitched or sent marketing materials. And another miracle happened in my relationship with my husband (while what I'm about to share might make you laugh, it was a huge deal for us). For over two years, I wanted to redo our kitchen, but my husband didn't see a need to do so. It was an ongoing discussion for years in our house. Well, can you guess what happened after my life-threatening Metta experience with Kelly? All I will say is that I might actually start cooking – that's how much I love my new kitchen.

Kelly is the perfect example of the entrepreneur who used to get paid strictly for her time. Everything she was doing required her to personally be with her clients because she's a licensed psychotherapist and yoga instructor, but she has a vision of sharing her expertise and insight with the whole world. She decided to create a program that can be delivered anytime, anywhere. This was the first step that allowed her to start taking her business international.

Kelly also teaches live retreats, and her vision is to create a certification program so other people can start teaching her retreats for her in more than one language. Here is a perfect example of a big vision. She brought the Metta teaching worldwide when many people didn't know what Metta was. Now is the time to take your share of the international market.

My vision for the next few years is to work with as many celebrities as I can because, again, they are already influencing the market. I want to take the fast way to deliver my talents. My talent is understanding languages and cultures and building international networks. My vision is to grow this business and work with clients like Leonardo DiCaprio Foundation. They have a very clear message about climate change – Leo's vision is truly global. Everybody should care about the environment, and everybody should be concerned.

My goal is to reach millions of people with messages like Leonardo's and get these people involved in such global causes. To do that, the message needs to be adapted to different cultures and different languages. There are a few main areas that generally concern most people: wealth and business, health, spirituality, relationships and the environment. I'm on a mission to work with world leaders in those industries to help them expand their impact and attract many more followers.

If you'd like further information, please go to my website, www. carmenring.com. You can schedule a call with me there. And if you'd like to email me, please do so at carmen@carmenring.com.

10

RESOLUTION

Engaging with and Supporting Children Today

By
Rize McGill

My name is Rize Lamont McGill, and I like to be known as one with the greatest heart and counseling. I've been a teacher and counselor for the last 30 plus years. It's been nothing short of rewarding and a positive experience, and it's been a blessing taking on this work even to the point of implementing additional services on my own.

I attended Arizona State University, where I received my undergrad in physical education. I continued my education by going to Wilmington College and obtaining my dual master's degree in education and special education. Upon graduating Arizona State University, I was going straight into teaching until I took another turn and went into counseling. I was a little saddened by what salary looked like and realized I wanted to make a little more money. I worked two jobs, sometimes three, to make up for some of my loans, and also to develop my skills as a counselor, thinking one day I may become a teacher.

It turned out to be a blessing because once I got into the school where I work now, I had the benefit of helping kids realize behavior was as important as education on the scale. If you are unable to achieve listening because of behavior problems, you'll never get to the lessons at hand. So, it turned out to be a dynamic experience because I was able to implement some of the positive social skills, and conflict resolution skills. I realized that if I wanted to gain any of my students' attention, it would be helpful by demonstrating the importance of listening and then the purpose of learning. I worked across the board: elementary, middle school, and high school.

In counseling, I created a stress management program. The benefits of getting my certification in hypnosis and stress management allowed me to create a video where it included going out to various countries and creating relaxation; from hot air balloons to time spent with animals, and soft and serene environments where there were babbling brooks and various ducks, geese that were landing – it was very beautiful. I also made an audio tape where I would describe various methods to achieve stress reduction, positive thinking, achieving sleep, and increasing memory skills.

It seemed like I had a pattern where not only as a counselor I used that to help students, particularly young teens, develop a stress management program for themselves through positive self-hypnosis, but to think differently and to think positively, and that included conflict resolution skills. Also, when I got into teaching, I began working with kindergartners, which was quite a positive and rewarding experience – teaching them how to read, as well as the methods that I've learned through obtaining my master's degree which I implemented a few years later. I realized that students with learning disabilities were struggling with all of my materials. I started creating visuals, drawings, and demonstrations to achieve further understanding for them, through each of the various modalities that children learn to retain information: by way of what they hear, what they see, what they touch, and sometimes I would even create some treats for what they taste. I was on all cylinders for them to achieve their knowledge and retention through reading.

Also, upon the later years, I've created an anti-bullying program. This involved making 3-D characters, putting them in a situation where they must solve problems, and then have in one way or another, conflict resolution. Many of the characters' successes were based upon what I could see working with my students. The rewards were visible in their ability to read as well as maintain a sense of responsibility through inclusion socially and what they were able to accomplish as a responsible young teen.

The Power of Support

In terms of taking all those years of what was working, what was successful, I also researched and described it by writing a book, *Can't Stop Crying*. It was about a small youth who encourages everyone he meets, and then along the way, he's followed by a bully. This bully creates this idea that because of the youth's success, socially, he must be some sort of sorcerer. The encourager didn't realize he was followed by this bully. Along the way, he's made a lot of friends, and he eventually meets an angel who needs his help. The angel calls upon him, the encourager, to help save the world – which involves rescuing a princess.

So, the book is filled with tons of positive support, social skills, and also both conflict resolution skills and confidence building. I wrote the book to support what it's like for teens that are dealing with areas of bullying across this nation, which became a big concern. Bullying itself motivated me to write this book, and it's to the point where it creates a sense of helplessness for many of the families involved. It's overwhelming in schools as are the fights that occur due to poor social skills and a host of adversity currently brewing in the US.

I was also at the point where all the successes further enhanced my mission because I had decided to make and free up a lot of time so that I could create, through this book, some speaking event workshops as well as a team of actors on a professional level. This team would then further display what conflict resolution, and social skills look like, and then act out these stories by way of a play, TV shows, through social media or speaking events. So, with the success that I was able to achieve, I realized that there's a learning modality that plays quite a critical role in the educational concepts to the point where I began to research some of the most influential people today, or throughout history – such as the educator, Benjamin Bloom, and his taxonomy through educational acceptance.

In the 1960's, Bloom was able to describe educating youth, and what I've gotten out of it not only is his style and his system of what works, it can also further enhance building positive relationships of trust and social bonds between peers – as well as bonds between students and teachers. Bloom challenges the freedom of what thought and examination mean because we know that teens are constantly trying to create a sense of independence. His style involves (A) putting their thoughts together to form a whole, and (B) through education and through design, the freedom to improvise by what they're able to implement by evaluating their ideas, and then (C) the analysis of one another in groups, as well as the analysis of the materials and concepts. Aspects of organizing structure are then further understood, and their only responsibility is to then make it understood among their peers.

Think about children with learning disabilities. They cannot learn simply through pencil and paper. Bloom's style allows these teens to be creative, to use skills, their God-given gifts on the level of presentation, and then through special needs, they can use their creative expression. If they're not able to write, they can say it and be graded as such, and then apply the concepts or compare it to real life situations – which is part of Bloom's taxonomy. They can solve how they see it graded through a point system of what they're able to create. If they're able to create how they understand a new term of any type of research on the individual, they can present it in their own words. This is invaluable because their retention level increases, this goes into how they're remembering and describing it to others.

When it came to creating my own books – and all my years of working with teens and children – while I was finding a ton of success, I wondered if people were underestimating how bullying can be just far too much of what's going on in their communities. Some people seem to accept it as some specific way of life; it very much is not. The repercussions of bullying and, not to mention, violence and abuse that goes on in the home does warrant major concern. All of us should take part in creating more of an environment wherein each of us is actively engaging and implementing support, patience, and modeling responsibility for our teens. They are our future, and how we should leave more support and encouragement so that they can eventually give all the positives, love, and support to their own children.

Some children turn to suicide, dying alone because of the various forms of bullying and neglect. That's the worst case, but no child should be left without some type of support. If you identify as the teacher, that child is sitting in the back of your room because of their skill level, and because of their fear, they are acting out because they don't want their peers to know their level of education, abuse, or neglect. These types of scenarios are real, and this continues on a level that inspires me to keep working hard on my contribution to help and build our children in our society. It's a responsibility for us all.

Sometimes when I've witnessed students in a group, I'd hear them talking and suddenly, because of whatever someone just said, their voices would get louder. Sometimes there's also a grouping that goes on by the peers involved, inciting words like "Fight, fight, fight," when it could've been an easy, solvable resolution based on a little reflection, and a little bit of time; in other words, if whoever triggered the other would simply apologize. Because of pressure from their peers, two people accidentally facing each other are now faced with changing their mood. They become defensive as the hands go up and people incite this violence because of these added triggers. Someone as a professional and/or themselves could develop these social skills to be a voice saying, "No there will be no fight, and this was an accident."

These are simple techniques where these students and children, between the community and in schools, could develop and realize that they can empower themselves and not give into peer pressure. There are real techniques, and we only need to understand the development of children, how they are raised, and our role as adults. When we bring a child into this world, there's a ton of bonding that goes on at home. Some parents do realize, and others could use more education to realize how they can empower themselves through their own nature by taking on the responsibility of tending to their child; feeding, changing, cleaning, bathing, adhering to time available for being there socially, and modeling communication skills.

There's tons of study that shows if a parent doesn't have any expression or continues to neglect their child, there's a disconnect. In many cases, caregivers already created an enormous amount of bonding with their child through years of being their parent. It's just now when these teens start to enter their age of adolescence; there's an adjustment where the parent no longer tends to their child like in the days when they were raising a baby. Now it becomes staying actively involved in different programs where the parent's role is now in the way of facilitator, providing education, support, and some of the experiences that they had at work or with the family that raised them.

Creating a support group for that teen will create enormous value. When the teen is left among their own peers, they're filled with lots of decisions to experience and make that work from the bonding built all along all the modeling that also came from the parent(s). Yet, still there's the challenge of fitting in which students tend to face; that seeking approval between their peers is pretty powerful. Positive developments don't necessarily happen through parental guidance alone, although awareness is very important. It also comes from all the professionals, all the people that engage in that child's life. If there was any history of abuse or neglect, these behaviors would multiply when the child gets to school; and, even though that child might be responsible at home, they might still have behavioral problems at school.

An Embracing Gift

This is the message I told myself in the mirror at a very young age (after feeling the hot-iron that made its way to me from a family of six): We all have a gift from above that is set before birth to connect, inspire, teach, help others, and share as it guides you onto a path to grow and flourish on an amazing journey and successful future! Our gift is a natural sense, easy and enjoyable, an instinctive quest like quenching thirst. It shows up like desirable free time, revitalizing your energy and spirit, as it connects with others and others connect with you! Other people will be dialed in as you hear sounds of value, appreciation, and gratitude!

If you don't know what your gift is, ask a friend, relative, or someone you trust. Once you discover your gift, keep your focus and encourage others to do the same through kindness along the way. There will be obstructions like debris, rocks, branches, sticks, with hints of old relics as others are also learning their way to rise to the mountain of success through discovery. A way to know whether there are any obstructions from friends, associates, relatives, and others is whether or not they are encouraging you to stay on your path to success.

Pay attention to those who are modeling success, like people who have been with you through rough times. Name those people in your mind such as your mother (like mine) and ask questions like who, what, where, and how. Keep an open mind, and do not be closed to ambitious people with similar interests to your own. You will realize their effect through your senses – such as listening to amazing hero-like qualities from others that uplift and cause you to feel positive energy, chemistry, and goosebumps of magnetic, electrical enthusiasm.

Saying, "No!" to a friend is a must sometimes, and if they value your friendship, it is respected especially when they motion a negative choice. You are not alone, so return gratitude and encouragement, and extend where they can stay on their path, depart gradually, and stay on yours! Later, they will appreciate you once they come to their senses. These friendships are long-lasting because they will be a leader for you, should you fall off your glorious path, they will do their best to return you to it!

So, it comes down to bonding and creating a level of communication for the teacher, communication for any relatives involved in the positive sense for the child, between all adults, coaches, care workers, and peers involved in their life that also play a role. There's a team, so to speak, that can surround this youth with a sense of inclusion and self-worth so that the students struggling with at-risk behavior, or any child can blossom and realize their potential.

The benefit that comes with paying attention (as a parent, a teacher, or anyone involved) is that you can then help the child on the path and guide them to their purpose and their gift. I believe it's important that every child has a gift – a gift from God that comes by what they did growing up, the quality time spent with building blocks or recognizing shapes, numbers, colors, through games, their free time, or their skills. Finding their gift is vital for growth. The various areas of coordination and quality time socially play a role in showing that child (as a parent) what works and what they seem to be attracted to, and then putting that child on their path so they can further realize their potential, guiding them into an amazing life, to see the world and have an amazing job or career because of it.

Another point that I want to make is that there has been an enormous number of killings, shootings, and attacks happening today. All of the threats, beatings, fights, and lack of direction are exhausting many communities, and the lack of communication between parents and teachers are the result of poor continuity and leadership. Any improvement will take the entire community embracing or engaging so that the child can fill their role – and having that child practice their role, in the case of various siblings. For example, the oldest child, or the middle child, by order of the oldest child, can gain a sense of responsibility through direction which the parent can provide. All this take is practicing consistency, describing the rules, and giving the child their chores, a sense of responsibility, and (if applicable) their allowance. That way, they can feel the value.

Keep in mind, children will make mistakes. By explaining the purpose and the reason for the mistakes that were made, they can understand and explain it to their younger sibling(s) who will then learn from their older sibling, receiving guidance and direction. This creates bonding which is invaluable. Some of the effects are long-term, so this can play an amazing role for any child to rise and become part of a change within a thriving community.

These children are our responsibility in all communities and on all levels. Abuse and treatment that children experience throughout school and within all communities, not to mention at home, those forms of neglect and/or sexual abuse are happening at alarming rates. Today, the statistics are staggering as 6 out of 10 children report forms of bullying in schools nationally. In the average of 20 states, there are 17 children per 1,000 suicides in these rural areas, and those children were ignored. With that in mind, as a professional, I put in 110%, working late hours. I put in tons of work throughout my pattern of working with teens, and even adults for that matter, as well as providing parental support and maintaining that work. This is why I started creating characters to describe what it's like to interact, and what it's like to actually put a team together. I can create a play, a show, or some real-life people to demonstrate how easy that can be. I can illustrate how a community can work as heroes, guiding, showing patience, and demonstrating what works by simply modeling ourselves through ethics – as leaders and as essential kings, queens, princesses, and princes.

Too often, these kids see a lot of negatives, and they model themselves from that. Even though they're in their worst behavior, they still see us as responsible adults. They will quickly label adults as a non-provider or someone who doesn't care, and it takes longer to change their thinking once we lose them as models and leaders. With that in mind again, I have worked many hours creating these characters. I put together a ton of visuals paired with my reading program.

We Are Not Alone

One night, I worked very late, and it didn't feel any different than the other nights of my regular job; but then creating these characters in those late hours brought a sense that I had to come to a stop. I literally felt that I couldn't move or speak, as if God was talking to me and said, "Go to the internet. Just go." I knew at the time that there are other people who are working as hard as I am, that there must be. As I scrolled down many videos, I saw one with a girl who broke her backpack. There were teens who appeared to be hiding, and when she came into the picture with her head held up, these other kids jumped her. They attacked her viscously and began to beat her. Whoever was recording kept the video running, and they were laughing.

That video touched me deeply because that should never happen to any child. The thought that these teens could create a video and feel that they can embarrass and cause terrible effects on this child is hard to conceive. Then, I went to another website, and I found another girl who was running a timeline of the date that she would commit suicide. It was heartbreaking, and I felt like there was nothing I could do. Personally, I've been there before. I've had experiences where I had no help, and I had to search for answers growing up. We all have a purpose and a gift. We do. We all have a sense of responsibility, and that should never happen.

So, we all have a part, and if we allow these kinds of behaviors to be way at the bottom where it's not being discussed, I want to make a point that we all have a sense of responsibility to help the children and model for these children. Once we're all gone, what we were able to teach them and model to them is what they will, in turn, take with them, sharing with their children and their children's children, through how much we've been able to help them. And at that, I just want children to know that they're not alone.

You're not alone. There are people around you, and you can turn to those people that are helpful; someone you trust; someone who models life for you; someone who cares about what you do and where you go. Talk to them, because you're not alone. There are also programs for people that truly want to help you. And I want you to know that I love you, and you don't have to make these decisions, because there is someone out there. If I can't reach you, someone will. So, that's my purpose, and that's my gift to society; it's how I've encouraged everyone I've met. My gift is having the greatest heart and the ability to listen so that children can be encouraged and make decisions that will bring them hope.

If you are interested in having me speak at one of your events, please contact me at RizeMcGill007@gmail.com, or visit my website, www. RizeMcgill.com. At my website, you will also find materials for the programs I've mentioned in this chapter. I am grateful to be part of a team of amazing authors, and I hope you find them as inspiring as I do. God bless!

11

THE WILDEST DESERT POPPY

Perfume is the Most Intense Form of Memory

By
Sharon Farsijani

My name is Shaghayegh, and I go by Sharon. My company's name is Desert35. We're a perfume company, and we customize scents for weddings, special occasions, and individuals. Who I am, really goes back to how I was raised. I grew up in Bensonhurst, Brooklyn, NY. When I was at the very tender age of sixteen, my father decided to move back to our country, which is Iran. While I was raised in NYC, I was actually born in Tehran; I am an Iranian-American. Returning to Iran was a complete culture shock from every angle you could possibly imagine: social, work, school, etc. I didn't even know who I was. My family is very Persian, and I was very white and American in my own sense; so, I felt very, very misunderstood and out of place.

From that time to now, I've launched my own company, I'm an entrepreneur, and I'm a super-duper big advocate of helping women and teenagers (especially young women) understand their full potential. I want to help them use their potential to really create whatever career and/or intention they have for themselves. I want to empower people. I want to help people grow. Right now, my company is growing, and I am growing alongside it – that's the greatest aspect of the process.

Nonetheless, my journey truly began when my father took me back to Iran. When the plane landed, I glued myself to that seat, and I did not want to step into that airport. I was no longer in Coney Island; I saw people outside in coats and burkinis. My father enrolled me in an international school where I was with girls of the same kind of background as myself. We all felt very safe at school; but whenever I left that campus, *Oh God*, I felt like a lost taxi driver wherever I went – it was just a maze for me. Still, it was with that black and white contrast that I really started growing as a teenager.

Eventually, because of my great communication skills, my energy, and my camera presence, I was discovered and hired to be an editor first, then a reporter, and then an evening news anchor at IRINN, in the English News Section – which is basically the equivalent to CNN in the US, or the BBC in the UK. While working in the Iranian news channel, I didn't quite fit in, *Of course*. Still, because I was so fluent in English, and I had high energy as well as good interpersonal/ communication skills, I quickly went up the ladder. Then, I was terminated after four years.

The main reasons for the termination were my open-toed shoes, my perfume, and my plucked eyebrows. It was the whole religious human resource aspect of the company that hit me at age 22, and I really went down a rabbit hole because of it. I didn't really fit in with the whole Islamic part of the Federal News Agency in Iran, which was okay; but, that really hurt me, and it really made me slide downhill – taking with it all of the energy with which I began. It left me in tears, and I cried for a whole week until there really were no more tears left to cry.

I went into an emotional coma that week, and this was at a time just before being hired by Channel 4, after working for Channel 6. I was a game show host for Channel 4, and we also had a late-night TV show which I co-hosted. Before working with Channel 4, I begged my parents, "Please take me back to where I call home, to where I don't feel out of place, to where I won't walk somewhere and feel like I'm something different." I felt like an alien, really. And soon, we did return to the United States. Mind you, when I came back, I was completely broken; I had a complete sense of identity loss.

I'm a very proud Iranian-American, and I say that with pride. Yes, 50% of me is white; I grew up here; I went to Elementary School and Junior High School. However, 50% of the blood in my veins is Iranian, so I kind of have both elements. Nonetheless, culturally, I was very lost when I was in Iran, and then when I came back, again there was another sense of loss.

Upon My Return...

I picked myself up rather quickly. I went to school. I got my degree. With me, everything is backward. First, I get the job, and then I get the degree. I worked in broadcasting when I was in Iran, and then after I returned to the US, I got my Broadcast Journalism degree. I was soon randomly hired by Lehman Bros. Lehman went bankrupt, as everybody might know; but while I was there, I decided to pursue my MBA as opposed to journalism. This decision took me to Paris and Buenos Aires. When I came back, I graduated, and then I wanted to open my first business, which was a coffee shop in Santa Monica.

One of my "coffee-shop" investors turned out to be a very good publisher, and he helped me publish my first book, which was really just a book of poetry. Because I was self-published, I set up my own book tour; I organized it single-handedly, calling coffee shops across Chicago, New York, and New Jersey, requesting an hour where I could bring a table for my books, and possibly do a little speech regarding what the book is. With the help of friends and family, we managed to get some sales.

At that time, I had just graduated from Pepperdine University in Malibu. I soon decided to write my second book, and through that project, I wanted to help teenagers who had a similar upbringing; who were brought up here – especially in a place like Brooklyn, super rebellious and opinionated – and were then taken back to Iran. I wanted to create an outlet for them to express themselves and really avoid feeling the way I felt when I was in Iran. And, I also wanted people to know what really goes on with teenagers such as me and how much of a culture shock it is.

While I was writing that second book, I had no compass and no direction; but having neither of those things actually is a direction, even though there are no apparent answers. Being very spiritual, I would meditate every day; *I can only see 200 meters in front of me. I would say to myself, I know there is something at the end of the road for me, but just the fact that I don't see it doesn't mean it doesn't exist*, and that would be my goal and objective.

So, I knew that I was extremely lost and headed on the unpredictable path of the unknown – which is the beginning of an entrepreneurial journey; you just know that you want to do something, or sometimes you know, and you have a product, and you want to do something with it. For me, it wasn't even about a product – I didn't even have one; I just wanted to express myself. After exploring the possibilities throughout January, within that confusion (which is a compass within itself), I started to understand that I was opening to the world of scents, and this eventually led me to launch Desert35 Fragrances.

Long story short, I came to New York to get the same vibe as I had growing up in Brooklyn, in order to finish writing my second book. After going through so many different hats in various companies, the last one that I parted ways with was Martha Stewart Omnimedia (MSLO). I left when they were bought out by a private equity; at that point, I knew that I wanted to do something with my life, rather than just simply being employed by someone, and getting a regular paycheck. I knew I had this huge potential in me that was just ready to be awakened.

Every day I stepped onto the subway or hopped on the bus, I saw people who were just trying to make a living. I would think to myself, *what about trying to make a life? What about really smiling and getting that paycheck? What about loving what you do?* I took a moment to myself, and I started thinking. *All right, who am I? How can I discover this?* After

I finished and published my second book (which is currently in pre-production for a film adaptation), I went to a couple of networking events where I met some people and found new ideas.

I began experimenting with perfumes. I remember making twelve categories about the different perfumes that expressed different aspects of myself; the Catherine Zeta-Jones in *Oceans 12* in me; the Meg Ryan in *Sleepless in Seattle* in me; the Angelina Jolie in *Tomb Raider* in me. I had these different parts of me which I then made into individual perfumes. In any sense, within that year, all of my experimenting with who I was and my approach to making perfumes all amounted to people liking it and wanting me to make scents for each of them as well.

Creating Desert35

. I took my approach, and I made a company out of it. Through my company, people could actually customize personalized perfumes. Further inspiration struck me when one of my friends asked, "Why don't you make the perfume gifts for my wedding with Desert35?" And, that started a whole new chapter. One thing led to the other, and we officially started offering services to weddings and special events. Since then, the company's really taken off.

When my business was just starting, I began with the thought, *oh my God, I need money for this. I need money for that.* Without a job, I spent all my savings (around $15K- $16K) on an app developer. And then, when the developer finished, I got the codes back and none of it was usable. I paid $35 to make the site myself, and right now, today, I'm using that $35 website; and I'm not using the batch of codes collecting cobwebs in a folder in my Mac; the codes for which I paid nearly $16K a complete waste.

So, that was my first lesson, and now I share it with the world: you don't need a lot of money to start a business. I built my site for $35. Today, it's fully functioning and running the whole company; whereas I went into debt, using my savings to compensate the app developer for a bunch of codes that really aren't usable.

Once I moved past those codes, I needed a new job in order for Desert35 to start flying, to spread its wings and become the butterfly that it is today. As I began searching for work, I was groaning within myself, *Oh my God. Man, I have to get a part-time job in order to help Desert35 grow*; but I was unaware that really, those full-time jobs and the part-time ones that followed were helping me grow as an individual from a management perspective.

It's really cool how everything – the black and white of Iran, the difficulties that I went through when I went there and came back, the challenges with my first book and trying to make the second – all of this has now interconnected and helped me build a business. My path helped me grow as a person, and that's what I value ... personal growth. Today, if anything bad happens, or if something that I think is bad happens, I know that it's really an opportunity in disguise.

If there's anything that I need to convey to anybody on an interpersonal level, it's that you should be yourself. Be unafraid. If you're Iranian, be Iranian. If you're American, be American. Be you no matter whom you're talking to, because only the truth shines, and your authenticity will bring out the best. Also, it's important to really love yourself – to know your full potential, that you're capable – and to really have a sense of gratitude for anything that happens along your route. On a realistic level, when you step into the society, it's important to welcome the lens that every challenge is actually an opportunity dressed as a challenge – it's all about perception.

My passion for being who I was led me to develop Desert35 because if I pretended that I wanted to be a managing director or a CEO somewhere, just for the sake of that title, believe me, I would not be happy. I reflect on myself. I meditate every day and focus on being grateful for having discovered this love and having had this gratitude along the way. I'm also grateful for the development of this lens that I've received through my experiences. This lens is one that I'm able to put on automatically for Desert35, or for the book, how I want to help people, and how I want to help teenagers.

Everyone is worthy of loving themselves, being persistent (I call it patience with a plan) and having perseverance. If you only knew how many times a door has been closed on me, just because they thought that perfume doesn't really express anything. When we first started Desert35, I went to every single lifestyle place in New York City, telling each of them, "We have a scent. Our scent expresses a lifestyle." We went to gyms. We went to hotels. We did events. And even though I say "we," it was really me, myself, and I. Nobody believed in the idea other than me. We even did speaking engagements, where I'd say, "This is a perfume, and if you mix sandalwood with oud, it could bring out the sensual side of you." These worked especially well when we did it in gyms and people leaving the locker-room after showering. After speaking with us and smelling some of our perfume, they'd say, "Oh, this is so cool, because now I feel something. My mood changes."

We wanted to educate people as to how scent can impact your lifestyle and your mood. My entire experience added up to me having this pool of knowledge, and then using it to help my friend with her wedding; making scents as favors and gifts for the bride, the bridal parties, their best man, the groomsmen, the mother of the bride, and the groom. We customized everything. We took them through an hour perfume brief, and then we created each of their custom perfumes from scratch (which takes two months in our factory), and then we bottled each scent. We engraved the bottles with the bride and groom's initials as well as their wedding date, and we sent it out to the venue.

In ten years' time, if they wanted to recreate that scent for an anniversary (a birthday, a bar mitzvah, a sweet sixteen), to remember that special day, they just need to contact us, and we can put the formula together again – and bam! It's the best form of memory. It's more powerful than any photograph or video because a scent is really connected to our emotions.

Desert35 has really taken off because we give the gift of memory; we take people down memory lane. We also offer our bespoke (customized) perfume services to individuals. We give them a unique gift to remember their special day; that's how we were built, and that's how much I'm connected to it. I love bringing smiles to my clients. They all love and appreciate their gift. And for me, their smiley faces say it all.

Desert35 Luxury Keepsake Gift Box,
Custom Fragrance, Engraved Bottle

The Reward

On a much deeper level, again, I've grown alongside this baby that I call Desert35. I've grown alongside my book as well. As I was building and building, I reached a point where I started thinking, *oh my God, I'm building. Now that I've created let me give back.* I'm giving back with places that speak to help individuals, through proceeds from Desert35 sales to a charity we support, or sometimes I teach math here and there. I do events on how we can blend scents, and how scents can impact our mood, bring out the sensuous part, bring out the simple part, the natural part, the confident part. Perfume has so many different angles and dimensions, and that's the beauty of it.

What I really want to get across in this chapter is that the process is the reward. It's the most important part of your journey. Listen to the process. Walk to it. Open yourself to it. When the caterpillar becomes a butterfly – Yay! – it's good, it's pretty, and it can fly; but when it's in the cocoon, and it's undergoing a massive transformation, that's the beauty. Once Desert35 cracked its cocoon and became the great company that it is today, the process of that was truly what mattered most to me. So, try to give love to your process. Try to understand it. Try to smile with it. Again, I wasted a lot of money on things that I thought would be profitable to me, like an app developer getting a super awesome website up. Nope, it didn't benefit me at all. And on top of that, I had a hard time asking people for help, not because I was arrogant, but because I would keep thinking, *oh my God, I could do it myself. I should have told myself, No, Sharon…you can't do it yourself, because, in this process, we're all connected. That's why people have different talents. That's why we tag each other to do stuff.* You can't do it all by yourself.

When you ask people for help, you can't have expectations that they'll do it for you. You need to ask politely, and you need to let it open up naturally. If a person is meant to walk on your path, they will; and, if they're not, say, "Thank you," and then focus on gratitude and move on. The idea of moving on is connected to the persistence that I want to instill in others.

The Origins and Future of Desert35

What I really want for Desert35 is for it to be a healthy, successful company. I want to grow. I want to increase my client base. We are currently focused on creating bespoke and custom luxury scents for weddings, special events, and individuals – bringing the beauty of a signature scent to everyone. Just like most products on the shelf – be it tissues, well-designed clothes, inspiring books, or prescription drugs I want my product to have a positive impact and lasting memory for years to come. Specifically, with weddings themselves, if you give it as a gift, it brings a smile to anybody's face – it's called positive fragrance technology.

My company name comes from when I was creating this business; I wanted something that would express who I was, just like the perfume expressed it, so I said, "Okay, it has to be something connected to me." My name, Shaghayegh, in Persian means "wild desert poppy"; a love flower found in the desert. We took the "desert" part of my name's meaning and combined it with my age at the time. As I was 35 years old when I was developing the company, it was officially dubbed: Desert35. The name has nothing to do with perfumes, although we customized our logo to make it connected with the world of scent. Honestly, at the time, I just wanted something that would really help me express myself. In the beginning, I laid everything on the floor of my base studio apartment in NYC. Basically, my apartment was an accumulation of a table, 10,000 cotton balls that I did my experiments with, and videos of famous perfumeries. I wanted to learn everything about the industry. I calendared and attended all of these perfume events in the city so I could try understanding the science of it; at the end of the day, while it's a fashion product, at the beginning of the day, it's still a science.

There's a science for making scents. There are psychological aspects to it, about what you're trying to achieve with every scent. It all started out with a bunch of cotton balls and boxes, and me definitely living on the low – because I thought I had to invest my money in something like an app developer. But then I did a little pilot launch here, a little pilot launch there, and I saw that while I might lose some money along the way, the most important thing I could do was really focus on my goal … on my product.

We also have another platform that we've launched for Desert35, and it's very much connected to my story and my background. It's called The *Poppy* Collection, The Power of Authenticity, and it was inspired by my memoir, *Shaming My Red Lips*. It's about my journey from when the world around me was changing, and also from when I was changing myself. As an Iranian-American born in Iran, raised in Brooklyn, and then forced to relocate back to Iran at the turbulent age of sixteen, in my young mind, there were two suitable reactions: fight or flight. Today, with my new collection, with both the story and emotion that I have expressed through my personal memoir and Desert35 Fragrances, I am sharing my fight for staying true to myself – and that's something every single one of us should be fighting for every single day.

Again, my Iranian name means "wild desert poppy," so each of the blends in my new collection is infused with natural poppy flower oil representing each of the four categories of fragrance, symbolizing various parts of any female's journey of self-discovery. The emotion connected to creating these unique scents fortifies one's belief: being your true authentic self, every day, all day. I share this path of authenticity with these fashionably blended Eau De Parfums named:

- *Poppy* Feminine & Confident
- *Poppy* Feminine & Spicy
- *Poppy* Feminine & Simple
- *Poppy* Feminine & Fearless

Staying true to yourself and standing up for what you believe in – no matter the consequences – is the greatest accomplishment you can hope to achieve. With this collection, I hope to empower others with the passion and limitless strength endured through any female's journey. I want that strength to be conveyed to whoever wears it. The Desert35

Poppy Collection as well as our private blend, Unrestricted, In The Now, will be available at Macy's Galleria, and each blend will be accompanied by a copy of my memoir as of June 2018. All of these blends will also be available on Amazon.com in June as well.

My memoir, *Shaming My Red Lips,* which is the inspiration behind Unrestricted and The *Poppy* Collection

In Closing

Know in your head that this is the nature of development; it's always a work in progress. Even right now – even though I have a great website, good people, someone who produces the product – it's still a work in progress, and that's the beauty of it. We're a butterfly transforming into a bigger butterfly. Personally, I try to keep myself alert and awake every day to the fact that my process is part of my journey. I need to really maintain gratitude. I need to look at everything through the lens of opportunity; even the downs are opportunities – be mindful of them.

When I was trying to get an agent for my book or trying to get some kind of an investment for Desert35, there was surely rejection. Over time, I saw that it was just redirection to a better path. I had stuff printed out around the apartment that reminded me that rejection is just redirection; that it's best to have gratitude.

So, keep on knocking on doors. Know that if you keep on knocking on all of them, one door will eventually open. If someone's asleep, then you keep on knocking. Eventually, they'll wake up, and they'll open the door. And then, they'll either say, "We are not interested," or "Hey, come and have a cup of tea." There's always an opportunity somewhere.

If you want to know more about my company, please visit our website at Desert35.com. There you can read through our scent journal, and you can also purchase our Unrestricted private blend as well as The *Poppy* Collection. If you'd like to contact me for any help, one-on-one, or speaking engagements, please do so at shfarsi.com.

With So Much Gratitude,

Sharon

12

BALANCING THE BAZAAR

A Lifelong Journey through Hospitality

By
Lori McNeil

I grew up in a very strong business family with a strong passion for entrepreneurship, but we didn't call it that at the time. Both of my parents had high energy and creativity for exploring new things and ideas, and they always encouraged my brothers, sisters, and me to not be afraid of trying new things. I love the fact that I was able to grow up in this environment where those things were supported and that my curiosity and my interests were encouraged.

I remember my mom owning several businesses from the time that I was little; including different restaurants as well as real estate. I grew up in an environment where I was able to witness how to approach people and a variety of businesses; all of this led to incredibly strong conflict resolution and problem-solving skills that I still use in my business today. When we were around seven-years-old, my mom showed us how to make barrettes for local Christmas bazaars. I remember getting to explore my crafting and creativity skills with a loom in creating these beautifully-colored barrettes.

In the 70s and 80s, Christmas bazaars were very popular, and many people used them more heavily for their Christmas shopping – and it meant supporting the local economy and local craftsmanship. I got to be a part of that, and it was so fun sitting and making all these different barrettes with different colors of yarn, and different little buttons and accents. Then, I remember bagging them up together in little sandwich bags, putting little price tags on them, and sitting, on many Saturdays… all day long, down at a bazaar. I appreciated my experience there, learning to speak with people, how to talk about pricing, and explaining how everything was made. I was able to really share my interests and my passion through this product that I put a lot of heart and passion into speaking with other people. I learned at a very young age that people want to support you; they want to be a part of your passion and your vision, and they want to understand why certain things are important to you.

Why was I doing this, and why was it so important to me? Well, part of it was that it was just fun, and it was different. More or less, I had my very own little business going when I was only in first and second grade. As a little girl, I was learning all of these really valuable business skills including how much to reinvest into colored yarns and other supplies. Also, I was simultaneously contributing financially to the family. The skills I learned in making all of those barrettes in that bazaar and interacting with my customers have definitely remained with me throughout my entire career.

My parents moved around a lot when I was young, and I remember being so excited each time we moved, as it meant I would get the old checks. They would void all the checks from the previous address, and then I would practice playing business owner, writing out checks the best that I could. Even this simple activity I enjoyed as a young girl, and it has impacted my skill building and mindset for entrepreneurship.

A few years later, I took a lot of those principles and skills and applied them to a new project. I wanted to have a lemonade stand. As many younger kids like to do, especially in the summertime, I wanted to set up a little booth. I had seen other kids doing it before, and I was a customer of theirs. I thought, *Well, this is something that I can definitely do*. I asked my mom, of course, if it was okay. I set up a little stand, and I had my little sign. I had quite a few customers who knew me, who were supporting me. At one point, the business had stopped; but then it dawned on me that in the summertime there were many activities going on and that there were lots of yard sales as well.

Because we were a large family that didn't necessarily have a lot of money, we shopped at yard sales a lot when I was little. Most of my clothes in my younger years were either from garage sales, or they were homemade. I was very familiar with how many yard sales were in my community each summer. It dawned on me that there were a lot of people that did that, just like my family. Other people and families would go from yard sale to yard sale, and in a small town, that was what many people did on weekends. I realized that's where the traffic was on those particular afternoons; there were a lot of people congregating in one place at each sale, or they would have a route that they would follow throughout the community.

I then continued forward with the idea of going to the customer, instead of expecting people to come to me. I didn't necessarily have ads in the paper or big signs around town or anything like that; I would just sit in my yard, and if they saw me, they saw me. So, I realized that if I put in a little more effort and creativity and had a little more courage to go to where the people were, I could potentially make more money. I would contact the homeowners or the people in the community who I already knew, or my friends' parents, asking them if I could set up my lemonade stand in their front yard and just be available for anyone coming to their yard sale. This proved to be incredibly successful.

I was so glad that I had the courage as a third grader to step outside of my comfort zone and try something new. I felt pretty comfortable just trying it and seeing what would happen. It was very, very successful. I then spent the rest of the summer setting up my stand all over town at various yard sales. It was just one more example of not only building those relationships with your customers, but this also gave me more opportunity to have conversations and practice with pricing and upselling.

While I had a price per cup of lemonade, I hadn't originally thought about negotiating for multiple cups in the same family. Would I still charge the same amount per cup, or would I give them a deal if they bought five cups? It really gave me a different opportunity to practice my business skills, ones that I continued to build upon that really helped to lay that foundation throughout the rest of my professional career. To this day, I still stop at lemonade stands to help encourage and support young entrepreneurs.

Leveling Up

When I was eleven, I took a bigger leap of faith. I decided that I wanted to become a business owner a little bit more officially. My younger sister and I had an idea for capitalizing on summer traffic. At the time, we needed money for school clothes and other things that we wanted to buy, and to capitalize; we wanted to set up a hot dog stand.

I remember my mom helped us take over for a hot dog vendor that was retiring – they were selling some of their equipment. We drove up to Washington to take a look at everything; it was in excellent condition, and it had this cute little kind of mural painted on the side of it. *It's perfect!* But the vendor told us that it was $3,500, and that was a ton of money as an eleven-year-old – I had a really hard time fathoming that.

While I was very passionate about the idea, I also had to trust my mom in telling me that while $3,500 seemed like a lot a lot of money, we could earn money back from sales. I trusted my mom's business savvy. She helped us co-sign our first loan so that we could buy this hot dog stand and some equipment to get started.

I'll never forget my mom excusing me from school on the big day. I had a note, and it was all planned in advance. She picked me up from class. She took me home, and I put on the nicest dress that I had with the fanciest little coat that I usually wore to church. She took me to the bank. I had a folder, and I had walked into this bank meeting with many important men – in the eyes of an eleven-year-old. I'd never been into an official boardroom of a bank before. The night before, my mom helped me prepare a one-page proposal. It was all my ideas, but she helped me type it up; a little bit of a budget, an outline, and a little story explaining why I wanted to do this. I made it very personal, and as professional as I knew how at that age.

They all told me, after the fact, that I not only did a great job but that they as a bank were absolutely excited to support my type of business strategy and entrepreneur spirit. They were excited to give me the loan and to support us in our adventure. I was very nervous. I sold my first hot dog, chips, and a drink combo lunch pack for $2. Customers had the choice of sauerkraut, chili, or just ketchup and mustard; but it was all the same price. Once again, I was learning to price in a much different way, and I was learning cost control, how much I needed to sell in order to make a profit and the cheapest place to get my supplies.

My skills were continuing to build on each other. I ended up making my $3,500 back in the first month. *This is super exciting!* That was the most money I had ever earned. Not only was I able to buy school clothes; I was able to participate in more fun summer activities. The next phase was learning and remembering to go where the customers are. I had a very good location for my hot dog stand downtown. In the summer months, there were more people, tourists, different parades, and different activities; this meant more potential customers. I had to remember the strategy that I used with my lemonade stand. I decided that I would again go to where the people were.

I didn't have fancy equipment. My hot dog stand was too heavy to just wheel up and down the sidewalk and the street. So, I took a cardboard box flat that soda pop cans came packaged in – it's about a one by two foot little flat box – I took a bungee cord, and I poked a hole in each side of the box, and I wrapped the bungee cord around the back of my neck so I would have kind of an old-fashioned tray balanced in front of me. I based my design idea off of the vendors at bigger stadium baseball and football games. I loaded up a bunch of different hot dogs and drinks, as much as I could pack onto my platform. I walked up and down the crowd where thousands of people would gather for parades and various activities. I actually sold more doing that than I did in my permanent location, just using the strategy and principles that I had learned when I was in first and second grade with the lemonade stand.

That worked very, very well. It was worth it to me to make several trips up and down the street, back to my cart to reload. It was worth it because I saw a large return on my time investment in doing that. It further reinforced the idea that you give the customer what they want, in a convenient way, because the customers didn't really move from their spot. They were already in their spot, so I would basically do all the work. I would hand it to them, lean over, wait, and leave after the transaction – whatever it took in order to be as convenient for them as possible.

Hospitality

I will always keep these experiences close to my heart from when I was younger, because they became the foundation for my complete state of mind, how I think about business, how I approach relationships, and how I think about customers and products. From that point forward, I truly believed in serving the customer, and I still do. Fast forward another couple of years to when I was thirteen-years-old; I actually had my very first job working for someone else outside of the family. I believed at a very young age that I wanted as much experience as I could get. I had a little bit of experience doing some of my own things, so I wanted to know what it was like to work for someone else and gain new insights and start to fill in some of the gaps in my own thinking.

I started working at a historical lodge as a housekeeper, and I absolutely loved that job. Most people might think that being a housekeeper would be gross or not much fun, a bottom of the totem pole kind of a job; but, it was fun. As it turned out, as a housekeeper, I interacted with customers all the time. I was part of a team that really focused on customer experience. When it came to taking care of the customer and preparing their room, the building, the lobby, and all the pieces as they walked on to the property, I loved knowing that I was a part of their experience – whether it was for the night, a weekend, or a special occasion. I loved being a part of building that memory for people. I loved being a housekeeper.

I also had the option of being a part of many different weddings and special events that actually took place on the property. That's when I really started to create a love and a passion for events and for hospitality as I put some of those pieces together within a specific business niche. I learned so much in working for someone else. I had a great boss, a great supervisor, and a lot of really great memories and great experiences. I was then able to add even more to my mindset, and I continued developing my own practices and my own business philosophies.

Fast forward again to my adult years when I was traveling and teaching internationally in several countries. I started out teaching in elementary and junior high. I traveled with many different teams around the world in order to really go where the people are – once again. I would work in one-room schoolhouses, in small villages, and all over. At the end of a teaching day, I would go out into the community where there were other kids who, for whatever reason, weren't able to be in school that day, and I would teach additional classes. I just kept going to wherever the people were in order to get them what they needed and what they wanted. I continued that strategy again, even internationally as I started my teaching career.

As I continued my teaching career, I became more of a curriculum developer. I would develop workshops, classes, and seminars – taking everything that I had learned over the years with business philosophy, and really coupling that with educational pedagogy. These two worlds really started to come together in a very strong, unique way during my adult years. When I was in my early twenties, these worlds started melding more so than before, and I was able to offer educational opportunities that were intentionally designed to meet specific goals, using the business philosophies that I had already developed.

Within the curriculum I developed from scratch, I'd teach on several different topics. I have developed over 100 different topics and programs within workshops, seminars, conferences, and keynotes. As I teach the importance of servant leadership, I taught not only what this means but what this looks like every day in real business and why it is important. It's important for those in business to understand the whole idea of customer service and hospitality. Customer service is when you offer a service; someone pays you for something, and you offer something in return. Beyond service that is primarily transactional, the difference between hospitality and being a hospitality-minded person is the experience.

It doesn't matter what kind of business yours is; if you're in the business of people, you're in the business of hospitality, because you're trying to build that relationship with people; you're trying to serve them; you're trying to create that experience that hits the emotional feeling which then causes that customer to have a connection with you. You can have a good customer service experience, but it won't necessarily result in an emotional response. In order to really dig deeper as a business, you need to continually evaluate and figure out how you can offer the best experience that results in a necessary emotional connection, resulting in a stronger relationship for both customer loyalty and customer retention. I've seen businesses struggle because they hadn't done a deep enough dive. I've had people tell me, "But Lori, we don't have enough_____," be it staff, resources, time, money, or customers. I always say to that person, "You're actually losing more time and money than you realize by not taking the time to figure this out on a foundational level to be able to launch your business forward in a much stronger direction." I always encourage businesses to figure out the resources needed to figure out how to actually create that time and invest in that time; they're missing out on so much more business growth than they might even realize.

Expanding My Reach

In 2001, I started taking business principles and educational approaches to larger organizations. From 2001 to 2005, I was one of the team trainers for Oregon State Parks (OSP). I did training in customer service, team building, leadership, communication, conflict resolution, and culture in order to help them really develop the overall experience for the customers visiting their parks and the state of Oregon.

I worked independently with a couple of the parks on the east side of the state to really work on these issues. This would lead to stronger experience, reputation, customer loyalty, return guests, and less employee turnover and visitor complaints. It was an amazing experience for me to be able to learn through helping a large organization in this way, getting them to where they wanted to be; and to share in their success stories. Time after time again, as they started to implement the new tools that they were being taught, they experienced massive results.

The last couple of years that I worked with Oregon State Parks, I started implementing one-on-one coaching. I would work with individuals, and we would focus on both personal and professional goals because it's very important that organizations understand how to best support and invest in their team members personally. An individual's personal life, their balance, affects the organization's balance. At one point, I implemented strategies that ended up being invaluable to one park in particular because their team members were able to actually support each other on a personal level.

My strategies led to greater productivity, communication, and overall personal investment in the organization's mission and goals. Their employees started feeling much more valued on a personal level, and this leads to stronger, healthier, teams overall, which in turn, led to stronger customer service and hospitality experiences for the clients/visitors. This concept developed into a special program I use today, which I call, "The 3 Ripples."

I often work with teams in understanding that connection between the personal and professional goal-setting that actually leads to stronger organizations and teams. This is what I've continued developing in my own personal and professional teaching and coaching business. I travel all over the world working with businesses and individuals, and I help them understand that connection between how the individual internally deals with things and how that can affect them professionally as well.

I'm continuing to develop more classes on different topics. I'm diving deeper into further personal coaching and really helping people understand the limiting beliefs behind their actions, and how that's actually holding them back professionally; how it affects the deeper vision for their life personally, and how they can start to move more in that direction with pursuing their personal and professional vision. I want to help people understand the difference between personal and professional goals. I want them to see how these goals lead to one ultimate life vision. I want to show people what's holding them back, how they can be in balance, and get them moving towards the purpose of their overall life. Once I guide someone through that process, a whole new world opens for them along with a whole new level of passion and purpose as they move forward with clarity and a deeper understanding for why they do what they do which ultimately is what drives them. Once I've guided them through the process, they are headed in a much stronger direction personally/professionally for the organization.

I teach and coach anywhere in traditional settings as well as online. I like to work with passionate entrepreneurs, managers, and owners who are serious about working on the internal and external balance of their business, the overall business wellness, and all the different pieces to figure out what they're missing. They don't know what they don't know. I help them tap into the tools and the understanding that they need to figure out how to move forward in a stronger capacity for greater success overall. I help them figure out their mission, their goals, and walk them through that process.

What I do is not just a one-and-done. I also do a lot of keynote speaking and trainings, but I truly believe in the long-term succession planning and accountability. I like to journey alongside businesses and ensure that they are completely set up for long-term success, not just listening to a seminar and then not knowing how to implement the new tools and concepts. The coaching and training programs that I have designed get results. I've spent my life developing my own philosophies, evaluating successful outcomes, witnessing how powerful the results can be for businesses that work with me.

Businesses need to approach this whole process differently and create a different mindset for doing things in new and improved ways than they ever have before. I love helping people and businesses accomplish those goals for greater success. I am an international educator and business coach and helping other people and businesses reach greater levels of success is truly what gets me out of bed in the morning.

My formal education resulted in my MBA, my M.Ed., as well as over 20 specialized certifications. As a lifelong learner, I have taken my entire journey and developed programs that are designed to get results. Over the past 20 years in working with people and businesses globally, I have a proven track record, and I have been featured on NBC, ABC, CBS, and FOX. More details on all my programs and live events can be found on my website. I invite you to visit me at www.lorimcneil.com to see how you can obtain greater levels of success – getting you from wherever you are, to where you want to be!

13

THE POWER OF RESILIENCE

Helping Children Bounce Back and Move Forward

By
Kate Lund

Imagine a little girl ice-skating with a hockey helmet on her head in the days before all kids wore hockey helmets. She hears her peers snicker as she skates by because the helmet looks funny to them, but she needs to wear it due to a serious medical condition. She looks different, and she feels different inside. Her peers act superior because they can skate carefree, without a worry or a cumbersome helmet on their heads.

Now, imagine a little boy on the playground today, in tears because the other kids are making fun of him for rooting for the "wrong" professional sports team. Or, a little girl petrified to read in front of her classmates. She has something called dyslexia, and she can't read as fluently as they can.

These are very real scenarios that play out in our schools each day, scenarios with the potential to impact a child's sense of self and sense of possibility in a way that can spark long-term negative consequences.

Experiences like these can prevent children from ever reaching their true potential. The good news is that we – parents, psychologists, teachers, coaches – can help children to rise above the challenges they face, get in touch with their inherent strengths, and move towards their potential. In short, we can help children to be resilient.

I'm a licensed clinical psychologist, performance coach, and mom. I was also that little girl wearing the hockey helmet, skating along while the other children laughed. The topic of resilience is at the intersection of my life as a child, my work as a psychologist, and my role of mom to 10-year-old twins.

My goal in writing this chapter is to provide an accessible, actionable, and practical roadmap for parents, teachers, and coaches – or anyone interested in building the resilience of their own children, or children they work with.

I was drawn to writing about resilience because I grew up with a medical condition called hydrocephalus, which set me apart from my peers in various ways and got me in touch with a need to bounce back and move forward, despite the setbacks along the way. I was helped in this process by a great support system that allowed me to see the person I was, as opposed to the challenges I happened to have. I came to see and focus on what I could do rather than what I could not do, and that was important. As time passed, I internalized the idea that I could do things. I could do most everything that my peers could do; only a few activities remained challenging, and in the big picture they were no big deal since I could do so much else.

My work as a clinical psychologist in a range of medical school, university, and private practice settings over 15 years has also drawn me to the topic of resilience. My experiences working with children and families to overcome challenges and create a new sense of normal, when things are anything but, have been powerful reminders of how vital it is to develop the skills to conquer challenges early in life and to find ways to not let the challenges define you. Watching my own children grapple with life's trials and tribulations has also contributed to my interest.

While we don't want to negate the reality of challenge in the lives of children – because challenge is an inevitable part of life – we do want to help children focus on the positive. For children, internalizing what they can do, as opposed to what they can't do, is empowering – particularly for kids who happen to face medical, learning, social, or other challenges. Helping children to shift their focus from what is wrong to what is right is extremely important.

It's also important to keep expectations in place for such children, just like it was important for me to have expectations for myself: that I would function fully in all domains of my life – as a member of my family, as a student, and as an athlete. With this approach, I was able to internalize the idea that I could do a lot of the things my friends did. By focusing on those activities rather than what I couldn't do, I was able to develop a positive outlook and an overall sense of self. Ultimately, I gained strength and understanding and emerged better equipped to tackle future challenges.

Bullying and Other Challenges

As a psychologist, I see people overcome challenges and come out stronger on the other side all the time. Inherent in this process is the idea of helping children build on the core principles of resilience, which include skills such as managing emotions, tolerating frustration, problem-solving, developing courage, navigating challenges, and figuring out, "What's another angle I might take? How might I look at this problem differently?" I'm often reminded in this way how powerful and important it is to build the skills of resilience early in life, particularly given the number of stressors (they're everywhere) that kids face today.

Why is resilience so important in helping kids to believe in themselves and maximize potential? Resilience helps kids move through and beyond challenges, no matter what form the challenges take, and we know that today's children face a myriad of challenges across the domains of their lives. Let's look at two examples: bullying and pressure to overachieve.

Bullying is a serious problem for this generation of kids, particularly in the internet age. Cyberbullying is prevalent and invasive. It's insidious, following kids wherever they go; in the classroom, on the playground, at home, and in bed when they're trying to sleep. Bullying in general, whatever form it comes in, can impact every aspect of the child, on every level – including their sense of self, self-esteem, and ability to cope – and has the potential to do significant damage.

The good news is that we can help build resilience on both sides of the bullying equation. We can try to stop children from becoming bullies by helping them to develop a strong social-emotional foundation from the get-go, based on the ability to understand and appreciate differences among themselves and their peers. A strong social-emotional foundation is created by helping kids to develop the skills embedded in emotional intelligence; these skills help kids to accept and embrace individual differences, using what they see as a vehicle for understanding as opposed to a means of ridicule and putting others down. Both as a psychologist and a mom, I believe that this is key to reducing the number of bullying children experience, cyber or otherwise.

Developing a strong social-emotional foundation also helps children who are being bullied to recognize their own strengths and use those strengths to their own benefit. This is not an easy process, but it can be a start for helping children, who are the targets of bullies, to get the upper hand and move beyond the painful experience.

Another important social challenge is the need to succeed at a high level – the need to be the best. This type of pressure can come from parents, teachers, other students, and society in general. For some, this can lead to never feeling good enough; never achieving, never meeting the expectations of themselves or their parents to, for example, get the best grades, be the best in a sport, and win at all costs. These expectations and challenges come at a high cost.

Helping to Build Resilience

How do we help children to become resilient in the face of these and other challenges? First, we need to see children for who they are and not for the challenge they happen to have, or the outcome we want them to achieve. We need to view children as individuals first, and we need to teach them to manage their emotions and tolerate frustration.

Next, we want to help children to navigate friendships and social pressures by helping them to better understand, appreciate, and accept individual differences. The inability to understand how we're different from one another, and how we can bridge those differences, is a big piece of navigating friendships and social pressures, and it's where friendships can really go awry for kids. If that fundamental understanding doesn't exist, friendships can suffer, and that comes with a whole list of additional ramifications.

We also want to help kids to develop the courage to fail and to try again. This involves encouraging them to be able to take risks knowing they can get back up and try again if things don't go right. Related to this is helping children to develop problem-solving skills. Building resilience in children this way helps them to get in touch with their strengths and use them to their advantage. Resilience helps kids to answer the question, "What is possible for me, and what do I need to do to get there?"

How might these challenges play out for kids with underlying differences that could intensify the experience of day-to-day challenges? Specifically, I'm thinking about the children profiled at the beginning of the chapter (the little girl with hydrocephalus, the little girl with the learning disability, dyslexia, and the child who was bullied for wearing the wrong clothes or rooting for the wrong team). For these kids, the challenges are real, just like they are for all kids. The different principles that we're laying out here can help these children to get in touch with their strengths and thrive through and beyond their challenge.

The Toolbox Approach

Let's delve deeper into what we can do as psychologists, parents, educators, and coaches to help kids build resilience and thrive. I like to think in terms of giving kids a toolbox of strategies they can use when faced with situations that require resilience. How can we help kids to develop and use the tools they need? Here are some ideas:

1. Manage emotions and tolerate frustration
2. Navigate friendships and social pressures
3. Develop a sense of focus and attention
4. Develop courage

Manage Emotions and Tolerate Frustration

All kids, regardless of their challenges, will benefit from learning to manage their emotions and tolerate frustration. If children are overwhelmed by emotion, or if they can't tolerate the inevitable frustrations they'll face, they will find it more difficult to get up and move forward following a challenge or setback. In fact, moving forward might be impossible, so this idea is key.

We can teach kids to manage emotions and tolerate frustration by helping them to develop mindfulness skills and the ability to self-regulate. This, in turn, can help them to build resilience to stressors in a way that can be generalized across domains of their life and can, in the long run, make them more resilient to any stressors they face. As a result, performance across the domains of their life will likely improve.

Navigate Friendships and Social Pressures

Kids need to learn how to be a friend, and a good one at that, and they also need to know how to stand up for themselves and their beliefs when friendships go off track. Here, self-awareness and the ability to assess and understand individual differences among peers are at the core.

We teach this through helping kids build the skills inherent in emotional intelligence, with the core skill being the ability to view individual differences with curiosity and understanding, as opposed to ridicule and put-downs. Helping kids understand themselves and how their behavior impacts others (and vice-versa) is a big piece of helping them to feel good about themselves, to be able to get up following a setback, and to be able to move towards their potential.

Develop a Sense of Focus and Attention

The ability to set a goal and to stay focused on reaching it is at the core of a child's ability to work towards their potential; without focus, it's too easy to get off track and stray from the goal and what's really important.

Develop Courage

Kids need to be able to take that first step forward when things are challenging or hard. We can help by encouraging them to take risks and not be afraid to fail. And if things don't work out, we can help them to problem-solve, get back up, and try again from a different angle.

The ability to handle failure is an important piece here because kids often put too much pressure on themselves to be perfect. What this really means is that they give up the opportunity to take chances, to take risks, because they don't want to fail. So, helping them learn that it's okay to fail is important, and so is helping them to manage their expectations for the outcome.

In the big picture, how can we help kids to believe in themselves and what is possible for them? This is actually the ultimate goal for my work and for my practice. We can do this by fostering resilience, by helping kids to push through limits within the context of a supportive backdrop, by helping kids to move through and beyond challenges, and by encouraging them to get back up and try again after a setback.

This process is really at the core of how we learn. It's how we get better at things, and it can help kids to believe in what's possible and understand what's necessary to get there, to achieve, and to live that possibility. In doing all of this (as parents, as psychologists, as teachers, as coaches), we need to provide a supportive structure or scaffold in helping kids to take these risks when things are scary, to move forward despite the fear, knowing that it's always going to be possible to try again.

It's also important to point out to the child when appropriate, "Hey, you did a great job with that. Look at the things that went really well." And then, within that positive framework, suggest in a constructive manner what could be done differently; what might be helpful the next time. This really helps the child to recognize that they have the innate ability to take that first step. It helps the child to imagine what's possible, and to start to understand how to get there.

The Importance of Optimism

A sense of optimism is important for kids. At times, things can feel hopeless, especially for a child facing challenges. These challenges are very real, so we don't want to negate them or downplay them. We want to help kids develop the tools and the skills to manage challenges so they can move forward. Within the context of developing optimism, this means helping children to get in touch with the things that do go well, the things that are good. We want to help them notice where they do have control and help them to take even greater personal responsibility in those places.

Personal responsibility is a very important concept for children. Helping them to get in touch with what they can do to impact their outcome and their situation is a large piece of the optimism equation. We also know that optimism tends to fuel motivation to try new things and to take that step forward when something seems difficult or out of reach. This is particularly important in building confidence because once a child is moving forward, they begin to experience success and no matter how small these might seem, they begin to foster a sense of competence over time.

A can-do attitude goes a long way in building resilience and helps kids master challenges. We need to help kids focus on the idea that,

"Yeah, this might be challenging, but I can do this." At the same time, we want to help them experience and name gratitude each day, as this really helps them to get in touch with the possibilities in their lives and to answer the question, "What is possible for me and what do I need to do to get there?"

This idea is significant because it's easy to just focus on the hard stuff. It's easy to focus on the things that went wrong. It's easy to ignore the good stuff, but this just stalls any momentum a child may have had and hinders them from reaching their potential. The hard experiences are inevitable, so it's important to help kids identify what is going well, what is right about their day, their life, and the bigger picture – as opposed to simply focusing on what's wrong, and what's hard. This can go a long way in helping kids to internalize resilience.

On the subject of optimism, I want to add that it's important to help kids accept and embrace challenge as part of this process. Often, we want to take the easy road; we want to find the shortcut. And, sure, challenge is not necessarily fun, but on some level, it usually presents some sort of opportunity. So, if we can help kids to look at a challenge with curiosity and a "What can I learn from this?" attitude, instead of automatically perceiving it as a big, nasty obstacle, we're helping them to develop resilience and essential skills that they can use across their lives. The second related idea is that of positive self-talk – something that is imperative for all of us, and especially for a child who is facing a challenge. It's easy to start picking ourselves apart when faced with a challenge. We think about what went wrong and what will never go right. It's important to shift this framework and help kids to pick out what did go well in a given situation, despite the challenge. For example, "How did I use a strength that I can use more next time?" Helping kids to identify their own strengths truly helps in fostering gratitude and optimism, and these, in turn, are important in the bigger construct of resilience.

The Long-Term Impact of Resilience

Why is resilience so important for children? Because teaching children the skills early on to bounce back from life's inevitable challenges will make things that much easier for them as teenagers and adults. Helping kids to develop a strong social-emotional foundation, to tolerate frustration and manage emotions, and the other areas discussed, above, are critical. The child who doesn't have these skills will find it harder and harder to get back up following a setback as he moves through life. Developing resilience early helps children to become successful adults by providing the core skills they'll need to move forward despite challenges across their lifetime.

So, what became of those children whose struggles began this chapter? As the girl in the hockey helmet with a serious medical condition, I persevered through some tough times as a child. With the support of my family, close friends, and teachers, I learned early to see myself as the child I was, and not simply as the condition I happened to have. It wasn't easy; in fact, it was hard. Still, I learned to focus on what I could do, as opposed to what I could not do. I then internalized my strengths and used them to work towards my potential, within my own unique context.

With time and a strong foundation in social-emotional understanding and skill-building, that little boy on the playground who was ridiculed because he was rooting for the wrong team was able to develop a sense of resilience and a fuller understanding of his own strengths. This allowed him to ignore the taunts of the other kids and to focus more on his own goals and how he could become stronger.

After a year of tutoring and mindfulness training to better manage her emotions and tolerate the frustration of her reading challenges (along with the encouragement of her family and teacher), the little girl who struggled to read developed the courage to raise her hand and read in front of her class for the first time. She was no longer afraid, and in fact, she felt proud of what she had accomplished. She felt good about herself.

My vision as a psychologist, a coach, and a mom is to help all children to develop resilience early in life, allowing them to maximize their potential within their own unique context. Inherent in this vision is helping children to develop a toolbox filled with the skills, knowledge, and understanding of what it will take to master challenges and keep moving towards their potential in order to thrive across the domains of their life.

I am available for consultations and coaching with parents, coaches, teachers and students, classroom programs, keynote speaking, and workshops. You can contact me at drkate@pugetsoundsportspsychology.com.

14

KEEP SINGING

Leading with Harmony during Times of Dissonance

By
Brenda Bowers

"Brenda, the show must go on, so just keep singing."

I can still hear my mother's voice ringing like a high-sounding cymbal with endless resounding waves. All I could see at that moment was my brother, Steve, out like a light on the floor of the stage on which we were singing, right next to me. I saw him fall straight back like a tree after a lumberjack yelled, "Timber!" You see, my brother would faint on stage, but he was the greatest voice of the seven children vocalists comprising the Singing Coles, along with both our parents, James and Erma. I hadn't started kindergarten yet, but I remember this event like it was yesterday, and it still holds a place that is so often very present before me.

How could my mother, who I knew was the nicest woman in the world, be so insensitive, seeing her son on the ground, seemingly totally unconscious, and then yell at me as I tried to help him back up? *He's our star singer,* I thought. Of course, I didn't say that out loud, nor did I say,

He's my brother. He's my hero, my protector, and he's my friend. How can the world go on, much less this song? But obedience was always our number one premise, to trust Mom and Dad limitlessly and unconditionally. And we did!

So, what did I do?

With trembling insides and fear enough to fill an ocean, I kept looking forward. When my part came, I sang just as if Steve was standing there holding my hand, giving me confidence and the assurance that everything would be okay. He always said, "It's just a song, Brenda." He would tell me, "You just give the people what they need to make them have a better day. That's what we do. We make people's days better." So, sing I did, and in a few minutes, that tall, thin, handsome soul was standing right next to me again; and the show did indeed go on.

Even the Dissonance

In the early 2000s, I attended a workshop by Dominic Alldis. In 1998, he founded Music and Business, which is an organization that provides inspirational learning events where he uses his broad knowledge of both classical and jazz music with the world of business. He uses the illustration of a symphony orchestra, a string quartet, or a jazz band and he brings music to life in a startling way that is highly relevant to business today. He creates inspirational learning events for business organizations through his metaphor of music.

Dominic himself is a conductor of a symphony orchestra, he's a jazz musician, he plays in bands, he's a composer, and he creates new pieces of music all the time. Music and Business provides extraordinary insights into leadership, collaboration, creativity, and personal development, inviting the corporate world to explore new ways of thinking about business and practice. His organization provides four different options:

1. An orchestra event

   - Focusing on leadership, collaboration, listening, and trust.

2. A jazz experience

   - Focusing on improvisation, creativity, adaptability, risk-taking, and change within a fast-moving commercial world.

3. A classical experience

   - Focusing on coordination and precision needed for high-level performances.

4. A fusion experience

   - Focusing on balance and the strategic alignment with creative independence.

I had an incredible experience with Dominic and his team at a healthcare leadership summit; I had an epiphany about my own life and its journey up to that point. The melody, the harmony, the consonants, and the dissonance brought me to the platform of conductor and KPI (a key person of influence), without me realizing it; it was very similar to that which Kevin speaks about in his first book, *Put a Shark in Your Tank.*

As number six of seven children – all singing before I came on the scene at the age of two – I had to learn quickly by sitting under the best in class, which were the previous five. I learned how to be in sync while singing "Johnny One Note" in such a way that our voices were indistinguishable. I also learned disunity or disharmony when even just one single voice was not the same nor even in agreement; however, in such cases, the listener experiencing the presence of us would still hear sweet music in their ears. Why was that? More importantly, how could that be? I concluded that difference is as imperative as similarity; my experiences, however, seems to show that my harmony is so disruptive to the predetermined melody of our society's sheet music, that elimination of the song, the artistry, the music seemed to be the only option that our culture offers.

Now, did I need to suffer the loss of my father at age 14, become a single mother at age 15, a widow by age 35, and diagnosed with a chronic, incurable condition before age 50? I'd like to believe that I did not; but, my past had led me to appreciate that reflective moment of my brother fainting – which did happen more than once by the way – when I was but a mere babe myself. My past continues to inform me that the dissonance itself is a KPI that has a perfect pitch and a killer business plan to seal the deal of success.

Today – as a Doctor of Philosophy, an academic, a healthcare executive with an additional doctorate in nursing practice, and an avid contributor to both my church as well as the broader community – I have a voice as an instrument of change, one that is worthy for consideration or even concert attendance. I work hard to ensure that the voices belonging to those who cannot get to the table or afford a ticket may still be heard. Have you ever felt like your biggest problem and greatest issue was much larger than the odds ratio of winning the Power Ball Lottery? Well, guess what. Me too. Well, actually, me most of the time.

A Guide to Making a World of Difference
(spheres of influence)

This chapter is not about the downstream of how you sell yourself, how you sell your products, your brands, or your business; all of these are critical; but you have celebrities like Kevin Harrington, Tony Robbins, Russell Brunson, and Rob Kosberg for that. My message is preparing you upstream so that when it is time for your downstream effect, you are ready to engage; you're ready to give, offer, and receive at your highest and best level of potential and power.

My movement is to ensure that you're prepared, ready, well-practiced, and playing in the first chair ... the second your time to shine shows up yes, I said second, not minute, hour, day, week, month, or year. We have 59 opportunities every minute to make the right and best choices. Unfortunately, we have underestimated the power of the seconds, so we have defaulted to sloth speed in a stealth-paced world. But, you can train your brain to function in one thirty seconds' time, just like you train it for three-four time.

So, those of you who really want, to not only play in the 1% but live in the 1% of the 1%, you need to start making success-second settlements. In order to play in that sphere, you must embrace success-second settlements. You need to become resolute in the shortest time possible; resolute in the things that yield the highest and best outcomes. Preparing you for this game of celebrity success is the first and foremost thing in this hierarchy and symphony of life. So how did I do it? Or better yet, how do I continue to do it?

I decided to write what I live by every day in my book, *World Changers and Difference Makers; A Comprehensive Guide to Transform Your Life and Mend the World One Sphere at a Time.*

I believe we exist in a minimum of a two-world universe, which I refer to as SL2-squared:

1. Self-life intelligence
2. Societal-leader intelligence

We have multi-billion-dollar products, but if we don't realize who we are, then why should anyone else? If we don't like or love ourselves, why should anyone else? I teach you in my book how to love and like yourself as part of the first of a two-world intelligence model SLi-squared.

Self-awareness is the first, largest, and central sphere to what I call our self-life intelligence world. If you don't have a stellar relationship with yourself, then how do you expect to build a killer list of contacts? I instruct on this topic as the second sphere of self-life intelligence. If you are so abrasive in your presence, then how will anyone get close enough to hear your fiscal freedom message? Then, in Chapter 4, Authorial Presence, this is sphere three in our self-life intelligence world.

If you don't organically know your ideal client – where they live, what they look like, their fears and frustrations, or their pains and their passions – how will you ever get your message to them? In the book,

I cured that chasm for you in a chapter called Organism Knowledge, or sphere four in the self-life intelligence world. If you have not done your homework and prepared yourself with the essential expertise that you need to be reputable and credible, then it won't matter how great and wonderful you are as a person. No one will schedule you to do their hip replacement if you're licensed to sell cars and not licensed to practice medicine as an orthopedic surgeon.

The final sphere in this first world of self-life intelligence is where you will discover your current expertise and how to develop others that are essential to your success. I will now share with you the five of several concepts that I cover in greater detail in my book.

1. Never let the song inside of you die.
2. When faced with rejection, stay in the game.
3. Learn your SEOTAKs.
4. What is your TAGline? Are you wearing your TAGS?
5. It's time to shine.

Firstly, never let the song inside of you die, even when it's only jumbled noise. Once the noise is sorted out, you will find that the answers lie within a separate note. You must be willing to un-jumble the chords, so the song doesn't die because of the noise. One person's noise is another person's splendor.

Secondly, when you are rejected, whether it's because of race, gender, ethnicity, socioeconomic status, intellect, excellence, whatever it may be and I have been rejected for all of those reasons – stay in the game. And if you can't play by the written rules, then write your own poetry, lyrics, melody, and your own harmony; and then follow your composition that was birthed from your pain, residing in your heart and defining your passion.

Thirdly, you need to learn what I call Seotaks (Self-Encounters of The Awareness Kind); you must have those. You need to become keenly aware of yourself first. This is always your #1 priority. Then as you integrate yourself, with other people, environment situations, and circumstances, the experience exponentially changes for the better. So, become aware of yourself, and experience yourself. If you were a one-person band, what would your dominant instrument be? Why? For every 59 seconds, how do you experience you? Is it typically a pleasant experience or an unenjoyable one? Why?

Self-awareness is the nucleus of self-life intelligence; all other spheres in our world are subject to its foundation and platform. We don't think beyond it, live beyond it, nor do we succeed beyond it. So, you see, no matter how genius we are in the generation of our ideas, if we lack proficient, mature, highly-developed self-awareness, our lid (the top of our potential) to realization and monetization will always be diminutive—it's the difference between those who can and those who should is those who do, investing in yourself.

Fourthly, what is your TAGline (Talents, Abilities, and Gifts)? Are you wearing your TAGS (Talents, Abilities, Gifts, and Skills)? When is the last time you listed yours? You can list truth without losing humility. Too often, we bury our own Taglines, so we don't outshine others. There is no reward for minimizing your talents, abilities, and gifts. Wear your TAGS. Boast in them! They are the gems you lend to this world. You must bring them to the forefront, know how to articulate them, how to speak about them in the manner you're branding yourself. Your talents, abilities, and gifts are the drivers for your TAGline.

Finally, it's time to shine. If you hide your stardom behind the Milky Way, it doesn't stop the star from shining; it just obscures its view. There are people who are wondering why you keep showing up with a 25-watt bulb in your lamp; they know that you're a thousand-lumen legend and wonder why you're oblivious to the obvious. During what I call my daycare-to-doctorate journey, there were many times I didn't even realize my heart as the lamp to my soul; but once I did, of course, I bought a 25-watt bulb...well, actually it was more like a 13-watt. I looked for a 2-watt, but I couldn't find one at the time. Life was just too hard. Life was too painful, it was too full of failures, it was overloaded with losses, it was disrupted with downfalls, and it was supersaturated with stumbling blocks; to the point that the last thing I wanted to do was shine.

Now, don't get me wrong, I still dreamed and wanted to be debt-free, get my mule and 40 acres, live on a private island (or at least the beach with nature surrounding me and horses and dogs anywhere I looked) with a home large enough for each of our children to have their own wing with privacy and luxury while yet being close; but the key words are "wanted" and "dreamed." And, when coupled with my nightmare of a lifestyle and decisions by the decade versus choices by the second, I knew I'd never have to worry about this fantasy coming true. I was my own worst self-fulfilling prophecy. While my dreams and wants haven't all been realized yet, what I can guarantee you is that I can see the reality of them coming to pass. "Wanted" and "dreamed" are no longer past tense, they are perpetually present! Are yours?

My husband, Bill, and I were both widowed when we met, but we've been married now for over 20 years. We wanted our total of 11 children to have the leverage to succeed in a world that predominantly was positioned unfavorably for them as part of a Black American family with a whole lot of baggage. He and I went on our own educational journey to role model the process for our children and for our small congregation, of which at that time 90% were on welfare when we founded the church. Our ultimate goal was to obtain the credentials needed to offer Christian education from daycare to doctorate, which would provide an option other than the public-school system – which also struggles in its success rates for Black students and those who excel beyond high school…well, the numbers are too low to even mention.

After we married, Bill and I both obtained associate degrees, bachelor's, master's, and doctorates; and all 11 of our children have at least a bachelor's, most have a master's, two have doctorates, one with a Ph.D., and the other with a JD. And their fields of success range from revenue cycle and healthcare, education, engineering, finance, nursing, healthcare administration, business administration, to clinical mental health. If Bill and I stopped wanting, dreaming, and believing, where would we be? If we chose to commit dream and desire suicide, it could have potentially killed generations.

Spheres of Leadership

In my book, I explain the characteristics, attributes, behaviors, and actions needed to draw out the leader in each of us, but at a different dimension for various purposes. For example, I consider sphere one in the second world that we exist in (societal-leader intelligence) as a novice/beginner, or the supervisor sphere. When you are new to a relationship, a role, or a career, this is the sphere you want to ensure you master with all of its values, behaviors, and actions – versus, the highest-level sphere (sphere five, which is the expert, executive, C-suite entrepreneur sphere), the behaviors for that person are much more refined, more matured, and perfected. The sphere five should bear the persona that a sphere one strives to become one day.

So, I'm a sphere five as a healthcare executive, for instance, and as an academic who contributes to the body of knowledge through executive coaching, consulting, research, public speaking, and other things; however, I'm a sphere one with specific regards to strategic marketing planning, mass automated emailing, social media affiliate advertising, and list creation strategies. Therefore, I need to know how to respect my sphere five expertise and defer to Kevin, Tony, Russell, and Rob in their sphere five space while I humbly learn and embrace the role of a sphere one when needing their celebrity expertise. There are five spheres total in the societal-leader intelligence world. I am sharing two of them at a very high level just to give you a flavor of what to anticipate when you engage in my SLi-squared strategy system for enhancing society by mastering yourself – truly, the secret sauce to success.

I am able to submit without intimidation, reservation, jealousy, envy, and unplugged circuits, so there's no loss of energy flow between what I've mastered in my self-life intelligence world and the nucleus of my societal-leader intelligence world – the heartbeat of how I make a difference on a larger scale is how I make a difference in myself every second. So, a key point in the societal-leader intelligence is our ability to be fluid enough to know when to contribute and to know when to recede.

We can welcome those who are smarter than we are, who have made it bigger and better than we have, who are the best in class, who are no longer just the generalist or the specialist, the experts, or the thought leaders who now reside in the space of celebrity. There might be areas or fields, and spheres where you reside as that celebrity; however, when we find our ability to free ourselves from always being that sphere five every second, we can open up intimate possibilities which we never even knew existed.

Opportunities reveal themselves when we master our self-life intelligence. Too often we jump into making social change and being big, strong leaders without working on our self-life first. I believe that each of us can make a world of difference, one second at a time by excelling personally and professionally by mastering our self-life intelligence world. This ensures we are excellent contributors to our societal-leader intelligence world.

One last point is to never violate your values or tolerate those who do. Surround yourself with people who do not share your opinion but do share your values. Don't be afraid of anyone who knows more than you; in fact, seek them out. When you share your values with another person, you don't need to waste time removing the noise from the conversation and the dialog. Tonality is critical even when harmony is strategic. Value violators are tone deaf and often quite disrespectful; they look for your hot buttons and push them with force, with the intent to cause pain. So, stop seeking their validation, support, and affirmation. Diversity of thought makes great music, but misaligned values engender crippling chaos.

In order not to remain stuck in this very common cesspool, create a list of values that define your philosophy of life. After you've created that list of values, ask three people you interact with the most – not whom you like the most, but interact with – and ask them if they agree with your list. I can help you strengthen those relationships if your values align, and I can help you get out of those relationships and replace them with value validators (versus value violators), which in turn will accelerate you accomplishing your desired outcomes.

A World of Harmony

I've had the opportunity to provide executive coaching, consulting, education, and training on multiple topics; a few of them include healthcare, leadership, physician and nursing development, coaching and training healthcare executives, religious leaders, governances and boards, women, women's conferences, organization and leadership development, and mentoring. I've been a keynote speaker at a number of events across the country and even internationally. I've also been a commencement speaker. I was once on a ticket with Gloria Steinem, who then attended my breakout session on lateral violence in the workplace. I am also a change and transition thought leader. I published my dissertation in 2006 on executive transitioning from a silo to a system-based approach in a complex healthcare organization: implications for continuous leadership development. In that same year, I received a Women of Influence Award in the area of inspiration by the Business Journal. I've since written multiple articles on developing leaders. I have a copy-written model on change and transition with an emphasis on the people impact of change. I've authored a devotional called "A Word for Youth, 365 daily meditations". I have numerous certifications in executive coaching, talent assessment, change and transition management, organization leadership development, life clarity and business coaching, and healthcare consulting. And I am still a daughter, a sister, a mother, and a wife.

But one of that greatest accomplishments and gifts in my life is an annual event I hold for my mother's birthday in February, Black History Month. Each and every year, we celebrate her as the matriarch, and we celebrate her story. All of my siblings come together to sing as part of the program, just as we did when we were children. Today each of us lives in different states, and we look forward to seeing each other when we arrive at the event. We never rehearse; but we know where to line up, which way to sway, who's playing what instrument, the songs we will sing, and who will lead. We get right up, and we perform; we do what's ours to do in that same unified obedience that we've had since I was two years old and for most of my siblings, way before then.

Without fail, we are over-showered with people asking, "When did you have time to rehearse? How do you sound so good? Why don't you get together more? We enjoyed you so much, the crispness of your stature, the respect and honor you give your mom. The spirit of obedience is so palpable." Well, my conclusion is that the magic is in the music, the victory is in the voices, and the hope is in the harmony. Celebration is not optional, coming together is critical, and connecting ensures constant creativity.

Networking is important for continued organic growth. Just because we are found in a wood of weeds versus an orchard of oranges, we can never stop sowing seeds; we can never neglect to water our good ground to facilitate healthy growth. So, through my obstacles, I was able to grow an orchard in the midst of wild-growing weeds. And because I know that I'm not a special case, and I didn't receive an extra dose of plant food actually, probably quite the opposite, but because of that – the proof is in the people's progress. I know you can do the same and even more.

I know that I can help you realize your wants and your dreams as I continue to realize more of mine. You deserve it! If not now, then when? And if not you, then who? If you want further information, please visit my website www.aword4u.com, where you can find my book as well as some free downloadable content about mentoring and leadership. For a free consultation, please contact  me at drbrendab@aword4u.com. I look forward to building a lasting relationship with you, and I'm sure we will make great music together.

15

THE WEB SURFER

*How I Got My Ph.D. from
the School of Hard Knocks*

By
David Stewart

I am the owner of SurfTheWeb.com and also Streamline Properties Incorporated. I've been an entrepreneur my whole life, and my main focus right now is working on launching SurfTheWeb.com. I have had some great success in business over the years, and those successes came about with some learning from, what I like to call, the school of hard knocks – I joke that this is where I earned my Doctorate. Honestly, even with the best education, you will also learn from that "school." As I share some of my story, I hope you can benefit and skip some of these lessons yourself! Being an entrepreneur is not for everyone, but it can give you a very fulfilling life, and if you do it right, you will have greater flexibility than you will ever have working for someone else.

I realized as far back as junior high school that I was interested in being in business; but I officially started when I was working with my father and my brother at the family equipment rental business, years later. As a junior-high-schooler, I wanted to be an entrepreneur and took all the business-related courses. My first project was during the gas crisis when I saw an ad for gas guards at wholesale, closeout price. This product was a cone-shaped coil that you insert into the gas filler pipe that would prevent anyone from siphoning your gas.

This ended up being my first lesson of the school of hard knocks: the product had limited life as the gas crisis passed – and if you're not first or second in the market it is really hard to get traction without a huge marketing budget. A similar thing happened with Razor Scooters. I bought a sample scooter that I had shipped in from China to compete against the Razor when they were just starting to get hot. Because it was required to order a container load, that stopped me at that time. A friend of mine did order a container load and had a hard time moving them because he wasn't the first or second to market – and everyone wanted the Razor brand.

Later, when I managed the largest division of our family equipment rental business, I soon took over managing the Party and Medical Rental division and built it up into the largest division. I found a separate location and negotiated the lease and grew the business. At one point my dad decided to start a one-way trailer system, to compete against U-Haul because U-Haul had a monopoly on one-way trailers after the close of an old company (Nationwide Trailers). I initially thought my Dad was crazy and couldn't do it, but now I am really proud of him. His success taught me you could start something big if you put your mind to it. Because of that, I know I can make SurfTheWeb into a national brand. I helped my dad with designing and implementing the computer programs to run the company. This was back in the early days of microcomputers, and we were working on an IMSAI 8080 microcomputer with dual floppy drives. Together along with my other brothers, we ran that whole company. I designed programs that would track the commissions, the trailer movements, and create the dealer lists, which required a lot of copy work – so I started my own copy service.

I started Quality Copy Service with $5000 dollars, which I borrowed from the bank; it was a considerable loan back in those days. And I leased a Xerox 9400 high-speed copier and an office space next to the county government center. My hope was that my Dad's one-way trailer system would be the major customer for my copy service. Well, as it turned out, the trailer business didn't work out after a while because a major competitor came on board; but my Dad was able to get the business going with the trailers nationwide, so I was pretty proud of him on that. Nonetheless, in the process, we started the copy business, and I ended up with two locations doing millions of copies a month. So, I just grew with it, and we became more profitable than the trailer business at one point. One thing I decided from the beginning was that I would not try to undercut other companies to get market share. Everyone else at the time was selling copies at 5 cents each. I opened the store at 6 cents and called the business "Quality Copy Service." I knew people were willing to pay for quality and I was right. When the other stores raised their price to 6 cents, I moved up to 7 cents.

During that time, I also started a computer dealership and became a Commodore computer dealer. When they came out with the Commodore 64, I developed a 10-key pad for it. I designed it, manufactured it, and marketed it nationwide. Through my dealership, we sold many Commodore 64 computers and sold some of the first computer learning networks to schools.

The School of Hard Knocks

From this point forward, I truly began learning from the school of hard knocks. My lessons were as follows:

1. Ensuring quality partners
2. The importance of non-compete contracts
3. Running background checks
4. Ensuring finances

I also became a Xerox selling agency, selling the Xerox copiers from 1985 to about 1997. The economy was in the downturn when Kinko's opened up their premiere store between my two locations. So, I ended up closing one of our locations, and I took on a partner so we could offer some additional services, one of which was document scanning. My partner had contacts in the Navy, and he was able to get many contracts with them, but document scanning was pretty new as an industry, and it didn't take off quite as well as we expected – still, the Navy kept us pretty busy.

My partner ended up buying me out; but not in a super-friendly way. This was my first lesson from the school of hard knocks: making sure you have a good partner and protecting your interests to ensure you can't be forced out. Still, overall, the copy business was good for me while it lasted. After 17 years it was time for a change anyway.

Right after that, I was able to buy Summit Golf. The company custom-manufactured golf clubs and marketed them nationwide via telephone sales with a return guarantee. When I took ownership, business was small at the time. I actually bought Summit Golf because it owned two domain names: (1) Birdie.com and (2) SurfTheWeb.com with my main interest in SurfTheWeb – even back in the late nineties, "Surf the

Web" had become synonymous with using the internet. My hope was to build a site that would become popular; that many people would start using SurfTheWeb.com.

Unfortunately, the golf club company turned out to not be what I expected. The business model we had with the return policy was not sound. While I did much better than the previous owner, there still wasn't enough cash flow, and I ended up closing that business down. During that time, I had a telemarketing room with 24 stations where we sold golf clubs nationwide. Eventually, my room manager ended up leaving Summit Golf to start his own business with six of my telemarketers. In hindsight, I should have made a non-compete contract with them. They eventually discovered that it's not as easy to run a business themselves, and they ended up not lasting very long.

Employees often look at the owner and think, *oh man this is easy, I could do this myself;* but the group that left me didn't last more than a month, as they ran out of funds and couldn't run their business. If I had that non-compete contract with them, I could have avoided that problem. With my Xerox business, my service manager left with some employees to start their own copy business, which also failed. It's really important to create non-compete contracts.

Something that also could have helped me avoid that problem is running background checks. There were two key employees at the golf club company who ended up being problematic; they were plotting to start their own business, and I discovered this as I was closing it down. And I also found out one of them had broken into our store shortly after starting up and he stole some computers, some antique clubs that belonged to one of our employees, and he made it look like a break-in. I learned after closing Summit Golf down that it was an inside job.

Another thing learned from buying Summit Golf, when buying a failing business it's important to ensure you have the money to carry it until you make a profit. Another lesson, spending money on a project before it's actually necessary can be detrimental. I've had several different projects where I thought I would begin right away, so I ordered things like mailing lists, but then the project would end up not happening, so that was a waste of money. Always monitor the use of funds and only spend when you are sure it is necessary.

Returning to my first lesson regarding business partners, I learned this lesson again after closing down Summit Golf. I had an opportunity to buy a resort up in Wyoming, and I brought on someone I thought would just be a financial partner, but he ended up being a working partner. We put up a down payment, we signed the papers, the previous owner turned the keys over to me, and I was then in charge of three small resorts; each of them had a restaurant and a bar, and two of them had lodging. From a shoestring budget, my partner and I were able to get everything up and running; but he was not a good working partner. My partner caused problems with employees as well as the National Park Service, which did not allow us to complete the contract to purchase the resort; as the resorts were on National Forest land, they needed to approve the transfer of the business. Working and running the resorts turned out to be both a good and bad experience. I learned a lot, and we were able to successfully revive each resort from a dead stop. We had about 40 people working under us, including students from South America on their summer break, which was our winter season. The problems between my partner and I, and those between him and our employees and our budget led to shutting down this business.

The Web Surfer

SurfTheWeb is now my primary focus. I'm more of a visionary, but I was able to build a team of tech people who are now preparing the technical side. SurfTheWeb.com will have social interaction based on topics: like basketball.SurfTheWeb.com, footbal.SurfTheWeb.com, or basketweaving.SurfTheWeb.com. And then there will also be localities: like LosAngeles.SurfTheWeb.com.

Each SurfTheWeb topic will have news, information, articles, directories, a marketplace, classifieds, and events pertaining to the topic or the locality. There will be a directory primarily for the localities. We will have a network of independent sales organizations (ISO's), each selling various services that we either own the rights to or that we have companies providing on a contract basis for us; everything from web hosting to SEO and web design, and so forth. Each of the topics and localities will have editors and executive editors, which will be paid positions. We'll have advertising, and our local ISO's will sell to local businesses to sponsor these various topics or localities as well. And, where Facebook is focused primarily on the individual, SurfTheWeb will be about the topics and the localities. From there, I'm confident that we'll be able to build up a very good product that people will go to for gaining information and socially interacting with that information.

We'll also have SurfTheWeb.TV. We have a content aggregator that has the system to create the equivalent to a ROKU, which will be white-labeled under SurfTheWeb.TV. We'll be developing that right away too. As far as I'm concerned, the beauty of SurfTheWeb is the branding.

Microsoft attempted to launch three search engines: Live.com, Microsoft.com, and now Bing.com. When they launched Bing, they spent over one hundred million dollars on the initial launch to get the Bing brand known. The advantage we have is everyone knows and uses the phrase SurfTheWeb.

My mission is to make this a family-friendly site, and turn it into a billion-dollar company, which is just one percent the size of Google; I think it's a very doable deal with our branding power. We will also use the power of name recognition and use celebrities to promote our site and SurfTheWeb.TV.

One way that we will develop content is through our members. To reward people for both content and interaction, we will be trading our own cryptocurrency or tokens through an ICO, which will also be a way to raise capital to launch SurfTheWeb. We'll have the initial coin offering of our ICO, which will raise upwards of $50M, and then people will be able to earn coins by interaction and commenting or providing articles and so forth.

This ICO system will create community and a reason for people to be involved because they can then spend those coins on products and services that we offer through SurfTheWeb. At the time of this chapter being written, we are raising our initial seed capital. This will hopefully be sold out by the time this book hits the print. Our initial offering is a 506(c) Reg D offering, so we can raise any amount from accredited investors. So, the second round will be our ICO – which will also be registered with the FCC as a Reg A+, allowing anyone to invest and the coins to be immediately tradable.

From the 506c and the Reg A+ rounds will give us the money to launch SurfTheWeb. We will also do a reward non-equity crowdfunding. Part of the purpose behind that is creating further brand awareness. People will be able to donate (as low as a dollar and up) and receive merchandise and other items, like a logo t-shirt or hat, and then different products/services we will be offering as well – which we will sell at a discounted price. Beyond that, there will be the option to become an ISO or even an editor of a topic.

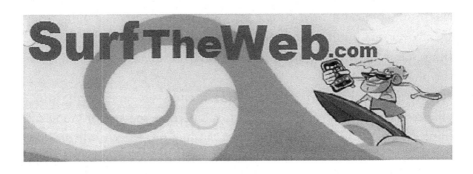

All in all, I believe our plan will take the new and dynamic website to great heights; it will become one of the best places to go to online. Until then, I would love to hear your stories and how you've dealt with the school of hard knocks, or just to talk with you. I will always be available through SurfTheWeb. You can find me under "contact us." So, just look for the link on that, send me a note, suggest topics you would like us to start with, and I will reply. I look forward to chatting with you.

16

UNLEASHING LATENT POTENTIAL

Are You Planning to Fail or Preparing to Succeed?

By
Karl Shaikh

• •

I believe in the latent potential we all have. I started my first of many businesses in 2003 (in London). Among other degrees, I earned my Master's in Finance in 2007. I have helped some very large organizations, as well as some of the most promising startups and non- profits, with their strategy, strategic thinking, and planning. I totally get entrepreneurs, and they get me! StrategicShift, my latest venture, works with leaders to help them address strategic issues and unleash their organization's latent potential.

• •

We are creatures of habit. We think somewhere between 60,000 and 70,000 thoughts in one day. We live huge parts of our lives on autopilot. We make very similar micro decisions day-after-day, and each decision seems to be pre-determined by our prior actions – without even realizing it. Our lives are full of repetitive actions;

yet, it seems we're in an ever faster changing environment. How can you unleash your latent potential?

If you're about to embark on a major change, commitment, or investment, you'll be tempted to make a plan to optimize the best return on your commitment. Yet, deep down, you probably know, that the plan won't play out as you expect. Mike Tyson, the American Boxer (who has now been inducted into the International Boxing Hall of Fame and the World Boxing Hall of Fame) is reputed to have said: "Everybody has a plan until they get hit in the face!" You also know that the vast majority of people who join fitness gyms in January, with a plan to get fit, soon return to their prior lifestyle by February or March. This is a dichotomy that causes entrepreneurs and leaders a major problem. We seem to need a plan (or something that provides the benefits of a plan) whilst having the flexibility to unleash the latent potential.

Why People Demand Plans from Us

When we plan, we do so for several reasons (including):

- Coordinating activities
- Planning resources
- Convincing employees, partners, investors, customers, distributors to join us in our endeavors.

Plans help people around us. These people expect us to know that we understand what needs to be done, and in what order, and plans make them feel comfortable. *It's kinda' what a leader is expected to do.* People want to see certainty in our plans. Ending the presentation with the words, "but this could all change tomorrow," usually won't win many supporters!

Plans also help our own confidence. Plans where we try to predict every detail give us the hope and/or delude us into believing that we can eliminate uncertainties with careful planning. Even though we all know the future is uncertain, the plan helps us feel like those uncertainties can be controlled if we have worked out the details. The more we think about a certain version of the future, we begin to think it's highly likely. Just because we've researched, analyzed, and studied this version of the future doesn't necessarily mean that this version of the future will actually come to fruition.

Plans are NOT the Answer
(being prepared is!)

Yes, plans can serve a function, but only if we acknowledge that they **may**, and most likely **will** need to change. The contradiction in the above two paragraphs is that in dynamic/disruptive environments, unless we explicitly articulate that the plans **will** change, our employees, our investors, our customers and other stakeholders will not be prepared for the imminent change in direction (potentially requiring additional funding). Without this warning, these groups of people will want the things to work according to plan, adding pressure on us to deliver as we predicted – to get things right the first time! Failed businesses have typically tried to stick to their plans and have become prisoners of their plans.

Let's look at some definitions:

• •

PLAN a detailed proposal (including a list of steps with timing and resources), for doing or achieving something.

PREPARE to make or get something or someone ready for something that will happen in the future.

• •

The distinction in the above two definitions may seem a little nuanced at first. What we'd like you to observe (for now) is that planning leans towards rigidity towards one's plans, whereas preparation leans towards adaptability. The definition of **Plan** commits us to a singular plan, whereas the definition of **Prepare** allows us to be ready for changes.

"By failing to prepare, you are preparing to fail."

BENJAMIN FRANKLIN

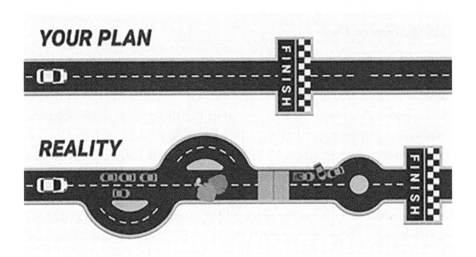

Planners unwittingly kid themselves that just because they have a plan, they'll be able to achieve the desired outcome. However, as can be seen in the image above, the reality is rarely a straight line to the finish line. In reality, that journey is full of surprises. The road is harder, longer, takes longer, and probably requires rerouting.

Preparers are nimble footed; they focus on resources in ways that will begin to influence the future immediately as the future emerges into reality, instead of resisting this emergence. Unintentionally, the employees within the Planners' business are set up for failure, and the table below shows how we can set up our employees for success.

From **PLANNERS**	To **PREPARERS**
Employees' targets are based on "time-based milestones." Employees have actions that must be **achieved by these specified times**.	Employees are expected to focus in on "**readiness**" and "**foresight**." Employees are expected to make the most of the **potential**.
Employees are **alert** to the pre- specified actions (Contrarian emerging reality can be easily missed).	Employees are **alert** to and pay attention to the emerging reality, whether consistent or contrary to the assumptions.
If/when the emerging reality is different from the plan, the employees are: often **blindsided**, can **resist**, tend to "double-down" and try even harder to achieve the prior targets they have been assigned in the plan.	The employees are orientated towards the emerging reality, **learning from the emerging reality**, adjusting/re-routing accordingly and make the most of the emerging reality.
Missing the targets typically result in **negative consequences** for the people, so the employees are strongly incentivized to preserver with actions that are not working.	Failures are considered as learning opportunities. Performance is reviewed relative to whether most was made of the emerging reality. Successes are celebrated.

As can be seen from the above table, employees in Planner Organizations are battling the forces of time! While employees in Preparer Organizations **influence** their environment as it emerges.

Importance of Rerouting

Most executives and business owners think of a map as a good analogy for a plan (including strategic plans). If we want to go from Dallas to Austin (Texas), then having a plan (knowing that our route will be I-35, and knowing the steps, times, and resources required along this route) will give a feeling of confidence. With a paper-based map, when traffic builds up, the first you know of it is when you yourself see the brake lights of the cars ahead of you come on, and you realize it is too late for you to exit the highway – and then you get stuck in the traffic!

The modern GPS systems have an Early Warning System (EWS) which works by monitoring the speed of cars way ahead of you along the route to your destination. If traffic builds up on your primary route, the modern GPS system will give you an alternative "next best route," often before you pass by the exit options. Although the paper-based maps have evolved to become the modern GPS, the strategic plans are still stuck in the past.

This chapter is designed to help you evolve the planning for your own business, set up your employees for success and be able to respond in a timely manner for any changing conditions on your business' horizon – unleashing your organizations latent potential.

Successful Businesses are Preparers

We looked back into business history and reviewed the old strategic plans of multiple businesses and categorized them according to whether their strategy succeeded or failed. Some businesses were added to both lists if we found that their business succeeded with one strategy at a particular time and failed with the same or different strategy at a different time period. For each business (irrespective of the group they belonged to) we identified either the explicitly stated assumptions or the implied assumptions the businesses, or the industry as a whole, had made within this old business strategy.

Then, for each business, we identified which of the above assumptions turned out to be better than or worse than expected and whether this deviation of the assumptions was instrumental in that businesses' success or failure.

We found that the successful firms were either a) lucky and the outcome was better than they had expected in their assumptions, or and more importantly, alert and attuned enough (knowingly or unknowingly) to the assumptions they made, and able react to the surprises of how the assumptions actually turn out. The unsuccessful organizations were doggedly pursuing their plans despite changing circumstances whilst successful organizations were able to reroute.

Clayton Christensen is a professor at Harvard Business School and a renowned authority on disruptive innovation. He notes in his best-selling book, *The Innovators Dilemma*:

"Research has shown that the vast majority of successful new business ventures abandoned their original business strategy when they began implementing their initial plans and learned what would and would not work in the market. The dominant difference between the successful ventures and failed ones generally is NOT the astuteness of their original strategy. Guessing the right strategy at the outset is not nearly as important to success as conserving enough resources… so that new business initiatives get a second or third stab at getting it right."

Kodak was founded in 1880. It was known for its pioneering technology and innovative marketing and was often rated one of the world's five most valuable brands. Despite popular belief, Kodak's demise was NOT because Kodak didn't see the digital camera coming! On the contrary, Eastman Kodak built one of the first digital cameras in 1975.

We believe that Kodak's demise was caused by its inability to monitor an Early Warning System (EWS). Their assumptions at the time were:

- Digital cameras market may or may not exist.
- The market will be certainly smaller than their existing market.
- The digital camera is a product that customers may or may not want.
- A business model will almost certainly give Kodak lower margins than their existing product lines.

In hindsight, those of us using digital cameras or smartphones, we know the first three of those above assumptions turned out very differently. Due to the absence of an EWS, as the reality emerged differently from their assumptions, they weren't able to re-direct – and they got stuck in traffic with nowhere to go! We posit that Kodak were planners and not preparers. They resisted the emerging reality and stuck to their original strategy to their detriment. We will now show you how you can become a preparer too.

THE SOLUTION

Preparing Your Business for Success

To unleash your organization's latent potential, don't doggedly stick to a plan (as you would have with a paper-based map); instead, prepare for changes as GPS mapping systems do. But how?

First of all, you'll recall from the beginning of this chapter; there was an emphasis on "Convincing employees, partners, investors, customers, distributors to join us in our endeavors." Unless you address their and your own expectations, an alternative to a plan will be rejected. Without changing these mindsets, the practical steps for making the change will fall on deaf ears!

- **Prepare** your financial investors to expect changes and prepare them to stick it out for the long haul.
- **Be prepared** by allowing yourself time for trial and errors.
- Do not overcommit your own reputation on the successful first try. **Prepare to learn** and iterate.

Secondly, the same section at the start of this chapter also explained that people demand plans from us for "coordinating activities and planning resources." Our solution for providing control includes two components:

- Not declaring what you will do, but instead declaring your **Baseline Hypothesis** of what you expect will happen (with influence by your organization).

    o   In other words: What cause and effect relationship are you expecting to influence as the basis of your strategy?

    o   What cause and effect relationship do you believe in and that you will influence to provide the outcomes (increased revenue, improved margins, higher ROI) that you expect to influence from a given set of initiatives?

    o   In this chapter, we'll consider the Baseline Hypothesis as your Strategy.

    o   Some people find this topic fascinating, and if you'd like to learn more about Strategy as the Baseline Hypothesis, see our forthcoming book.

- **Preparing** to reroute your strategy like your GPS mapping system reroutes you upon discovering excessive traffic on your primary route.

    o   Develop an Early Warning System (EWS) to review your progress to determine how the reality is unfolding, as compared to your assumptions (the focus of the remainder of this chapter).

How to Develop an EWS for Your Business

We will first describe how you can develop an EWS, and then we will do a deep dive into the two areas that are the most challenging in this development. An EWS can be developed in the following six steps:

1. Explicitly Identify Assumptions within your strategy
2. Prioritize the Assumptions in terms of likely impact
3. Identify the Indicators to monitor priority assumptions
4. Articulate the IFTTT (tripwires to alternative action)
5. Take action and adjust actions as tripwires are triggered
6. Upon major adjustments, repeat the above cycle

STEP 1: Identifying Assumptions

Identifying assumptions give you a foundation and ongoing grounding in how reality is unfolding. And, like many things in life that are both simple and hard, your payoff for careful attention to assumptions will many times exceed your investment. No organization possesses a crystal ball to know exactly what will happen in the economy, financial markets, or competitors' next bold moves. That means assumptions are a necessary evil.

So, grab a marker, get to a whiteboard, and start to brainstorm: what are the biggest assumptions that your success relies on? Why are you assuming that? Is there anything being taken for granted? Are there beliefs that you are ignoring that you shouldn't? What beliefs are leading you to this conclusion? What were the areas that you had the greatest discussion/debate when forming your strategy? What areas caused the most passionate resistance? (Note: differences in perspectives within your team are a good clue of the assumptions to monitor.) What can you learn from taking different perspectives?

STEP 2: Prioritization

It goes without saying that some assumptions deserve the closest attention. However, organizations have trained themselves (without realizing it) to trivialize the assumptions that might not agree with the plans. Assumptions that don't support the intended plans are the assumptions that organizations' antibodies most like to suppress; yet these assumptions may make the biggest impact (positive or negative). Recall Kodak's story! To succeed, confirmation biases (that we all have) must be overcome – seek different perspectives and ask different people to help prioritize assumptions that might have the biggest likely impact on the future.

STEP 3: Identify the Indicators

Once the assumptions are articulated and prioritized, they need to be monitored, by first identifying specific indicators that are measurable and representative of how the reality is emerging along these priority assumptions. Ask yourself which indicators (when monitored) will provide early warning on whether each priority assumption is turning out as predicted (unlikely) or better or worse than expected?

STEP 4: Articulate the IFTTT

The secret trick to this entire EWS process is to then identify "tripwires" that may adjust/tweak your actions. We call these tripwires IFTTT (*pronounced IFTee*) statements. IFTTT statements support the hypothesis statement of your strategy and follow the following format. "IF THIS should occur, THEN we will do THIS__." We suggest you have between 3-5 IFTTT statements to account for the priority assumptions that would have the biggest impact on the future outcome of your business.

Articulating the IFTTT statements acts as a quality control tool to ensure the EWS is robust before you embed the EWS. The IFTTT statements improve the quality of the thinking that goes into developing the EWS. However, the reality will probably surprise you (unless you possess a crystal ball), and your actual decisions (upon the tripwires being triggered) will need to be adjusted in real time – and you shouldn't feel limited by the decisions when the IFTTT was articulated.

STEP 5: Take Action

Take action, monitor the indicators, and adjust actions as tripwires are triggered in real-time.

STEP 6: Upon Major Adjustments, Repeat the above Cycle

Some of you may have observed that in the past decade or so, the concept of Lean Startup has taken the technology startup world by storm. One of the central mantras of Lean Startup Philosophy is to Build → Measure → Learn → Build → Measure → Learn, repeating cycles.

The Preparation model that we have shared with you in this chapter is also cyclical as each cycle of the "be prepared" model is essentially an experiment to test our strategy on an ongoing basis. Instead of the traditional approach of: create a plan, publish it, and be married to the plan until its safe enough to admit that the plan is out of date and that a new plan is required. We propose a cyclical iterative process of experimentation towards exploring a better future.

DEEP DIVE

Beyond Superficial Assumptions

First, there is no universal set of assumptions, or questions to unearth the assumptions relevant to your strategy, because all markets and organizations are unique. As inspiration for you to identify your own set of assumptions, we provided some example questions earlier. Below, we provide some more examples. In either case, please don't limit yourself to the questions provided here. It's very important to ask yourself other questions – which shared obviousness do you need to challenge?

- Will our competitors truly respond that way?
- Has this ever worked?
- Will funding continue to be available?
- How good are we, really, at implementing big ideas?

Second, dig deeper by asking yourself: "**Why does this assumption matter?**" and then, "Why does that matter?" and so on. This repetitive WHY inquisition on each answer is called the "5 Whys?" technique and can unearth very valuable insights.

Third, it's NOT just a matter of going deeper, but also understanding the **sensitivity** to those deeper assumptions. In other words, what happens, if these assumptions materialize only partly? What if the assumption materializes in a different flavor than you had assumed?

Indicators for Your Business

When I ask entrepreneurs to think about what indicators they might want to monitor as part of developing an EWS, I find that most leaders initially gravitate towards revenue/profit/ROI as the primary metrics of interest to them. Of course, they want any change to have an effect on growing their business, so this first answer is understandable. However, the problem with these is that (a) they are lagging indicators (i.e., it tells you things too late) and (b) they are too generic of an indicator (the revenue growth/decline could be caused by many factors other than your intended change project).

Using revenues as your indicator would be like Waze (an app that helps you navigate through traffic) using your **speed** to tell you if you're stuck in traffic. Your speed is (a) a lagging indicator (you know after you are **already** in a traffic jam), and (b) likewise, it's a generic indicator (your speed may have slowed down either because there is traffic, or if you have run out of fuel).

In order to help you develop your own indicators (both lead and specific) to enable you to be prepared, let's briefly look at a few simple examples.

EXAMPLE 1:

Our prior management consultancy business had decided on fast growth and was embarking on scaling up the business operations, both with new clients and with new consultants. Amongst the metrics we measured were the rate at which we were attracting new consultants to join us (this indicator doesn't directly lead to revenues, but we felt it would be both an early lead and a specific indicator). Better than expected figures of consultants (of the right caliber) joining us signaled that we had a valuable proposition that others wanted to be a part of. This gave us the confidence to increase our marketing budget aimed at winning new clients, which then had a positive, vicious cycle effect on winning clients and also on attracting other high caliber consultants.

EXAMPLE 2:

A non-profit organization that I have helped over many years decided to expand their footprint by establishing additional chapters (think franchisees). Some of the board members were rightly skeptical that we had the resources for this expansion, so we decided to measure the actual resources required as we expanded. We monitored the actual hours used to develop processes and systems to manage additional offices. By the time we got to the fifth such chapter, our tripwire had alerted us to know that we hadn't found economies of scale, and we knew that without economies of scale we wouldn't have the resources/capabilities to manage an expanding chapter network.

This lead to a second, passionate discussion – and that lead to an interesting new idea! We decided to reverse the previous strategy and decided to merge with some of the chapters. The most active board members from the chapters joined the main board, making the core organization's board much stronger which was a fantastic outcome.

Being prepared is more than a 6-step process to create an EWS –it's a mindset change! This change in mindset from **planning** to **preparing** is hard to embed within organizations, particularly if the planning approach is deeply entrenched. As you achieve the mindset change throughout your organization, performance will be easier to come by, as your employees will no longer become prisoners to their own plans and will feel empowered to experiment and learn towards a better future.

Likewise, the change in mindset alone won't deliver the results either. The change in mindset needs to be complemented by our "Being Prepared" framework that we call Early Warning System (EWS). Our "Being Prepared" framework, outlined in this chapter, addresses each of the above reasons why people demand plans from us – (a) convincing employees, partners, investors, customers, distributors to join us in our endeavors, and (b) coordinating activities and planning resources – while also preparing us for the ever more dynamic world; one wherein, if we are not the disrupter, we can easily become the disrupted. We need to stay ahead of the game!

Amazon is a prime example of an organization that has exhibited phenomenal growth through their ability to experiment their way to a better future. Many members of the Echo team were previously on the ill-fated Amazon Fire Phone team.

• •

It's worth noticing that a strategy doesn't always get us to where we had intended. Like Columbus, we can find new land, which can be a better outcome. Success and failure can't be measured relative to our intended plans. Instead, the success/failure should be measured by what we achieve by landing where we land.

• •

A repeating cycle of experiments will ensure you constantly evolve and grow as an organization. That's how entrepreneurs like you can be the disruptor, not the disrupted! And it's how you can have a better future! Not only for yourselves, but for your employees, your families, your business, or non-profit organization, or for your community.

• •

We coach leaders…

- to develop a LIVING strategic planning process
- to develop an organization-wide learning environment that outsmarts your competition
- to unleash your organization's latent potential through regular self-reflection.

• •

You can reach us at KHChapter@StrategicShift.co

17

AMAZING WISER VISOR

*Helping Prevent Accidents and Saving Lives
by Keeping the Glare Out of Your Eyes*

By
Annie Lane

My name is Marianne, but my nickname is Annie. Later, when I entered the profession of childcare, people began calling me, "Annie the Nanny." The children loved it, and their parents remembered me, so the name stuck. Lane is my maiden name, which I started using again after my children both graduated; I wanted to at least give them the courtesy of having the same last name as they have while they were growing up, to prevent confusion.

I was born and raised in Southampton, Pennsylvania. I am one of four girls. I had a wonderful childhood. My parents didn't have much money, but there was a lot of love so that more than made up for it. I am a mother of two awesome children. My oldest, Cindy, is happily married to a great guy named Chris. They have blessed me with two beautiful grandchildren; Autumn and Nathan. My son, Michael, is a Staff Sergeant in the U.S. Marine Corps. He has been serving for fifteen years already and just signed for another four. His plan is to make it his career. I am extremely proud of both my children and the joy they have given me. As a child, when I was asked what I wanted to be when I grew up, I always answered, "To be an exceptional mother," and this has been my greatest accomplishment.

Professionally, I have had a very diverse career from being a program director for Jenny Craig to an award-winning salesperson in the Jewelry Department of Bon Ton Department Stores to staff manager and head hostess at several exclusive bed and breakfast inns along the Delaware River, in Upper Bucks County, Pennsylvania. When my children became adults, my love of people caused me to shift my career path to one of caregiving, and I became a nanny for a few prestigious families – hence I came to be known as "Annie the Nanny." I did a lot of eldercare as well. I took time off to care for my very sick mother, who was suffering from ALS until she passed away. I have always enjoyed working directly with people, and as you see my life's path has given me the opportunity to strengthen my ability to help others.

My Inspiration

I love being by the water, especially the ocean. It was during the trips back and forth to the beaches of New Jersey, and my constant motherly errands and nanny runs on the narrow, hilly, and twisting roads of Bucks County where my sensitivity to bright lights and sun glare got the best of me. The constant flipping of the visor back and forth in an attempt to prevent temporary blindness and vision obstruction became such a distraction from actually focusing on what was ahead, I thought, *why doesn't somebody come up with something better, that covers the side, front, and the corner of the windshield, more efficiently all at the same time?* Then I thought to myself, *Why not me?*

All vehicle accidents are frightening, but I remember one in particular, which I believe took place along the turnpike. It was approximately a forty-car plus pileup with several fatalities. A truck was transporting mirrors, and the sun was reflecting in those mirrors, causing such a glare that nobody could see – it was crash, after crash, after crash! It was horrifying that something like that could happen. It all had to do with the sun reflecting, and if the drivers involved had something in their vehicles that could remove that glare, like my Amazing Wiser Visor, then many injuries and fatalities could have been prevented.

I, personally, was involved in a vehicular accident coming down a curvy hill in a road, while facing into the sun. As I traveled down the hill, I came around a bend in the road, where the sun reflecting off the snow bounced off the corner of my windshield (the area the visor did not cover) and temporarily blinded me. The glare was so intense, and I drifted slightly across the center lane just as the other car came up around the bend. I should have seen him coming, but the glare restricted my vision for a second, and I ended up sideswiping the oncoming car.

My two children had their seat belts buckled in the back seat of my car. Luckily, they were not hurt, but I sustained some injuries. Out of precaution, the EMTs loaded me onto a backboard and slid me down the icy hill to the ambulance waiting approximately 20 ft away. Yes, it was also very icy conditions. My children thought this visual was quite funny, literally watching their mother sliding down a hill, from one EMT to the next – I believe they actually asked if they could have a ride! The point is, if I had a visor which protected that corner area, I would not have been temporarily blinded, and that accident could have been avoided.

In 1924 a man by the name of Hathaway invented the first rotating and pivotable sun visor arm for vehicles; proving even then there was a need to block sun glare from the front as well as the side. When heading around a bend or making a turn, the position of the sun would change, and the visor would offer protection from only the front OR the side – but not both! Hence my invention of the Amazing Wiser Visor, which blocks the sun from the front, side, and corner – all at the same time!

Trivia question: What year was Hathaway's visor **patented** and by who?

Any guesses?

Hint: It was the same year Superman first appeared in comic books.

Eleven months later Batman made his debut.

If you guessed 1938, you would be correct. And do you know who patented it?

That would be Henry Ford.

According to an article written by Ray Massey in the *Daily Mail*, sun glare causes thousands of accidents ("Glare of the Sun Causes Nearly 3,000 accidents a Year," Ray Massey, October 15, 2013). And while you would think there would be many more accidents attributed to glare, either from the sun or high-intensity headlights, the truth is that "glare" is not a defense for the cause of a vehicle accident. Drivers must be in control of their vehicle. According to the Associated Press at *Syracuse.com*, "Turning toward the glare of the setting sun doesn't qualify as a traffic emergency that excuses ordinary negligence, according to New York's top court." (10/13/2011)

According to Mainetti, Mainetti & O'Connor, P.C. (www.mmolaw. net), "We humans cannot change the weather; we are expected to adapt. This is exactly what New York courts will say about sun glare. Encountering sun glare is not sudden, nor is it unexpected, according to the court. Motorists know that the sun will impair the ability to see during the morning and evening hours. As such, drivers are expected to adapt and respond reasonably to the situation. Sun glare will not absolve or excuse motorists of liability in the event a car accident happens." (04/24/2015)

Donald A. Redelmeier and Sheharyar Raza wrote the article, "Life-Threatening Motor Vehicle Crashes in Bright Sunlight." According to them, "Bright sunlight is a natural factor in aerial perspective because it increases the contrast, resolution, and luminosity of surrounding landscapes. As a consequence, distant terrain can seem unduly close, and travel velocity may feel deceptively slow for drivers traveling in bright sunlight. The faulty impression could then lead drivers to compensate by accelerating faster (particularly for individuals on uncongested roads with seemingly easy driving conditions). Without a conscious effort to recheck the vehicle speedometer, therefore, a driver might inadvertently increase their risk of a life-threatening motor vehicle crash when traveling in bright sunlight." (01/10/2017).

In general, sunrise and sunset are the worst times to be on the road; particularly 4-5pm when people are traveling home – it's not quite sunset yet, but the sun sits right at your eye level. Two other factors that play into the danger of this time of day are blind corners and making turns into oncoming headlights. Somewhere along the line, somebody designed sun visors that are able to block the glare coming from directly in front and off to the side; but there still is a gap directly in the corner– does anyone really want to constantly be adjusting a visor as they drive down a curving road? That is just an extra distraction none of us need.

So, nearly ten years ago, I started tinkering with designs and putting things together to find a solution to this problem of glare. At one point, my design was just two solid pieces of material, and it was connected in the middle so you could fold it and put it back up when not in use as you normally would with a regular old visor. I realized for some; this design inhibited the driver's ability to properly see the road. I received feedback from some drivers, "I am really tall, so if the side piece is tilted this way, the front piece has to be tilted that way, it will not work, because the front piece will then block my view of the road."

Taking all of this into consideration, I realized both pieces needed to be transparent, able to block the glare, while still allowing drivers to see through it. Part of my developmental process has been to collect other kinds of visors and compare the functionality of them. Taking my working model, I met with about eight people from the American Inventors of Philadelphia. Each one had a different specialty, and they took my model. They pulled it apart, showing me the weaknesses and the strengths of it.

Since that point, I've made the improvements to my design model. Now I know what I want it to look like and I know exactly what I want it to do. I currently have a patent application (US20110057471A1). My visor is something that will benefit all drivers of vehicles. I have used the working model in my own vehicle, and it works very well. I certainly am not an engineer, but I know how it should best function and what it should look like. Now I just need the knowledge and capital to complete the manufacturing process and bring the Amazing Wiser Visor to you.

The Future of My Visor

In my efforts to raise capital, my main obstacle is disclosure. I feel I need to be cautious as to what information I should share and with whom. Because of this, I am having difficulties in accumulating finances to complete this project on my own. Back in January of 2015, I fell on ice and was hurt so badly I am now on Social Security for disability, and I have not received any income in over eight months. My savings have been almost completely depleted in just paying the normal monthly expenses we all have, as well as the extra medical expenses resulting from treatments after the fall.

It took me a long time to see that there's nothing wrong with asking for help. I always figured if I couldn't do it myself, then it couldn't be done. Once I realized I needed the help, the next step, I found out, was determining whom to ask. As it turns out, this is much harder than it sounds. You need to know the right people to talk to, and unfortunately, I did not, until now, which is why I am part of this book.

The Amazing Wiser Visor can help prevent accidents and save lives. It is obviously an aftermarket product; but when people see how well it works, it will be something every driver will want to have. So, if you're making a turn and the sun comes into view, you are still covered from any blinding glare. Since all areas are protected at the same time, the driver does not need to worry about repositioning the visor – distracting them from concentrating on the road ahead.

My plea is for assistance in raising capital, and I am looking for ideas and investors to help fund this project. Also, I have several other inventions that are presently in the napkin stage, if anyone is interested in getting involved on the ground floor and helping me promote them. If you have any questions or advice to further the Wiser Visor along – be it suggestions or financial help – you can reach me at WiserVisor@gmail.com. To my fellow entrepreneurs and dreamers, there is a lot of helpful advice in this book, and it's worth the read. In the meantime: stay strong, keep your momentum, and keep the sun out of your eyes.

Works Cited

Massey, Ray. *Daily Mail, Associated Newspapers, Ltd.* 15 October 2013.

Web. 15 April 2018.

Press, The Associated. *Syracuse.com.* 13 October 2011. Web. 15 April 2018.

Mainetti Mainetti & O'Connor, P.C., https://www.mmolaw.net 24 April 2015 Web.17 April 2018.

Redelmeier, Donald A., and Sheharyar Raza. "Life-Threatening Motor Vehicle Crashes in Bright Sunlight." Ed. Abdelouahab Bellou. *Medicine* 96.1 (2017): e5710. PMC. Web. 17 Apr. 2018.

18

CREATING CHAPTER 2

By
Troy Aberle

I am the creator of Troy Aberle International Inc., a company of like-minded people dedicated to Business Acceleration. I am a certified coach from Tony Robbins and a facilitator at Pacific Institute. I also have mentors like Brian Tracy, Bob Proctor, Brendon Burchard, and Napoleon Hill, just to name a few of the many I respect immensely.

My mission is simple: I am determined to help people learn the habits that result in success rather than the habits that cause failure.

I know about these key habits as a result of studying people and their businesses to find out how the techniques and mindsets affect the result of the various challenges put in front of them. These habits and beliefs are in the minds of the most successful people in the business community and can be learned by those of us looking to not reinvent the wheel in our own lives. Keep in mind the top performers know that business success is made up of strategies that are about 80% mental and 20% action.

My extensive business experience combined with the education of my mentors, taught me the value of systematic practice and study, combined with hard work, will keep me in the top of my category. And because of my rural roots, I am able to understand the value of combining this experience with the values I was raised with and how I am so lucky to have the opportunity to pay that forward to other people searching for the same answers I was.

What I've experienced during my own time in business management can be summed up in three words:

1. **Failure** – because I had no outcome or purpose, and because I was using habits that kept me from my goals. As well the people I was surrounded by had a poor influence and no similar inspirations that supported mine, and I became the same as them.

2. **Stagnation** – because I became comfortable with the level of certainty and accomplishment that I had. I was fearful of failure if I grew anymore because I worried about losing and questioned whether or not I was worthy of more reward.

3. **Success** – which was the result of starting a whole new chapter in my life, surrounding myself with inspiring mentors, and deciding to end old habits. I became obsessed with learning and implementing new habits and goals which were way out of my normal comfort zone.

I have worked for privately owned companies as well as large corporations of shareholders, including those operating in the agricultural industry, supply management, solar manufacturing, oil and gas, and safety. I have always held positions in management and sales at the places I have worked. I was often given the opportunity to be a leader of a department, a location, or a large section of the company because I enjoyed finding new opportunity and challenging the stagnant and reserved approach.

Being a leader has always been very satisfying for me as I was always able to relate well to people, primarily the people who already set good examples for others and teach what has been tried and tested. During that period, I always had the intrigue, the desire, and the passion for talking to people who were wiser than me; who had many more years of experience (whether it'd be with failures or successes) and could really teach me. This very much ensured that I wouldn't continue making any of their same mistakes, which I knew would help my development and my success so much faster than the people who were present around me. Crushing goals, and achieving targets that are not imaginable, are what drives me passionately. During this time, I committed myself and a large number of resources to taking courses, studying companies, and attending countless seminars. All of this was done in search of how leaders and high achievers became high-performance people. I owe a great deal of gratitude for what so many role models have taught me, shaping me into the expert I am called today. This approach has credited me with a great reputation and inspiration for people to want me to coach them with their careers and their companies. I am successful when I help people develop growth strategies, look at the company's direction from a different angle, and challenge what is working and not working for them.

My journey wasn't easy; I had to apply my learning to my own life and journey. I had struggles just like you and everyone else creating that next chapter in their life. Even though it appeared that I was successful, growing and excelling, I was dealing with depression, alcohol addiction, stress, worry, and both financial and life tensions of creating a family and running businesses simultaneously at a very young age. Often, it was tempting at many times to just give up and live a non-goal-oriented life. Being committed to the mindset of determination has caused my outcome to be a win each time I decided it would be! Having my wife's support and coaching has also been key to my own outcomes of success. I often guide my clients through this teaching: "If you want to understand what the most successful people have done when they start from nothing and end up doing awesome, you need to know it is because they understand that changing your identity and your focus is a must to change your outcome. These people also had to realize that their habits and focus needed to change from the limiting hurdles to a completely new path with clear direction and a mind shift that is prepared and laser focus of the ultimate outcome. Having the goals known and committed to is key to creating the visualization of achievement.

"Success leaves clues."

– TONY ROBBINS

All of us in business have experienced that numbing and sickening feeling of stress as a difficult situation arises, and it seems like there is no easy path to choose because of the hurdles we see in front of us along the path we are on. We have a choice: we can just give up and allow defeat to be our outcome, or we can choose to see the possibilities past the hurdles. The top 1% of successful people will confirm this because they understand that defining goals and being committed to achieving them is what earns results. Sadly though, most people are ok with learning to accept failure, as it just seems easier to not face the fears associated with trying and pushing past your comfort level.

Because of my own journey, I developed a very simple set of systems that worked well for me and kept me on the track to success. The first systems helped me define the actions and habits that were keeping me from my goals and reminded me what the repercussions were when using them. I needed to commit to a new set of habits that were going to get me to my goals and identify why it was so important to achieve them and who would be affected by the new outcome.

My problem was common for many of us: "How do I really commit to this exciting new life if I am still dabbling in the old one?" It seemed like such a hard question to solve, so I decided to share my gifts of learning to help people learn how to live the life they deserve and wish to commit to as their identity. In my experience, the people winning in business are often good at doing the following:

- They have a conditioned state that enables them to show up for the audience with positive and constructive conversation.
- They are committed to building a relationship that is mutually beneficial.
- They build rapport and trust with people and display how a future relationship will look like if they agree to a commitment to the business.
- They inspire people to want to work toward an outcome that is clearly defined.
- They are constantly double-stacking value to over-deliver and make the customer outcome greater than expected.
- They understand the human needs of people and want to help them achieve them.

I believe that business is the transfer of emotion, and when there is no emotional exchange, then no business will occur. You must know your goal, breathe your goal, and have only that outcome in your mind. Sadly, however, most people focus on the hurdles in front of that goal and fail because they are not determined in their mind emotionally. When you are not emotionally committed how would you expect a winning result? I am inspired and honored to write this chapter for you and hope that you can apply these teachings throughout reading this book and enhance your personal and business life!

How Can My Expertise Help You?
(peak performance coaching)

I am so thrilled to have the opportunity to serve people as a coach, mentor, or advisor because I simply love to help people be their very best. There is no better feeling than getting a call from someone that can't see past the hurdles on the track, and you guide them to smashing them all down and winning. I have several people on my team that offer specialized services such as; business coaching, life coaching, corporate workshops, sales training, real estate coaching, and investment coaching. The calls are 55-minute sessions and are primarily via telephone, video, or in person. Group strategy sessions are great for your company or workplace and can really get everyone involved in the discussion. And I really enjoy training someone your company to continue facilitating customized material all of the time for your team.

During our call sessions, we really dive deep to get the results that you must have. Whether it's a public speaking event or coaching session, my strength is being able to deconstruct the big obstacles you perceive as being in front of you, and I help you break these down into small, little chunks and accelerate your business very quickly. It's the bullshit beliefs you are telling yourself that is holding you back and my job is to make sure you see that fear is your enemy and that your own self-talk is the vehicle that keeps delivering that emotion. The majority of people have goals, but they only see mountains to be climbed in order to get there; and thusly, they start mastering these negative beliefs that limit them from even trying. The really high performers have mastered the strategy to focus on the reward on the other side of that mountain without allowing stress, fear, and possible negative outcomes to be the reason that they don't try the journey.

My programs are being shared and used by many people and coaches, and it's been proven, time and time again, to be very effective strategies. The people I help today are primarily corporate executives, managers, entrepreneurs, bosses, salespeople, and real estate professionals. All of them have very big goals that are very relatable to my past experience.

I've been blessed with the opportunity to always be on the top leader-board of the companies I've worked for, and to attain the results for which I was hired. Again, my reputation comes from very solid rural roots where I grew up on a farm and learned from a very young age that working hard, working with integrity and determination is paramount to keeping yourself in it for the long haul. My instinct is that there's a big factor with the 80/20 Rule: 80% of people only give 20% effort.

If you have a business that is stagnant, failing, or without any purpose, meaning, or direction, I want to work with you too. I personally know that it doesn't take too much work to make a massive change if you have a plan and the right people supporting you to achieve those results.

To this end, I created programs that can be learned through personal coaching, or by enrolling in one of my online courses. These programs include:

1. Creating and Living Chapter 2 of Your Life
2. The Good Boss
3. How to be a Rockstar Salesperson

Creating and Living Chapter 2 of Your Life

This program is a powerful system that I encourage everyone to go through, whether it be for your business or yourself personally. What we are doing in this exercise is agreeing that the journey up to today is chapter 1 of your life or your business's life.

On the top of a page, write "Chapter 1" and below add the following:

1) Identify your goal/outcome you want to achieve at the top of the page.

2) Identify the actions or beliefs that are keeping you from your goal, and how that impacts you and the people who rely on you to achieve that goal.

3) We agree on what of those items are going to stop being performed because of the negative result.

Then we start a new piece of paper and add the heading "Chapter 2."

1) Re-write that goal or outcome at the top of the page.

2) Identify and create actions that you know will move you toward the goal (these are usually the opposite of what was identified in Chapter 1).

3) List why these new actions or beliefs will bring you to your goal and who it will be having an impact on.

We must commit to the fact that Chapter 2 is the new blueprint that our life or the business's life will be lived and that we are no longer going to accept living the limitations of Chapter 1. You can't erase what happened in the first chapter of your life; you need to accept it and realize that these experiences have given us clues. Some of those clues created a positive outcome, and some of them created a negative outcome. But you cannot be halfway; you must create a very serious list and know that change is a must if you want a different outcome. Do not let fear stand in your way – all of us at some point have a fear of failure, the fear of success, or the fear of lacking self-worthiness.

To achieve success in this exercise, we must realize that there are 3 very important things to check in to calibrate our mental preparedness. These questions are as follows:

Key #1: Our State

- How are we showing up in this new chapter to be executed?
- What are we focused on throughout the day in our personal and professional life?
- Is our physiology showing our level of interest and energy (body language)?
- Is our verbal language portraying our message?
- What are our mental thoughts and self-talk?

Key #2: Our Story

- Why are we doing this?
- Why is achieving this a "must"?
- Who is going to be impacted because of our efforts?
- Why must we be in Chapter 2 of my habits?

Key #3: Our Strategy

- Be educated on the best actions to achieve the goal.
- Master the habits and mindset.
- Execute what we said we would to serve others.
- Empower those around me with inspiration.
- Be surrounded with only supportive people.

Writing answers to these questions on paper is very powerful because it really programs the emotional attachment that you have to each of the keys above.

The Good Boss Book

I am proud of my 1st book, *The Good Boss,* which is a product that reads very simple and methodical and supports the teachings I offer for the Good Boss Academy I have created. When I wrote this book, I wanted it to be simple and almost point form so that people could read it simply and remember it as quick answers to their own subconscious challenges. For the last 17 years, I did an intense amount of research into various companies, whether they be solopreneurs or large corporations, and everything in between. What I started to realize very quickly was that the companies I was studying seemed to have common habits taking place every single day. And these were really bugging me because you could tell these habits were developed from a very old chapter of the business; their strategy never changed.

There were many key elements that were not in place to support the current needs and wants of the employee; I will now refer to six of them, which I learned from my mentor, Tony Robbins. Every single person in this world needs to have these specific needs met in some way. And so, when I was looking at how employees were showing up, how many people actually understood what was going on in the business, who understood their job properly or felt really satisfied to be working there, the range was quite alarmingly low when the following needs were met:

1. Certainty
2. Uncertainty
3. Significance
4. Love connection and friendship
5. Growth
6. Contribution

Turnover of employees is extremely expensive and depressing. Clients hiring me were saying, "Our turnover's too high, Troy. Our staff is miserable, and we don't know where to start with the basics to begin the repair, and we are unable to execute the strategies and goals that we want to. Now, what do we do? We are so bad internally that we look bad externally to our customer!" So, I would literally start writing notes of things that needed to be done. At first, it started out to be point form, but I started to realize that this doesn't have to get really detailed, or rocket science level. These were very basic things that I taught bosses, and they were giving them good results as I did so.

I look at a guy like Henry Ford, a personal inspiration. He hired people, much smarter than himself, to be around him to execute goals. I think a lot of bosses still think that if they don't do it, it'll never be done properly. To this, my question is, "Why do we hire all these people if we won't inspire and help them be absolutely awesome?"

The Good Boss Online Program is available for purchase now, and it's also supported by my coaching and helping you find clarity in your business, specifically.

How to Be a Rockstar Salesperson

How to Be a Rockstar Salesperson, was designed for salespeople of any industry, whether it be product services, real estate, and many bosses enjoyed going through this as well. It is a successful video series that I produced and sell on my website. It walks you through items that show you how to prepare yourself mentally and emotionally for a sales meeting; how to conduct yourself in a meeting; how to build rapport and really understand the client's needs. In terms of sales, one big thing I fully relate to is that people either purchase things for one of two reasons:

- Gain pleasure
- Avoid pain

You really need to dive deep and get inside the person's psychological state to understand why they're purchasing any given thing. You can then help them in making a very consultative decision about whether or not what you have to offer is something that can solve their problem. The best way of implementing that for them is through their investment of emotion and finances to you being reciprocated by the closure and the experience they were hoping to find when they purchased what you offer.

I think there's a lot more to it, that if you actually show that you give a crap about someone, they will actually trust you more and want to continue buying from you. Not only will they be that satisfied customer; you can slide them into that category of loyalty because they trust you. And yes, when you do make mistakes, they won't just dump you because of it; they'll dump you because you no longer care about their being satisfied. So, I developed my course so that people could either start out in a sales role or they could grow into the sales role. Many who purchase the program are people going through really bad lulls. Lulls are when you're selling on fire for one or two months, and then you crash for one or two months.

During my sales career, I am honored to say that I have sold over $300 million dollars in products and services. I am a professional sales trainer that has been trained by great people who taught me how to be the best. That is why I am delivering the strategies that rewarded me beyond imagination. I can proudly say that my sales training systems have made people enormous amounts of money and created long-term success for companies of people that are demanding the best results.

Similar to this program, I also developed the Real Estate Masters Academy to help people in that industry. This is currently in development, and we are planning on launching it at the end of summer, 2018. If you want to be a part of the beta program, please reach out to coach@troyaberle.com.

Conclusion

Surround yourself with the people you want to be like or do business with. I keep repeating this and never understand why people cannot see it. You wouldn't go to a baseball game expecting to see a wrestling match. So, go to the arena that has your interest, and play the game too. Omit the garbage that doesn't interest or serves your needs. That is what I had to do, and it feels a lot better being in the arena I am in, which is supporting people to become awesome and inspiring them to do it for others as well.

My company is focused on business consulting and coaching people around the programs I've developed to help people be ready for that sales pitch or business offer. I want people to be happier at work and going home satisfied. I do develop programs that are specific or customized exclusively for a client; and at some point, some of those might be offered to the general public and business community. In addition to a variety of coaches, we have people that help our clients with branding, marketing, web design, and social media campaigns. A large percentage of our clients have horrible marketing occurring, and often in just one session, we can really streamline their efforts and have a huge impact on whom they are trying to get attention from.

My best compliment?

"Troy has such a wide range of knowledge and perspective; he really cares about the people he serves and delivers tons more than he promises. His team is just as powerful, and you can tell that they really love working together to make a huge impact in any industry."

My experience supports how I break down the big hurdles between clients and their goals, and how I get them to those goals. I look forward to anyone approaching me for coaching or for a discovery session. If you really want to be the best of the best, train like the best and master your success potential!

I am extremely passionate about enhancing people's lives, and I want to show you how simple making the right choices can be. There is no better feeling than helping people become their best. Please reach out to me and allow me the opportunity to show you personally how to create focus and the meaning behind it, and then let's build a strategy system that empowers with the best strategies to become a Master of It!

Find out how Troy Aberle International can help you, your business, or your career, and accelerate yourself to the next level that you deserve!
www.troyaberle.com

19

DEFEATED BY THE IMPOSSI-BALL®

Lessons Learned by a Patent Attorney

by
John Rizvi

I'm the founder and leader of The Patent Professor®. As a patent attorney and adjunct professor of patent law, for the past 20 years, I have seen too many people give up on their ideas because they don't think their ideas are big enough. They believe that in order to see a patent attorney, they need to have invented a time machine or a fountain of youth. Nothing could be further from the truth.

I started out my practice working at the New York City law firm of Fish & Neave. If you don't know who they are, these are the lawyers who represented Thomas Edison with his patent on the light bulb, Henry Ford and his automobile, Alexander Graham Bell with the telephone, and the Wright Brothers with their patenting of the airplane. Fish & Neave is to patents what Muhammad Ali is to boxing – the greatest of all time. But for me, something was missing. I wanted to work with inventors and startups with new ideas. Instead, the Fish & Neave of today mostly represents huge, multi-national corporations. All my meetings were with lawyers and MBAs; not once did I meet with an inventor.

My dream was to quit and start my own patent law firm, focusing on early-stage ideas, and the garage inventor. I wanted Steve Jobs and Bill Gates before they became Apple and Microsoft. I did just that when I started my own practice and branded myself as The Patent Professor®. At the age of twelve, I was on a mission. I took apart a Rubik's Cube with a screwdriver, and I destroyed it. My dream and sole ambition in life was to create a round Rubik's Cube (you can tell the nerds early). And one day, my mom took me to KB Toys in the mall. I went, as I always did, to the aisle where they kept puzzles and games, like the Rubik's Cube, and what I saw there on the shelf crushed me. Someone had already made a round Rubik's Cube, and they came up with a better name than "Round Rubik's Cube." They called it the Impossi-Ball®, and in my twelve-year-old mind, they had stolen my idea. I fought so hard not to cry in front of my mom, and I succeeded, except nobody knows you like your mom.

She saw me fighting back the tears, and she had seen my sketchbooks with page after page of drawings of my round Rubik's Cube. When I looked at her, she was the one who started crying. So, I grabbed my mom by the hand, and I dragged her out of the store. The staff had seen plenty of mothers dragging out their crying kids. I bet this was the first time they saw a kid dragging out their crying mom.

Children cry when they don't achieve their dreams, and do you know why? Because they actually believe that achieving their dreams is possible. But, something happens to us as adults. We let people convince us that our big, beautiful, bold dreams are just fantasies, so we dream small and dream safe. We stay confined within the boundary of that comfort zone that President Roosevelt referred to as "the gray twilight." People will try to keep you in that gray twilight if you let them.

Oprah Winfrey was told that she was too ugly for television. Walt Disney was fired by a newspaper editor for not having enough imagination – imagine that! How many of your dreams have you not pursued because someone convinced you that you didn't fit the right mold, you didn't look the right way, you didn't go to the right schools, or you didn't have the right connections, money, or social background?

What would happen if you had pushed ahead anyway? Having known, firsthand, the shock of seeing my round Rubik's Cube on a store shelf, while my designs lay hidden in a sketchbook under my bed, I know the pain of not taking action fast enough on a new idea. Little did I know at the time, helping inventors patent their ideas to prevent them from being stolen would become my life's passion.

What is a Patent?

A patent is a right granted by the United States to an inventor to exclude others from making, using, selling, or even importing their invention into the United States without their permission. In its simplest form, a patent is a monopoly granted by the United States to an inventor, enabling them to exploit their creativity by providing them with the security that they will enjoy the fruits of hard work and ingenuity; patents encourage innovation. In the famous words of Abraham Lincoln, the patent system added the fuel of interest to the fire of ingenuity. The founding fathers of our country, for the first time in the history of the world, decided to provide every citizen with the incentive to create and invent. They placed great confidence in the inspired ordinary citizen.

A patent right is a legal right to limit competition. It is often the most valuable of assets owned by a business. Some of the largest corporations in America today were started by individual inventors who decided to seek patent protection and then exploit the monopoly granted by the United States government. The airplane was the creation of the Wright Brothers, two bicycle mechanics in Dayton, Ohio. The electric light was the creation of a farm boy who never completed high school, Thomas Edison. Whether you're looking at AT&T, Dow Chemical, Goodyear, Eastman Kodak, Xerox, 3M, Hewlett-Packard, Apple, Google, or Amazon, it doesn't matter; the fact is that most of America's greatest innovations started as ideas with very humble beginnings. There is truth to the statement that today's big ideas are tomorrow's big businesses.

Patents are valuable property. Like other property, a patent can be sold outright, and of course, patents can also be licensed – for a percentage of the sales price. Over a billion dollars of patent rights are licensed every year. One question I receive often in my practice: How do patents differ from other intellectual property (such as trademarks or copyrights)?

Well, a trademark is a word, logo, design, or even a combination of these. The trademark identifies the origin or source of a good or service. It is valuable because consumers identify the mark with a particular quality of the goods or services. Examples of trademarks are Band-Aid for bandages, MacDonald's for fast food, and Coca-Cola for soft drinks. What about copyrights? Copyrights protect the literary, artistic, commercial, or other original expression of an idea. Unlike patents, copyrights do not protect the function of an item. For example, a copyright might protect the look of the screen of a website, but a patent would be able to protect the way the software actually operates.

Now that we've had that brief overview of other types of intellectual property, let's look at the different types of patents that are available:

1. Utility
2. Design
3. Plant

As plant patents are very rare, I won't be covering them in much detail. First off, utility patents are what the vast majority of new inventions are protected as. A utility patent protects the function of an invention. They are granted for any new, useful, and non-obvious process, machine, manufactured article, or composition of matter. Patents are also granted for new and useful improvements to existing inventions. The term of a utility patent is twenty years from the date of filing. For those twenty years, the inventor is given the power to exclude anyone from making, using, or selling their invention.

Unlike a utility patent, a design patent is not concerned with the function of an invention. A design patent protects the overall appearance of an invention and is granted for any new, original, and ornamental design. The term of a design patent is shorter than that of a utility patent and is only valid fourteen years from issuance. A design patent should only be chosen if the specific appearance of an invention is important. Otherwise, a utility patent is the type of protection that should be sought.

Practical Steps

What should an inventor do the moment they have a new idea? There are some things an inventor can do immediately to help protect their idea. These steps cost close to nothing and give some protection to an inventor before they're able to file a patent application. You do not need a patent attorney in order to complete these initial steps. The first step is to begin making detailed records of the invention. Ideally, you can do this in a bound notebook, or it can be done on a computer, as long as you have a way to date stamp the different entries. You may have heard the term "inventor's logbook," and that is where you keep detailed records of the progress you make with your invention. The inventor's logbook can also record any purchases you've made in the process of developing a prototype.

Now, one thing that you don't want to do when you have a new idea is to mail yourself a self-addressed envelope. This is a myth, and it's a waste of time and complete nonsense. These self-addressed envelopes are sometimes referred to as a "poor man's patent"; but they truly offer absolutely no protection. This brings me to the next topic, and that is disclosing your invention, but more specifically, the risks of disclosing your invention.

The possibility of having your new idea stolen before you have applied for a patent is something that has haunted every new inventor. As such, it is important to keep the details of your idea secret until you have applied for a patent. Prematurely disclosing your invention would jeopardize your ability to obtain patent protection.

In the United States, there are certain deadlines which an inventor must meet in order to avoid the loss of patent rights. What if you think you may want patent protection in other countries as well as the United States? If you are interested in foreign patent protection, the need to avoid public disclosure of your invention is even more important.

In most countries, a patent application must be filed before the invention is in public use or on sale. There is no grace period. With that being said, what about revealing your invention to your patent attorney? A registered patent attorney is bound by the canons of professional conduct and the attorney/client fiduciary duty. Anything you discuss with your attorney is attorney/client privilege and confidential, and disclosure to an attorney does not constitute public disclosure.

One thing I would like to share with you now is about non-disclosure agreements. A non-disclosure agreement (sometimes called a confidentiality agreement) is used by an inventor to reveal an unpatented idea to a party. The inventor has the other party sign a document that says they will not disclose any of the information to anyone else nor will they compete with the inventor. I strongly discourage revealing your invention until you have filed a patent application, even if you have a non-disclosure agreement. Non-disclosure agreements should be used sparingly and only when disclosure of your idea to another party is required. It is far better to discuss your invention in general terms and do not reveal how it works than to reveal important details and rely on a non-disclosure agreement.

Remember, to enforce a non-disclosure agreement you might need to go to court. Although you are eventually likely to win, this will cost a lot of time and money that should be going towards the development and marketing of your product. You can keep the details of your invention secret while still satisfying inventors and venture capitalists; keep in mind, they are more concerned with whether your product has marketing potential and consumer appeal than the intricacies of how it works.

Many inexperienced inventors believe that they can sell large companies on their idea and protect themselves with a non-disclosure agreement. This is a myth. Most established companies will refuse to sign an individual inventor's non-disclosure agreement. In fact, many will only accept new ideas if they are patented or if a patent has at least been applied for.

Provisional Patent Applications

There is a lot of misinformation about the provisional application, and I would like to help clear some of this up. Filing a provisional patent is cheaper than filing a regular patent application, and a lot of inexperienced inventors rush to file provisional patent applications. Keep in mind that a provisional patent application will expire after one year. If you do not file a regular patent application within the one-year period, your provisional application is thrown away by the Patent and Trademark Office, and you will have no legal protection for your invention.

It is important to note that a provisional patent application is not reviewed by the Patent and Trademark Office. It just sits there until the year is up and then it is discarded. Also, keep in mind that a provisional patent can never issue as a patent. Because the costs involved in filing a provisional patent are low, and there is no review of the provisional patent application, many fraudulent marketing companies and document preparation firms (with no lawyers on staff and no worry about being sued for malpractice), will offer to file a provisional patent application on behalf of unwary inventors who believe the application will give them substantive protection.

Because there is no review of the application by the patent office, document preparation companies will often file whatever you give them and only charge a couple hundred dollars for this service. Be careful. If someone is only charging you a few hundred dollars for a provisional patent application, it is extremely unlikely that the application will be properly written – and it won't entitle you to a real filing date. You might be paying for a false sense of security.

Having said that, when is filing a provisional patent application a good idea? A provisional patent application can be a lifesaver when you are under extreme time pressure to secure a filing date at the Patent and Trademark Office. For example, let's say you want to display your invention at a trade show in three days and there isn't enough time to file a patent application. If you use a provisional patent application under such circumstances, remember that it will be useless after a year unless you follow up with a regular patent application. It is best not to wait until the last minute to do this. Other times when a provisional patent application makes sense include protecting ideas that are in the early stages of development which might undergo changes during the following year.

With a properly filed provisional patent application, through an attorney, you can include those changes prior to the filing of your regular patent application at the end of the year. When properly filed by a registered patent attorney, a provisional patent application can be a secure and safe way of obtaining a filing date and becoming patent pending. Ask your patent attorney if filing a provisional patent makes sense in your case.

What's Patentable?
(and what are the requirements?)

In the US there are four classifications of patents:

1. A machine
   - (a device or apparatus)
2. A manufacture
   - (a manufactured article)
3. A composition of matter
   - (a combination of ingredients, i.e., chemicals)
4. A process
   - (a method of doing something, i.e., software or app patents fall within this category)

What are the requirements for patentability? An invention must be useful, novel, and non-obvious. And it must be adequately described in a patent application. We will look into each of these areas separately.

Useful

In short, this means that your invention should work. This is fairly simple. Your invention cannot be inoperable.

Novel

In order for an invention to be novel, it must be new, as described in the patent law. This means that the same invention has not been known or described by others in this country, or patented, or described anywhere before its invention by the applicant.

Please note: if the inventor describes the invention in a printed publication, and uses the invention publicly, or places it on sale, they must apply for a patent before one year has gone by. Otherwise, any rights to the patent will be lost.

Non-obvious

What if the exact invention is not shown in the prior art? What if there are small differences that your invention has over what is already known? This is where the requirement of non-obviousness comes in. The patent law does not permit a known invention to be patented; however, the law goes beyond that.

It also does not permit the patenting of an invention that is so close to something that is old, that the differences would be obvious. Obvious to who? Obvious to someone skilled in the art to which the invention pertains. This is an oversimplification of the non-obviousness standard. Indeed, entire books and treatise have been written on the non-obviousness requirement in the patent law, and a lot of litigation surrounds this area.

The Road Blocks

I strongly believe that a person has a right to profit from their ingenuity and that their ideas and inventions should not be subject to theft. Now that I have gone over the basics of patents, I want to address a couple significant roadblocks that I have seen preventing inventors from moving forward fast enough to secure their ideas. The first roadblock is the ease at which we can stay inside our comfort zone and avoid failure and the harsh judgment of others – again, this is what Roosevelt referred to this place as the gray twilight, and here's the full text of that famous quote:

"Far better it is to dare mighty things, to win glorious triumphs even though checkered by failure, than to rank with those timid spirits who neither enjoy nor suffer much because they live in that gray twilight that knows neither victory nor defeat."

As adults, we learn to give up on our dreams and decide to stay in the gray twilight. The key is to think back to your childhood and harness that ability to dream and the confidence that if an idea came to you, then it was meant for you to bring forward. And when it comes to launching a new idea, speed is everything.

In my 20 years as a patent attorney, I've seen too many inventors lose out on their ideas because they hesitated in moving forward fast enough out of fear that they were not the right person to bring the idea forward. They might believe they are an outsider to an industry. An example would be if someone who is a dental patient has an idea for a better way to take dental X-rays, but they aren't an expert in the dental industry. A more general example is someone who thinks that because they've only finished high school, they cannot contribute to an industry with a new idea because they lack the necessary educational background. Another example is someone who doesn't have the right connections or money.

I understand these concerns because I'm not immune to them either. I faced the same self-doubt as I was writing my first book, *Escaping the Gray*. I was an unknown author at the time, and this had me questioning whether I should move forward; but then I put things in perspective. *Well, nobody knew who Helen Keller was either.* Helen Keller was not the only blind or deaf person in the world, but she was inspired to write about her struggles. Anne Frank was not the only Jewish person suffering due to Nazi Germany, but she was inspired to write her diary.

Another common roadblock for inventors is questioning whether the timing is right for them to move forward. Having practiced for twenty years, I can tell you that ideas never come at the perfect time. I've had clients who didn't pursue an idea because they were going through a divorce at the time; they had lost their job; they suddenly found themselves expecting a child; they were audited by the IRS; they were college students barely scraping by. One of the hardest things in my practice is to meet with these inventors and see the evidence of their idea and tell them I can't do anything for them because they didn't file for a patent. I learned this the hard way as I spent too many years at the prestigious patent law firm of Fish & Neave, doing work for corporations that didn't interest me. I wanted more than anything else to quit and represent inventors directly, and help them secure their ideas, but I was scared.

It's hard to quit when you're at the top. Leaving the prestige and stability of Fish & Neave to go out on my own seemed like jumping off a cliff. I didn't know what to do. I started writing weekly emails to the smartest person I know: Dad. And it was a family affair. I also included my mom, my two sisters, and my brother. Week after week for two years, I shared my thoughts on quitting, and I would give my family an update on my decision – which was always no decision.

It's hard to jump off that cliff. The weekly emails were like a private diary of my innermost fears, except it turned out not to be as private as I thought. You see, I had one little letter wrong in my dad's email address. Instead of sending the emails to my dad, for over two years I had been spamming a total stranger with my thoughts about quitting until I got a reply one day: "Stop freaking emailing me."

He was frustrated at my decision, and then he really took the gloves off in his next email:

> *"You have neither the balls to start your own law firm nor the brains to give up."*

Something told me this wasn't dad. This single email from a stranger was my tipping point, and that evening I mustered up the courage to speak to my wife, Saba, about quitting. It took courage because the timing was terrible. We had a one-year-old daughter and another baby on the way. "Honey, I want to quit my job and go out on my own." We had no savings. I had no clients, no revenues, no staff, no office, and huge student loans to pay back. "Will you trust me with taking this chance?" I looked at my wife, and do you know what she said?

She said to go for it.

The greatest blessing in this world is to be married to someone that thinks you can do anything. Sometimes this can be a curse too, but that is for another book. So, with her behind me, I did it. I quit and started my own law firm. That was seventeen years ago, and it was one of the best decisions I ever made. And it all started with tiny, irritating emails. If you're on the fence about pursuing a dream that you have or launching a new product, let this chapter be your tipping point that gets you over the edge.

If you would like a free copy of my book, *Escaping the Gray*, or *Think and Grow Rich for Inventors*, please email me at JohnRizvi@ ThePatentProfessor.com. In your email, please mention this chapter from the Kevin Harrington anthology, and I will be happy to send it to you.

If you need help determining whether or not your idea has wings, or if you find yourself stuck in the gray twilight of your comfort zone, please visit my website (www.ThePatentProfessor.com) and request a consultation with me. Anything we discuss will be completely confidential and attorney-client privileged, and I will waive the initial consultation fee for any readers of this book.

20

BECOMING YOUR OWN SHARK THROUGH CROWDFUNDING

Attracting Millennials and Other Aspiring Entrepreneurs to a New Lifestyle

By

John Galley and Adam Ackerman

The days of working forty years for the same company, a retirement party with a gold watch and chain, and a nice retirement benefits package all lie dead on the dustbin of history. Millennials and Gen-Xers will need to fend for themselves. They must choose between a series of jobs – satisfying or otherwise, and with no built-in retirement security – or taking their lives into their own hands and both embrace and embark upon a full-time or part-time "life of the entrepreneur." The great news is that many Millennials and Gen-Xers are recognizing and embracing this new reality containing tremendous potential and opportunity for them. At the other end of the spectrum, there are many older, capable people who have been downsized or outsourced. Out of necessity, they too are looking for an entrepreneurial path that has an "easy entry" with low financial risk. Online selling of physical products is an attractive entrepreneurial avenue. Many people have become extraordinarily wealthy in a short period of time while building successful, sustainable businesses for themselves.

This path is providing financial and personal freedom on many levels. In the growing world of the internet and selling physical products online, a fundamental challenge is finding the necessary seed money; it's hard to make bricks without straw. There is also the issue that – as interest and competition increases in this attractive category – there are some tactics previously taught, initially bringing an experience of success, which no longer work as well today; alternative strategies are needed and are being sought.

Is there a newer path to the success of online physical products? One that requires very little initial money, with good odds for success, and when done right, almost zero financial risks, and a clear path to a bright future? The answer is a resounding "YES!" And it is not only viable for the new generations, but also for the older ones as well. Fortunately, there is an affordable, alternative entry path to selling physical products online that can be just as (or more) effective than what may seem more obvious or popular. It does not require "rolling the dice" on product selection, nor does it require spending serious money that people do not have on inventory for both sales and promotions.

Crowdfunding
(the fascinating jump-starter for product and business success)

Unlike loans that must be repaid – or selling equity in a business idea (think Shark Tank and Venture Capital) – crowdfunding is a less onerous path for both the beta-testing market acceptability of a product and the raising of money to capitalize on the success achieved. Once the seed money is attained, it's time to go forward to a "life after crowdfunding"; in a manner of speaking. This is a chance to become your own shark. Crowdfunding is a way to introduce the prototype of a product to a crowd of people (often called "early adopters") who enjoy being among the first to have a new product or product modification. Essentially, they pre-order the product and pay for it now, eventually then receiving their actual product at some point (usually several months) in the future. The two most popular websites for this activity are Kickstarter and Indiegogo. Crowdfunding is the ultimate entrepreneurial incubator for physical products! Contrary to what is believed by many, launching a successful crowdfunding campaign does not require some scathingly brilliant, creative idea. Most seemingly new products are the result of building incrementally upon existing ideas. It's a fact. Existing products with clever modification, differentiation and positioning are regularly achieving crowdfunding success (sometimes over $1M!) and this approach to product creation is becoming the crowdfunding norm.

As an industry, crowdfunding is in its infancy! There are proliferation and segmentation taking place as more choices and uses enter the field and "drill down" with greater focus; the possibilities have barely been scratched. In 2015, over $30B were raised with crowdfunding. With the typical platform user fee of 5%, that amounts to over $1.5B in crowdfunding platform revenue. A report in Forbes opines crowdfunding will account for more funding in 2016 than traditional venture capital. Amazing! Crowdfunding is the future wave of raising capital for new ideas. It has ever-growing appeal because it is democratic and simplistic and not elitist compared to venture capital.

The Tech Turkey
($348,449 in 30 days: breaking a category record on Kickstarter)

In the interest of full disclosure, when John began his first crowdfunding campaign, he didn't know enough about the subject to be dangerous. Yes, he previously heard of the concept and did a little research about it online; but he never spent any serious time on any crowdfunding website, nor had he ever "backed" or supported any campaign. He was as much of a raw rookie as it is possible to be.

About

Support

Pledge $1 or more

Our undying thanks for helping us bring our
sunglasses to the consumer market.

ESTIMATED DELIVERY
Sep 2014

37 backers

Pledge $5 or more

A handwritten "Thank You" Note from Orion
creator and patent-holder, Kirk Kreutzig.

ESTIMATED DELIVERY SHIPS TO
Oct 2014 Anywhere in the
 world

9 backers

John decided to create a sunglasses product using a special technology an acquaintance patented and successfully sold to the U.S. Defense Department in the form of several products. Together, their intention was to sell this commercial version of his technology on Amazon – and perhaps other internet platforms in the future. Making necessary changes to their technology, to ensure its suitability for consumer use as sunglasses, as well as an illness in this acquaintance's family, brought delays to their efforts in successfully launching on Amazon. During this delay, John made the decision to personally take the bull by the horns and beta-test the product on Kickstarter by himself.

Crowdfunding platforms are uniquely designed to accomplish this important market-testing activity. In this unique setting, it would be possible to make a case for this special eyewear, to pre-sell the product without already having it in stock and having the capability of it being immediately delivered. John's limited preparation for the campaign consisted of:

- Reading two books about crowdfunding
  - ➤ Both ordered on Amazon.

- Attending a local boat show
  - Where he showed people a military version of the eyewear and passed out fliers about the upcoming campaign on Kickstarter.
- Shooting a simple primary video for the campaign
  - With a local marketing videographer
- Writing the project page for the campaign himself.

Basically, that was it! John did reach out to a handful of family and friends; but at the age of 75, at least 40% of his lifetime friends were "on the wrong side of the grass." There wasn't a lot of traction to be gained there despite the typical advice offered by most of the so-called "crowdfunding gurus." After some last minute administrative scrambling due to unfamiliarity with the platform, John launched his Kickstarter Campaign on August 12, 2014. Literally within seconds, the first "pledge" arrived in his email inbox, and more of them just kept coming. John reached his goal and was funded within one day. By the second day, Kickstarter named his project as one of their coveted "Staff Picks." The momentum continued to build –pretty soon, pledges were rolling in at the rate of about one every 12 minutes – and steadily continued for 30 days; all of this totaled to $348,449! Needless to say, John was overwhelmed! He honestly expected to do reasonably well, but not to this extent. In part, his expectations were based on the fact that the technology really does work; even though people could not try them out personally, he had testimonials from serious people who said it worked. Overall, he never expected this kind of support.

It quickly became obvious that the vast majority of this support was coming from people John didn't know; he only occasionally recognized a name from among the many backers who were lining up to support him. As Butch Cassidy and The Sundance Kid (Paul Newman and Robert Redford) kept asking each other, "Who are those guys?!" John asked himself the same question. It was in that reflection that he learned an important secret which none of the gurus presented as he read their material. Knowing this secret – and how to unlock and activate it – is one of the most important components of a successful crowdfunding campaign.

Along with the other platforms, Kickstarter has profiles of the people who back featured projects. There isn't much on these profiles that initially appears particularly useful, and many people use assumed names and nicknames of some kind, but you are shown how many projects each person has backed in the past. As John looked at these numbers, he was astounded! A clear majority of his backers had backed 20-80, and even 100 projects in the past.

The inescapable conclusion was that these legions of backers were, as he came to call them, "Kickstarter Groupies" (or more generically, "Crowdfunding Groupies"). They are part of the internal, organic traffic to be found on any crowdfunding platform. Again, these are the ones marketers refer to as "early adopters"; they simply enjoy being among the first customers to have something new which interests them. They are like many of us as kids, wanting to be the first on the block or in their group to have the newest Lone Ranger Secret Decoder Ring and the like. Some people never outgrow this mindset and urge.

These Crowdfunding Groupies periodically (in the cases of many, even daily) visit the crowdfunding websites they follow, and then they cruise and peruse the most recent offerings and campaigns to see what interests them. And, if they do see something that interests them, they pledge to that campaign and support it. The numbers that John generated conclusively showed that these people are considerable in number and potential; they number over 3 million people on Kickstarter. They are the sleeping giant that everyone needs to awaken in order to assure the success of their crowdfunding campaign. If you can do this successfully, they alone can be enough to carry you to the winner's circle.

The Crowdfunding Novice
($440K raised, 4,000 new customers)

NASA-INSPIRED CHEF KNIFE

PATENTED TECHNOLOGY

CLOSED

KNASA Chef Knife Inspired by NASA Technology

NASA and Caltech's patented alloy reinvents the Chef Knife. The first knife innovation in 200 years!

PROJECT OWNER

Adam Ackerman
Newport Beach, United States
2 Campaigns | More

$566,112 USD total funds raised
2230% funded on December 16, 2016

Adam's story is similar in many ways. In 2016, after selling successfully online for a few years, he was introduced to a company that specialized in making kitchen knives. This group had an amazing technology but was struggling to bring their idea to market. While they had each of the components of a great brand, an amazing product, and a great story, they had no idea how to tell that story. Adam proposed a partnership with them and remembered his good friend John had recently broken a crowdfunding record with his own campaign.

He called John up, and they spoke about the knives and decided that crowdfunding would be the perfect place to launch Adam's new brand, Habitat Housewares. So, they launched it, and 45 days after the campaign ended, it raised $440K, and they sold 6,000 knives, acquiring 4,000 new customers – not bad for their first 45 days in business!

Adam has since launched an additional campaign for his knife brand and raised over $1M for the Habitat brand in a little over 16 months using crowdfunding as a revenue strategy. He and John have now arranged seven successful crowdfunding campaigns, raising close to $2M from their efforts – only a handful of people can claim to have done that. This Tech Turkey and the Crowdfunding Novice aren't foolish enough to claim they know everything, but they know a lot – and they've certainly paid their dues to learn it.

The Four Areas of a Crowdfunding Master

If you want to succeed in crowdfunding, you must master four distinct areas of the process. If you fail at any one of them, you will reduce your chances for success; if you master them, then you will succeed. The four areas are as follows:

1. Product quality
2. Product page
3. Traffic
4. Pledge fulfillment

1. Product Quality

A good product is simply a must. Let's be frank and honest, if you have a "crappy product" – either as an idea or in its execution – you likely have a fatal flaw. Keep in mind, this isn't as hard as you might think.

2. Product Page

You need to construct a compelling product page on your chosen crowdfunding platform; this is your crowdfunding version of show and tell. Your page is where you can show potential groupies what you have, why it matters, and why they should care and want your widget. Yes, gentle reader, this is salesmanship; but this too isn't so hard when you learn how.

3. Traffic

You need to drive online traffic to your Project Page in order to succeed. What if you threw a party and no one came? You might have a wonderful product and the most beautiful project page with every "whistle and bell" imaginable; but if you don't have eyeballs seeing what you created, then it will all be wasted. Frankly, this is the step that gives a majority of people the most trouble; but there are tactics you can learn – and these will help you reach that all-important goal of being funded!

4. Pledge Fulfillment

Once you are funded, you must fulfill the pledges you accepted–
and then you need to prepare for "life after crowdfunding." Your
campaign is not over when it ends on the platform, and they
send your money to you. Now your product needs to be made
and delivered to your backers. And then you begin your "life
after crowdfunding" for a successful product, in which you take
it into new productive sales channels with your new proof of
product viability, and your sales success.

There is almost always more to something than first meets the
eye, but that is life – and crowdfunding is no different. Still,
do not worry. Many people have done this successfully, and you
can too if you make an effort. Imagine sitting at your computer,
watching pledges regularly coming to your inbox. They represent
an affirmation of your ideas, product, and effort – and they
represent money! It's one of the biggest adrenaline rushes that
John and Adam say they've ever experienced – and it can be for
you too!

Getting Started
(the great idea you've always had)

Some people will ask, "Where and how would I begin?" Well, the likely
answer is right in front of you. Just think about it. Haven't you had an
"idea" for something that you've never been able to shake from your
mind? But you never got around to doing anything about it? And then
perhaps as time passed, you saw your idea out there in the marketplace,
and it was finding much success, while someone else was making serious
money from it? And didn't that bug you all to hell? Well, no more!

Now, with crowdfunding and simply learning the straight-forward
steps of how to do it well, you can become the person "in the catbird
seat," watching the money roll in daily and building a business of your
own that can last for years. And if you don't have some product idea,
now there are steps you can take to create a modification – also called

an "iteration" by the crowdfunding platforms – to something already existing, and that can be your path to crowdfunding success.

Building Your New Business
(with OPM, you never need to repay)

Imagine building a new business for yourself with Other People's Money (OPM) which you never need to repay. Most people would say, "No Way! That's not possible!" Well, there is a very viable way, and we've already been exploring it. Interesting physical products will always be a successful path to a rewarding business; every day, more and more, the internet is the place to conduct that business.

You could do what many have done these past few years: (A) You pick an interesting product – find a wholesale manufacturer who will private label it for you – and then (B) you buy inventory and send it to Amazon to be sold on your behalf. There are techniques you will need to learn, but this technique is making serious money for many people today. If you want to control your future (instead of being controlled), you should give serious thought to doing this too.

However, the better path is to use crowdfunding as your first step. You take your good idea, but you don't spend money on inventory without knowing whether or not you have a winner; you take your product to Kickstarter or Indiegogo and beta-test it for a small amount of money. If you are successful, your backers will pledge to your campaign, allowing you to recoup your campaign expenses, and to have money to fulfill your pledges as well as money for Amazon inventory – perhaps putting thousands, if not hundreds of thousands into your own pocket!

Now, isn't that a better way to start a business?! Using Crowdfunding and OPM to do it is the smart path to business success in today's marketplace. This is truly the way to becoming your own shark!

John Galley operates a Membership Website for experienced and aspiring Crowdfunding Creators. You can reach him at www.crowdfundingtribe.com. And Adam Ackerman has a full-service agency assisting Crowdfunding Creators with campaigns. You can reach him at www.fullyfunded.com.

21

TRULY "SUCCESSFUL HABITS OF THE RICH!" ™

Helping Americans with Their Finances in an Improving Economy

By
Ray A. Smith

I'm the President and CEO of Trycera Financial, a publicly traded company that started in 2004. We provide financial and credit educational programs for consumers who are seeking loans and can't qualify due to bad credit or no credit. I grew up on a dairy farm in South Dakota, and we worked hard. Farming and ranching is all about community and helping each other; it's about neighbors helping neighbors. I've used this life lesson as the basis to build our financial products because it is nearly impossible to navigate this broken financial system alone. Everyone needs help at some point in life. We've positioned our company to be the go-to place to learn about money and credit because there are no education programs in public schools teaching people how to manage their money and deal with credit – we certainly weren't taught that on the farm either!

As I got into the business world, it was an eye-opening experience. When you're in business and trying to make payroll, pay vendors, and make ends meet it's very difficult if you don't have your money and your credit in order. So, I had to learn everything about good money management the hard way. In 1998, I moved to Las Vegas where my partner and I opened up a credit card processing center. We processed credit card applications for a bank out of Chicago and dealt primarily with people who had bad credit. That's where I really learned how this whole financial system works, and how broken it is. By dealing with thousands of people, I came to a good understanding of how our financial system, credit bureaus, and banks work. I also realized how uneducated people are about this whole system, at no fault of their own.

A typical scenario we would run into is when we fixed someone's credit and helped them get credit cards or loans, within a few months, they would be back asking for us to help them fix their damaged credit again. After researching and trying to find the root of the problem, we found the reason they would return was that they hadn't changed their habits. People tend to just look at their bank account, see how much money is in it, and then they spend it. There's never a real spending plan for people to utilize and it isn't even something people are in the habit of creating. Since people don't spend wisely, they miss critical payments and damage their credit, which causes their interest rates and deposits to soar.

This typical situation is the basis behind our entire production, "Successful Habits of the Rich!" ™, which we provide to consumers. It has three components:

1. RichMoney™
2. RichCredit™
3. RichWealth™

We need to focus on money first. If we don't have our money in order, we really can't take care of our credit because the credit system is so fragile – this is where the educational components come into play. We primarily work with mortgage companies, auto dealerships, auto loan providers, auto refinance companies and furniture stores. People who are unsuccessfully applying for loans, they are our best clients. Once we have their undivided attention, we can help guide them, and they will listen to us. We look at where they are today, and we put a plan together for the future. We tell clients that 5% of their wealth is cash, and 95% is accessed through credit. If they don't have their cash in order, they get locked out of 95% of their wealth capabilities.

Most budgeting programs start with how much you make, and then they try to create a budget. With our RichMoney™ program, we have you list all of your expenses in a 12-month period. Typically, there are 12 cell phone bills, 12 power bills, 12 water bills, and 12 rents; car registrations happen one time annually, and insurance payments sometimes are paid quarterly. So, there's a finite bucket of expenses, and we have you, the client, input these items into our system. Then we ask how frequently you get paid (i.e., monthly, weekly, or bi-weekly). Depending on your answer, we tell you how much money you need to have each pay period in order to cover your bills.

The amount owed per period is critical because if it's bigger than the money you make, you have two choices: (1) you can go make extra money, or (2) you can look at your spending and trim it down to match your income. That's the difference between our program and most programs out there. After you've input all this bill payment information, we then print out a calendar for the next 12 months. We show you your target balance each day, and which bills will be coming out for the next 365 days. You can then print your calendar, put it on your fridge, and now, as a family, you will know where you are with respect to money. The calendar becomes an important informational and conversational piece. By doing this, our goal is to help you eliminate the stress and worry caused by the unknowns – now that your money is in order, you won't miss payments, and you will maintain great credit!

Once your money is in order, we now focus on your credit. We look at errors and mistakes on your credit, as well as any missing items such as your rent, water, utilities, and insurance payments. You make those payments every month, but they aren't reported to the bureaus. Part of our "Successful Habits of the Rich! ™" program is our patent pending process wherein we add those items as positive trade lines to your credit report. That's also what sets us apart from the competition; we're not just a myopic-focused program, we look at all three aspects – the money, the credit, and then the wealth building – which are like legs of a stool because they all lean on each other.

Finances Today

Our Company and its products were featured on Worldwide Business with Kathy Ireland®, and we showcased our vision of helping Americans navigate this broken credit system. The economy is coming back. People are getting more excited to use credit to make new purchases. Entrepreneurs want to open up small businesses. The time is now to start focusing on building and fixing your credit as it takes time. Bad credit doesn't happen overnight, and neither does getting back good credit, which is why we want to get in touch with people today and have them start working on it NOW.

We have different ways of reaching out to get clients in contact with our professionals. We've created a first-to-market LIVE Agent Kiosk which we place at car dealerships, mortgage companies, or places like furniture stores where consumers apply for credit and get turned down. These credit turn-downs simply go over to our LIVE Agent Kiosk, lift up a gold handset, activate our proprietary app, and one of our live agents, our professionals, come on the screen. We speak with the client via video conference. We see you, and you see us, which makes it more personal – we're bringing back the personal community help aspect which I mentioned earlier. We are there to build a trust and comfort level with each client and then be there every step of the way, from today and onward, for the next six months. You always have a support team to help you.

In addition to the kiosks, we're setting up independent agents across the country, much like AAA and insurance companies. People can set up their own business with little overhead and much support from Trycera Financial. We call this our "Business in a Box" model, but you don't need to have the employees. We have the employees. You just become an affiliate, start marketing, start enrolling people in our program, and then you earn money.

Our main focus and inspiration is knowing that we can get in and help a family or individual change their lives. Money management itself is so important. People can maximize and take advantage of this economy today because the banks are loosening up their requirements; lenders are becoming friendlier to consumers. Everybody had damaged credit because of the financial meltdown from 2008. If no one works on your credit, it will never change. We want to empower people, bring back their confidence and eliminate the shame they feel by having bad credit.

People look at the FICO score as a character reference score, but it's not. If you have a low FICO score, it doesn't mean that you're a bad person. The FICO score is just a computer-generated number. What we want to do is help put the data points in the computer system so that when that loan officer runs your credit report, your score is where you need it to be in order to qualify. We want to take the guessing game out of applying for credit.

By putting your money spending information into your hands via a calendar, you know exactly where you're at – you can log in and see your bank balance, look at the calendar, see your target balance, and see if you have extra money. That's the power we give back to the people. We take the guessing game out of spending money. Spending money is a requirement. Everybody needs it. The bad thing is we're all impulsive spenders, and we spend what we have, not what we need to spend. And then people think that they deserve bad credit. No one deserves bad credit. The financial institutions use the laws in their favor because, when you have bad credit, they get to charge higher interest rates. That's what they're all about: making money.

A 30-day late payment stays on your credit for seven years. The law states that a negative cannot stay on your credit for more than seven years, but the credit bureaus turn that around, and they do exactly that. Why? So, your score is low, and the banks can charge higher interest. We want to remove those negatives as soon as possible, or at least update them, so they have the least impact on your credit file. With bankruptcies and public tax liens, these stay longer than seven years – they stay for 10 years.

Collection agencies, that's another area where we focus on helping consumers. Collection agencies have no right to collect money from you. There's no legal agreement between you and them. For instance, let's say you have a credit card with a bank for $2,000 and you stop paying on it. That bank reports you 30 days, 60 days, 90 days, 120 days late, and then they eventually charge it off. That's on your credit report and is reflected in your credit scores. You've already been found guilty, sentenced to seven years of bad credit. Then comes along a collection agency. They buy that debt for pennies on the dollar, and then they mail you a letter. And in the fine print, it says if you do not dispute a portion or all of this within 30 days, "we will deem it to be valid."

These agencies wait the 30 days, and then they report another negative collection account on your credit file with the three bureaus. So, now you've just been sentenced twice for the same crime of not paying a bill. They typically will mail you a letter that says we'll settle for 50%. People are self-conscious, they want to do right, and so they think, *Well, I'll send $1,000,* but that $1,000 comes out of your family, and it goes to a collection agency that you don't owe the money to. This is exactly what we're trying to stop. We want to empower you, the consumer. We want to give you vital information and education to change your life today and start taking advantage of the financial situation and the financial institutions.

My partner and I are working with Congress to try to pass legislation to stop this. Donald Trump's administration Supreme Court Nominee Neil Gorsuch was appointed to the Supreme Court. In his very first ruling, he decided a case regarding collection agencies. He and the majority of the Supreme Court ruled that they do not have a legal right to collect money from consumers because there's no existing business relationship, which is part of the do-not-call law – there's no legal agreement.

We want to get this information into the hands of consumers so that you can keep more of your money for your family and spend it in your community. Part of our product package includes helping send cease and desist letters to these collection agencies. We tell them to stop contacting our clients, and if they reported negative items to the bureau, they need to delete it immediately, or our clients will have the right to take legal action against them.

Trycera

Our services are offered online, through our LIVE Agent Kiosks which are placed at various businesses including car dealerships and mortgage companies. We have affiliate programs. Our app works on all iPads and

Android phones, so you can talk to one of our live agents via your phone or any computer via our website. Anybody who is seeking financial help, we want to help them. We want to put information and education into your hands so that you can change the environment for your family. If you're willing to put in a small amount of the work and the effort – and it's not that much – we're willing to do the heavy lifting and be there every step of the way.

Some of our customers were paying 29% interest on their car loans. After completing our program, some are now paying less than 10%. One of our affiliates is an auto refinance company, and 83% of their applicants get denied because of their credit score. Their credit score has to be 660, but they're not. For some people, it takes very little to get them up over the 660. For others, it takes a lot of effort on our part; but it's still the same amount of effort on the consumer's part – not very much. We get a copy of the credit report, analyze it, do a complete audit, and then we send you the audit report, so you know what we will work on every step of the way.

By missing one payment, your FICO score could drop 100 to 150 points. If we can get your FICO score up over that threshold from 640 to 660, a 29% interest car loan can drop down to 10%, saving you $100 a month. Over a three to five-year period, we're saving you thousands of dollars just by simple corrections in your daily habits. If you go through our program, it's $640 financed over six months; $189 the first month, and $89.95 for five additional months.

The biggest problem is there's the stigma about credit repair, and there's a lot of misinformation out there. Many people have "expertise" knowledge in this industry; I question that. How many reports have they looked at? What have they done for people? How many clients have they helped?

We've helped thousands of people over the years. We see thousands of reports. We see the changes in the credit industry. We know what the bureaus are doing. That's why we feel like we're the expert. When people file their taxes, some go to H&R Block, Jackson-Hewitt, or a professional. Why? Because those companies and professionals know the laws; consumers don't have this awareness because the laws change all the time. We want to be the professional organization that helps you with your finances and your credit. We want to take the fear and worry out of you and your family.

We want to empower you by providing you the information and the tools that you need to navigate a broken financial system. We want you to have a personal connection with our professionals by looking into their eyes. We're holding your hand every step of the way during our six-month program. Whenever you get in a bind and have a question, you contact one of our agents standing by to help. We're always here to help. If we can't, we will tell you. We'll then tell you to contact an attorney or someone else if you're in that bad of a situation.

Over the next few years, we're looking to place up to 25,000 LIVE Agent Kiosks across this great Nation. We want to have up to 10,000 agents on the ground, knocking on doors, setting up their own business in little communities, and starting to help their own community thrive in this booming economy – with low unemployment rates, and with less and less regulations happening on a daily basis. Now is the time to take advantage of the situation and take control of your life.

You can find us at www.Trycera.com. Sign Up Today ... and start Living like The Rich! If you'd like more information, please contact me at (949) 705-4480 or rsmith@trycera.com. If you're interested in becoming an affiliate, go to our website and click on "Become Affiliate"– it's that simple!

22

MILLION-DOLLAR MARIJUANA INVENTION

The No. 1 Selling 2017 Harvest Product

By
Wade Atteberry

I am Wade Atteberry, founder and CEO of Original 420 Brand– we launched our world famous Hot Sauce in 2012. We've been in the CBD industry since 2014. Currently, less than about 20% of the people know what CBD is. We are reaching a quantum leap in getting people the correct information. I think once we get to that 30-40% threshold in society, CBD sales will really take off – the 2018 CBD market is expected to be close to a billion-dollar industry.

As a two-time cancer survivor, I have firsthand experience with the benefits of Cannabis helping me through the painful side effects of chemotherapy. When we started selling CBD in 2014, almost nobody knew what CBD was, making business very difficult because you had to explain the whole product. Salespeople try to make sales, but instead, we found ourselves trying to educate people. Our sales have actually started picking up recently as the news has really started picking up on CBD. Some states have actually outlawed CBD now, which is just amazing because it helps so many people with epilepsy, cancer, and many other ailments. It's an amazing product for so many people, even from just a headache to any type of pain. It's also an anti-inflammatory which really helps a broad spectrum of people, and it's non-psychoactive.

"Cannabidiol" or CBD is a compound found in the cannabis plant that can't get you high but has many medicinal benefits. "Apoptosis" is the process of cancer cells committing suicide, which is induced by CBD and THC. CBD on its own is an anti-inflammatory and protects against neurodegenerative disease – on which our hypocritical government currently owns the patent! Look it up: Patent#6630507 (also known as the 507 Patent).

CBD also helps with Multiple Sclerosis, as Montel Williams will attest to. It has therapeutic potential to help with schizophrenia, epileptic seizures, anxiety, pain relief, and rheumatoid arthritis. It relieves nausea and both increases and regulates appetite, which is very beneficial to patients going through chemotherapy. It helps to lower incidence of diabetes and high blood pressure while promoting heart health – I personally have been able to stop taking Lisinopril by replacing it with CBD and THC. It helps to treat depression, inflammatory bowel disease, and it helps to protect against bacteria, mad cow disease, and even toenail fungus.

CBD helps promote bone growth and helps broken bones heal faster and stronger. It reduces Dyskinesia, helps with insomnia and substance abuse disorders, acne, and psoriasis and many other diseases and ailments. CBD is one of the more than 80 cannabinoids found in the cannabis plant. It can be taken alone; but to be more effective it should be taken with some THC, this is called "The Entourage Effect." It turns out Mother Nature had it right all along as mankind has had an extremely close relationship with cannabis for well over 10,000 years of documented use with no known deaths – EVER!!

When I was a young kid, at 15 years old, I got arrested for growing over 100 marijuana plants. I never looked back. I've been growing my entire life because (A) I believe that we should have the right to grow a medicinally beneficial plant, and (B) there's no scientific reason to outlaw it – again, to this day, nobody has ever died from marijuana. Marijuana overdoses have the same record as unicorn deaths; so, it's a pretty safe product. Overdosing on marijuana can feel like the worst day of your life, but it has no lasting physically harmful effects. The best thing to do is take a healthy dose of CBD, drink some lemonade, and go to sleep.

My Not So E-Z Journey

I was a general contractor, growing up in a small town, and I raced all over the race tracks in New Hampshire. And then I raced all up and down the east coast from Florida up to Maine. It was hard for me to sell my cultivated marijuana in my hometown; I couldn't tell anybody there that I grew, due to the law at the time. So, I would sell it at the racetracks to other racers, of which many were prominent town's folk or general contractors who were in the same position as me; however, in their case, they couldn't buy from their local dealer because they didn't want anybody to know that they grew or smoked pot. So, I had a great group of guys that I sold to, and in return, they didn't wreck me on the racetrack – an added bonus. Selling marijuana helped support my racing habit, which was the greatest thing about it. It was an easy way to come up with money at the track every weekend, win or lose – it was just a bonus when I won.

I've had other endeavors aside from marijuana and CBD. In my earlier days, I invented Doggy Sunglasses back in the 90s. I went to Las Vegas and I won Best Pet Product Award at the International Invention Convention. I sold 10,000 pairs immediately, which I produced in Taiwan. And, then the downturn in the economy just tanked the pet and novelty industries, along with everything else when the Gulf War broke out – it was a pretty big drag on the economy, and it took away my investor, so that was the end of that company.

I also invented the E-Z Foam Glove. I won Best New Car Care Product at the SEMA convention in '08. This played out similarly to my experience with Doggy Sunglasses. I had a great investor (who was heavily invested in real estate…), and everything seemed to be going really well. I lived in Thailand for a year, working and getting the manufacturing process down. And when the economy went bust during that time, my investor ran out of money and I had to come back home and completely start over from zero again.

So, I've had my fair share of obstacles as an inventor and as an entrepreneur. I also faced obstacles in the CBD industry – the most difficult obstacle of which is legalization. We ship CBD to all 50 states currently and have since 2014. Today, there's still some question as to the legality of CBD. The 2014 Farm Bill Act basically says that if you import CBD made from hemp stocks with less than 0.3% THC, from international sources, it's legal here in the states. The common belief is that if you grow CBD strains in a state where it's legal, you can't transport it over state lines; but if it's imported you actually can. So, it's very convoluted. It is ridiculous that our farmers cannot legally grow hemp.

It would be really great for our government to just legalize a natural medicine that's never killed anybody; that we've been using for 10,000+ years. We just need to encourage them to go with the will of the people. In most surveys, over 94% of the American population agrees that marijuana should be available medicinally. If it's grown here in a state, it can only be sold in a dispensary to somebody with a medical marijuana card. As of 2018, we've legalized recreational marijuana in California – everyone of age therein can buy any CBD/THC products.

Banking is another huge issue, not just for us but for the entire marijuana industry. Obviously, Original 420 Brand is in the CBD industry. We are also in the picks and shovels industry for the marijuana business (we make tools), but our bank accounts routinely get closed down because of our name. They see the "420" and shut down our merchant accounts, where we take in our credit cards. We lose these accounts a lot more often than our bank accounts. So, now we're subject to dealing with high-interest merchant accounts which want to charge 7-12% on every transaction, plus a transaction fee, plus a monthly and a yearly fee.

We're being taken advantage of by the financial institution which is basically run by big pharma – they pay the lobbyists. We don't really have enough money in the marijuana industry to counter their influence. There aren't enough big companies to make any real dent in the lobbyist system yet, but that is changing. As more lawmakers become educated about cannabis, the laws will change to the public's benefit.

Our biggest primary obstacle to entering the marijuana business now is the regulations. These recently changed here in California in a way that benefits the biggest growers. That really hurts all the small mom-and-pop growers that have been doing this in the hills under threat of jail or having their kids taken away for generations now. It's harsh on the small people the way new laws have just been rewritten at the last minute. It was supposed to benefit smaller growers, but that's been changed, and many of us feel betrayed. As it typically plays out, big money came in and rewrote the laws, getting rid of their competition: the small people who actually care about it. Many families depend on being able to have a cottage industry; they've depended on this for 10-30 years now. So, it's devastating to a lot of small families here in California, and across the country.

The DeBudder Bucket Lid

In the hopes of doing my part of an evening out on the playing field, I invented the DeBudder Bucket Lid. Several tools on the market introduced in the last year or so to pull the buds from the stems – which for the last 30+ years was done by hand with scissors. It takes about an hour to get a pound of bud off the stems by hand. My DeBudder Bucket Lid snaps onto a five-gallon bucket and has notches in it. When you pull stems through the notches, it gently pops the buds off without damaging them. At that, you can do 8-10 pounds an hour, which is an absolutely incredible amount of time saved. From the smallest to the largest growers, this saves an incredible amount of time.

It's a very short window of time that you have between getting the buds out of your drying room and into airtight containers to finish curing the product; you literally only have a few hours. So, with the bigger growers or even a family home grower, you often need a bunch of extra help, which of course is a security risk and it's a financial burden to get everything into buckets immediately. With regards to the rest of the growing process, you have weeks on most other windows of time, like with cloning, where you have weeks between the plants popping roots to transplanting. With a harvest, you have up to a week-long window. The shortest window of time is when they are in the drying room and are perfectly dried to a 58-63% humidity level. Growers immediately need to put everything into airtight containers, so it doesn't dry out too much. You still need to trim the buds so they will continue to dry during this process.

The DeBudder Lid has saved a lot of small guys from bringing in help. Now, they can do it themselves. And the bigger companies and growers often spend $4,000 to $90,000 on DeBudding or Bucking machines, but it's the same speed, and it still takes a worker to feed the machine. Now, you can do the same amount with the DeBudder Lid. So, you can spend either $29.99 on a DeBudder Bucket Lid, or $4,000 to $90K on one of these fancy machines – big price delta there. This really helps the small guys and any big operations that don't want to spend the money on any complicated equipment that needs electricity, or that could break down at any moment. These are used every harvest which then results in lots of maintenance when it comes to cleaning them. Marijuana trichomes are very sticky; they're like glue, and they build up resin. So, anytime you have moving parts in a machine, they get covered in resin, and they tend to not want to keep moving. I'm not knocking these machines; most of them are very well-built.

From Concept to Shelf

When I developed the DeBudder Bucket Lid, I actually had a 3-D prototype printed. I found a guy who gave me a great deal on the CAD design, so I was able to go from concept to testing the product before making 10,000 pieces in China, and then having them shipped here. I air-freighted 500 pieces as soon as they came out of the mold because sales were taking off so fast! I was on the market in less than 100 days, from concept to being on a store shelf, which is pretty amazing turnaround time to be able to do that.

For the mold to be made in China, it was maybe 20% of what the mold was to be made here in America. It was the same with the units. I had $13K out of my own pocket invested in this project, and I borrowed $5K from my sister. If I were to do it here in the States, it would have cost over $50K which would have put it out of my reach. By utilizing China to produce a product, it was less than a dollar for each unit, versus the US where it would have been at about $4.00 per piece, which wouldn't be cost effective. I experienced a $29 economic boost here in America for every dollar I spent in China – that's not just a great ROI; it helped me grow the company and hire people.

Original 420 Brand now has about nine employees because of the cost delta from being able to do it here in the U.S. versus doing it in

China. So, I've been able to hire nine Americans and give them work, a paycheck, and help them support their families. Currently, we are in around 400 shops out of roughly 2500 hydroponic shops in America – so we have a lot of room to grow. We've sold 20,000 units in a 60-day period, which is phenomenal, and it feels great.

Recently, I ended up signing an international deal. International sales were originally out of my reach. We were focusing here in the U.S. when I was approached by this company on the stock market. My friend Landon L. told them about me. They're a pink sheet company now converting to a fully reporting company – it's very exciting for us to be looked at. When we signed the deal, they gave me a large number of shares in their company which has doubled our company's valuation. They are spending their money on marketing, advertising, and sales of the product overseas. I still get a percentage of every sale on top of the initial payouts. This is one of those dream come true things for a small-time inventor with a small business. You always hope that something like this will happen, and when it does, you're just grateful and amazed. We're always working on new products, and that company will be financing any new products that they like, which really helps. We like to reinvest in our families, our employees, and their families. We're trying to get benefits, and insurance for everybody at the company – keeping the economy moving forward, as we say.

Anybody Can Do This!

The biggest thing I'd like to point out to people is that anybody can do this. In the marijuana industry, there are many people who have been doing this underground for so long, they have great ideas and have worked on their own products, but they haven't taken action yet. I'm encouraging people to look at my story and see that with an $18K investment, I was able to create a company that's now worth over $2.5M. Anybody can do this. It's not difficult; you just need to do it. And, you need to take it day-by-day. Plan out your steps, and when your steps change – as they consistently do – you then adjust. Day-by-day, every time something comes up, you need to readjust. You must overcome whatever is thrown at you. It gets a little stressful at times, but if you just keep going at it, you will make it.

Lately, we've been shooting videos in our office space, but nobody knew how to edit the footage, so I called around to find an intern at an Audio/Video College. I was very surprised by how easy it was to talk to the Program Director and how receptive she was to get us some students to work with. We started right away and produced a video fully-edited with custom music and great camera work.

The first video project was entered into a contest to get on "The Next Marijuana Millionaire" T.V. Show. The video was so well-produced that I got a call from the Casting Director – I was accepted to go to the next phase! Anybody can do this! What do you need? Make a list and find a school in that field and give them a call. It took me 5 minutes to get an appointment with the Program Director and after a 30-minute meeting and a tour of the campus we had 6-7 students who wanted to be a part of our project.

Need an Engineer? Find an Engineering School. Need a Photographer? Find a Photography School. There are plenty of free resources available, and in my case, it was a win-win situation. We provided the school with our own feedback report that will help their students get better at real-life projects. You can find mentorship clubs that charge very little to nothing at all. Usually, they have CEO's or managers with a lot of experience that want to give back to the community and will help you for free. You can find ghostwriters who will work for whatever budget you can afford. I've had 200-300-word articles written by experts in the field for $50! With all the resources available on the internet there is no excuse not to be moving forward right away with your next venture.

I've learned how to tap into resources that would normally cost 10's of thousands of dollars, and I'm giving you this information so that you can be successful too. Make a list of what you want to achieve and work it backwards to make the full to-do list. If you want to be successful, find successful people and ask them for some advice.

We recently launched our Original 420 Brand Hemp Wheat Mango Beer. I didn't know anything about the Craft Brew Industry, so I started watching hours and hours of videos on YouTube about different topics in the industry. I reached out to friends to find out if anybody knew anybody in the beer industry. I received a phone call from a millionaire in the industry, and he gave me some great advice – for free! I had several questions ready for him, and I got the answers I needed to know. One of the questions was, "Should I just get my own distributors license or just go with someone who is big or small?" His advice was to get my own Craft Brewers License and self-distribute. Then, he explained all the benefits of doing it as a licensed Craft Brewer.

Original 420 Brand Today

Another project I'm working on is a padded armrest for trimmers. Hand-trimmed marijuana will always be in demand by connoisseurs. Trimming a pound of good marijuana by hand takes an average of 8 hours! That's 8 hours of resting your arms on the edge of a table all day. Some people will roll up a towel which will soon be full of sticky trichomes and can start irritating your arms – that's why I invented the Trim Pad™. It's ergonomically designed so you can rest at an ideal angle for trimming. It has two positions so you can lean in or sit back. It also has a holder for your cell phone, so you can listen to your favorite music or your favorite podcasts.

First, I found an engineer who works from home and has his own 3-D Printer, so he was able to make a prototype. I then found a Styrofoam company to make me another softer prototype to show investors. I had less than $1,000 in the project, and I was able to find enough money with the prototypes to fund it further. I always tell people to get a bunch of NDA's so people can sign them – so you can tell as many people as you can about your ideas! Nobody will rip it off! The only things that get ripped off are the successfully proven products – so get yourself a provisional patent! It's good for one year and costs around $200. You can then work on your idea for one year, see if it sells, and then you need to file for a full patent in one year, or you lose the patent protection rights. Now that's motivation!

I've just recently launched our High-Value Crop Bio Char after researching several companies that make and sell it. I bought 1 cubic yard and tried it myself – wow, was I impressed! After researching Bio Char, I realized it could actually save the planet. Basically, by taking any biomass and heating it to well over 1500 degrees in a low oxygen environment, it will turn it into carbon, and the "off" gases can be used to run the machine. This process is called pyrolysis. We can turn anything from human waste to woodchips into Bio Char.

Bio Char can soak up toxins in wastewater, so if we put it in drain basins before it enters our waterways, we can reduce the toxic runoff that pollutes our streams, rivers, lakes, and oceans. Bio Char helps the dead soil to become alive again by charging Bio Char with microorganisms such as worm castings, bat and bird guano, or just any compost it gives a "home" for microbes to live in. Bio Char looks just like the charcoal you buy at the store; it's just a more highly refined product. When added to soil, it helps to retain water and to aerate the soil. When added to concrete, it makes it harder. It has so many uses, and I highly recommend you do your own research on it!

If you have further questions about Original 420 Brand, the DeBudder Bucket Lid, or the industry in general, you can contact me at wade420brand@gmail.com.

23

DAY CAMP HORROR

Itching for $UCCE$$

By
Steven Greenspan

For the past 45 years, I have dedicated my life's work to specializing in the safe eradication and removal of poison ivy, poison oak, and poison sumac plants. I've also been teaching people who don't know much about these plants, how to safely go about identifying these poisonous-to-the-touch plants so they can keep themselves and their loved ones safe and out of harm's way. I had my first bout with poison ivy at the age of 16 years old. I can remember it as though it were just yesterday.

I was working as a camp counselor at West Hills Day Camp situated on Long Island. I walked barefoot every day, everywhere I went. Little did I know, I was unwittingly walking through densely overgrown fields covered with poison ivy. I did absolutely nothing to protect myself or my bare feet nor any of my other exposed body parts from making direct contact with any of these poisonous-to-the-touch plants to prevent what soon became the ravages of what they were already known for causing. Nor did I make any ill-fated attempts to immediately wash or decontaminate any of my several previously exposed body parts. Unbeknownst to me, I was covered with an invisible thin layer of urushiol – the potent plant's resin responsible for causing the itching, blistering rash that led to my poison ivy near-death experience. OMG!

STEVE GREENSPAN.

My very first week as camp counselor found me extremely busy, whereby all my free time quickly evaporated leaving me little to no time afterwards to ever first take notice, or silently discover for myself what was responsible for causing my itching blistering rash to first occur that it now should be covering much of my entire body. In hindsight, it never occurred to me that poison ivy existed as a possibility for causing my still greater discomfort. I made no effort to study or learn how to identify these poisonous-to-the touch plants, nor did I know or have enough sense to safeguard myself against making physical contact. The plants' vengeance was now about to unravel itself upon me.

As if but overnight, I could not help realizing that suddenly, without warning, I had developed a rapidly spreading rash that spread between each and every one of my toes. As my rash continued spreading itself, it was accompanied by incessant itching that prevented me from sleeping that night and most other nights ahead. My rash of unknown origins had now escalated into a burning, itching, oozing, blistering rash that persisted by lasting upwards of four weeks.

My seemingly unexplained rash started its rapid ascent upwards spreading by itself covering much of my body. First, it started on my bare feet. Next, it spread to and covered over both my ankles. Then, it was silently crawling up over portions of my lower legs. Soon, it was on to my calves, behind both my knees, and it was traveling upwards towards my upper thighs. Before I knew it, much of the remainder of my entire body was covered by this persistent blistering, itching, oozing rash.

In fact, what amounted to just a few short hours, my rash had escalated and continued spreading itself farther still, eventually encompassing my entire chest and rib cage, the back of my neck, my hands, between all my fingers, and all over my upper arms and armpits. My entire body had become completely engulfed, and the rash was accompanied by a persistent itching, blistering, oozing, and a burning sensation. No part of me was spared or left unscathed, nor was any of it considered sacred by the rash. My eyes were by now welded shut from a dried and caked yellow ooze.

Still, I held no clue as to what was responsible for causing me to experience such extreme physical body impairment, discomfort, and disfigurement. The only thing worse than not knowing the cause, I had no idea how to relieve all of my still greater rash symptoms. I remained sleepless. I was hopeless.

At workday's end, I would return home from camp only to find myself physically drained by the incessant itching which resulted in me continually scratching my entire body in places I never thought you could possibly have an itch. Come night time; I first placed a large white beach towel on top of my bed mattress to absorb all of the yellow oozing fluid that was steadily pouring off of my body. At daybreak, my mom entered my room to awaken me so I could get ready for work. She and I were both easily able to identify the presence of a pale-yellow halo outline in the shape of my body which had formed on the towel from the night before.

Both my face and outer extremities were left so badly disfigured from rashes and oozing blisters that I closely resembled a fire burn victim. Even my own mother's love (of me) found her wincing and quickly looking away when just moments before she first laid her loving eyes upon me to provide me with her own consoling sympathies (as her flesh and blood). It was at this moment that I became acutely aware of how difficult it was for me to breathe.

I was immediately rushed to the hospital ER, whereupon entry I was first diagnosed. I was told by the attending ER staff that I had a severe case of poison ivy rash (allergy). I was also informed that I was dying, as I lay there drowning in my own sea of bodily fluids that were now accumulating inside my lungs as a direct result of my poison ivy rash. At this time, I became overly concerned about how much of my body was affected. This rash was equally held responsible for welding both my eyes shut, and for spreading into my mouth, along with my gums, and inside my throat. It also spread through my ear canal and ran up into my nose.

After needlessly enduring many painful sleepless nights accompanied by nonstop itching, I later healed myself. I went on to learn much from what my near-death lesson had just taught me. I came to realize that my poison ivy allergy suffering was not unique to my allergic response. I was not alone in all my shared ignorance, nor was I able successfully to subdue all the resulting painful itching burning and scratching sensations.

My eureka moment arrived when I quickly realized not only did I survive my near-death poison ivy rash, but similarly, I realized I was no longer alone in all the frustrations stemming from my painful, agonizing experience. This resulted in me dedicating my life's mission to educating people about America's most dangerous plant – POISON IVY! This has become my great business opportunity of significant economic proportions, which is why I made poison ivy, and the art and science of stopping the resulting itching, rashes and ooze the objects of my business. While my first experience nearly killed me, it left me itching for $ucce$$.

The Rules of Poison Ivy

No one ever should go through life, needlessly suffering, nor should anyone have to endure what I forcibly went through alone. Poison ivy nearly caused the death of me, and yet this stupid plant is so common and prevalent throughout much of the US environment. Poison ivy rash allergy adversely affects 85% of the entire US population, which equals 310 million people who annually remain at risk for contracting poison ivy rash.

According to the American Skin Association (ASA), 50 million cases of poison ivy allergy skin rash are reported each year – for which there still is no cure! For those affected, poison ivy often results in rashes lasting two weeks or longer, which includes countless sleepless nights, time lost away from work or school, lost wages, worker compensation claims, greater loss of worker productivity, and out of pocket economic loss due to paying for poison ivy-related medical bills and aftercare.

Poison ivy rash is avoidable! You just need to properly identify it so you can avoid making contact. Educating the masses as to identifying these plants is now at the forefront of my life's work.

A growing list of evidence supports the presence of increased global population, accelerated climate changes, and an increased presence of atmospheric CO_2 gas, poison ivy plants (over all other weedy vines) are growing much larger, faster, and more virulent than ever before. The poison ivy leaves are now growing 60% larger than what previous history records already demonstrate. If you'd like to know more for yourself, please read climatecentral.org's article, "Global Warming and Poison Ivy" (06/11/2014), as well as Weed Science's article, "Rising Atmospheric Carbon Dioxide and Potential Impacts on the Growth and Toxicity of Poison Ivy (Toxicodendron radicans)" by L. H. Ziska, R. C. Sicher, K. George, and J. E. Mohan (Issue 55, 2007, pg.288-292).

Coupled with these facts, people are spending much more of their free time engaged in all sorts of physical outdoor activities, which places this same population at risk directly in harm's way. With a growing frequency of at-risk populations comes an increased demand for these same individuals to positively identify poison ivy's presence themselves, which forms the annual basis for human tragedy unraveling itself. This is my greatest shared concern and greatest business opportunity yet. Poison ivy is the cockroach and scourge of the plant kingdom. These plants have amazing adaptive and survival capabilities and are now not only able to grow but thrive in some of the harshest of extreme outdoor environments.

Poison ivy remains difficult to identify due to its polymorphic shape-shifting, making it America's most dangerous plant. The itching, blistering, oozing rash has no known cure, and this plant grows almost everywhere. This means that positive identification and avoidance is our best means of poison ivy prevention and keeping ourselves safe. To this end, I have developed PoisonIvy. App (which remains in beta) that allows users to obtain verification of poison ivy's presence in real time. The first step to avoidance is the proper identification and making use of this app to assist the end user in steering clear of it.

The simple rules of identifying poison ivy are easy to learn and fun to remember:

- When you see a plant has **leaves of three**: Leave it be!
- When you see vines growing vertically up trees trunks or building structures, and they look like **hairy rope**: Don't be a dope!
- When you see a **hairy vine**: It's no friend of mine!

Poison ivy rash starts slowly as an itching or blistering rash. It will quickly escalate in the first several days by spreading over more of your body. It will become systemic once inside your body, making getting rid of the rash very difficult once the blistering and itching starts. Once you've showered and vigorously scrubbed your skin surface clean after your initial first contact, you've decontaminated yourself. Scratching the rash once it develops will not cause it to spread, nor will breaking your own resulting blisters.

Here's the caveat: Anything that you wore the day you first made physical contact with this plant must be immediately and thoroughly washed using strong laundry detergent soap and lots of hot water. If laundering items are not possible, then discard those still contaminated items! The resident oils that continue to remain embedded on these used items or garments will easily cross contaminate and continue to give you a rash.

Similarly, if you have a pet that is allowed outside and comes into direct contact with poison ivy, they too will continue carrying the poison ivy resin urushiol on their fur coats. Once they're inside your house, they will readily transfer the urushiol to you and furniture in the same way as if you had just made direct physical contact with this plant yourself. By owning a pet, it is possible to contract poison ivy by never stepping or going outside your house. If this becomes your case, you must vigorously shampoo your pet immediately!

Poison Ivy First Aid

Poison ivy leaves, from years gone by, previously measured a mere 2-4 inches in length and diameter. Poison ivy leaves as of today (during an era of rapid climate change) have been measured attaining sizes of 12-18 inches or greater in both length and diameter. Yikes! Also, urushiol, the plant's toxic resin, develops in more concentrated form within these same plants as compared to years before, making this plant not only America's most dangerous plant but a menace and hazard to human health. The poison ivy, poison oak, and poison sumac are each ubiquitous within their range and can be found growing within 42 of the 50 states.

Poison ivy identification is something most people never satisfactorily achieve. To that end, below are some tricks of the trade that I learned by attending the Poison Ivy Rash School of Hard Knocks, and by silently itching over time. As shared at the beginning of my chapter, the first time I got poison ivy rash, it nearly killed me. Since then, I developed my own three-step formula for successfully identifying poison ivy and avoiding my previous mistakes:

1. Avoid the plant at all costs
2. Identify these plants
3. Decontaminate your body within 10 to 15 minutes of first making contact with any of the plant's parts

• •

Please note: To decontaminate yourself and pets, you need lots of cold running water, and a strong detergent soap – preferably a poison ivy removal soap specifically formulated for removal of the urushiol toxin.

• •

The best way to remove poison ivy plants is by physically removing these viny plants by hand. This is no easy task, nor is it safe. Poison ivy removal is what I specialize in performing (PoisonIvyRemoval. com). I perform this as a paid service to local and state governments, as well as commercial and residential entities, landscapers, golf courses, parks departments, phone and cable companies, and airports. I also train individuals how to identify these plants, how to protectively suit themselves up safely, perform selective physical removal techniques, and how to decontaminate themselves following removal.

Using toxic herbicides to first kill poison ivy before removing it is a bad idea, and I do not recommend it. All herbicides chosen or used to kill weeds are toxic to mankind, pets, and the environment. Herbicides end up being more toxic than the actual urushiol contained within the poison ivy plant. Why needlessly place yourself and loved ones at risk when physical removal provides immediate results that are 100% effective and safe? Do not risk placing you or your loved ones directly in harm's way.

When herbicide is directly applied to poison ivy, this doesn't necessarily mean it will kill poison ivy plants immediately, nor entirely – if at all. Often, herbicide usage results in repeated reapplication of the same toxic herbicide spray in order to successfully kill these plants. Herbicide sprays are never safe due to the resulting spray drift which causes known physical damage to existing nearby landscape vegetation. Besides, toxic herbicide usage never physically removes dead poison ivy plants from the landscape; it still requires physical removal to be performed later as an additional step towards ensuring one's own safety. Herbicide sprayed poison ivy plants will always remain poisonous-to-the-touch even once they turn brown or die. Dead poison ivy plants will continue giving you a wicked rash as if they were still green and alive. This is the reason why it's so important to physically remove poison ivy first without resorting to using of spraying herbicides and/or weed killers.

• •

Please note: All poison ivy debris generated must be carefully removed and disposed of offsite.

• •

My Mission Today

Poison ivy exposure is the second leading cause of worker's compensation claims. People with the rash will call in sick due to ill health, they will not be able to sleep properly (due to the itching, oozing blisters), they will lose time from work or from school, and this contributes to causing them to incur an economic loss factor. Since poison ivy is avoidable, I am designating each June as National Poison Ivy Awareness Month. By doing this, I can bring about greater awareness towards the ravages this plant now causes upon the greater population at large, how to safely identify these plants, how to avoid getting the dreaded rash upon any contact with these plants, as well as poison ivy first aid (what to do next in the unfortunate event of making contact).

The astounding growing annual pool of poison ivy rash sufferers lends credence to people's own miserable failing at adequately identifying poison ivy/oak/sumac in order to avoid making physical contact with any of these toxic plant's parts. The first means of poison ivy prevention is through proper plant identification; ironically, this is something most people fail miserably at – they never first learn for themselves, nor do they satisfactorily achieve any level or degree of success at conscientious competence at identifying. If you need help with this, please check out my Poison Ivy Identification app, PoisonIvy.App (again, this is still in beta).

Beyond the app, under development is my poison ivy skin protectant. Currently awaiting FDA approval (expected release March 2019), this skin protectant must be applied like suntan lotion. It will protect and safeguard your skin against making physical contact with poison ivy plant's known toxic oils. And – for those with nerves of steel who are brave enough to tackle performing on their own physical removal of these plants – please purchase my Poison Ivy Removal Kit (professional grade). My kit contains all the necessary items to ensure your success and safe removal.

Should you have any questions or concerns regarding poison ivy/oak/sumac, you can find me at PoisonIvyRemoval.com. And, if the need arises, you may email me about anything I've shared in this chapter. Please feel free to reach me atinfo@poisonivyremoval.com.

"I'm just 'itching' to remove your poison ivy."™

24

FRESH OFF THE BOAT

From $600 to $1,710,000 on eCommerce

By
Ellen Lin

I am the unlikely entrepreneur. I was born in Taipei, Taiwan, in 1982. I immigrated to Los Angeles, to the United States, in 1996. I came here with my family and started learning English and everything else in the US, which was difficult as English wasn't my first language. I definitely have some bully stories from when I was going to high school, but we won't really go into those details. And aside from those moments, I was lucky. I was accepted into UC San Diego, one of the top schools in California, and my parents were really proud of me.

I studied Computer Arts in college, pursuing my life's career dream of making video games. After graduating, I was employed by a famous game developer company called EA Games. So, that's how I started my whole career. I thought, *Okay, this is everything I wanted. I want to make video games.* I thought it was so awesome that people could see the title and then see, "Oh, Ellen made that video game." I was accomplishing my dream. I worked in that industry for four years, from 2005 to 2009. I was laid off because the economy crashed. I know a lot of people got laid off during that period of time. I never thought it would be my turn because I kept thinking, *Okay. That's just other people. So, it's never going to be me.* But nope; I lost my job.

My whole career dream got crushed. I totally lost myself; I didn't know what to do and what to think because I felt like it was the end of the world. Thinking back, it was actually the beginning of my whole entrepreneurship journey because two years after being laid off, I started trying eCommerce business. Many people ask me why I chose to do eCommerce instead of my dream; back then, I had many friends who just started their e-commerce businesses —*Okay, maybe this is a good opportunity.*

Also, during that period of time, my father's company was severely impacted by the economy crash; he needed some help. He was running a traditional wholesale business. So, he thought, *Okay. We should make something new together to help us. Otherwise, we'll probably starve on the street.* So, that's what we did. In 2011, we flew to Taiwan, to my hometown, and we made it into a business and leisure trip. We researched some factory manufacturers which we then visited in person. We really liked one of the factory's products, so we spent $600 US dollars buying 20 or 30 different products. We put everything in our luggage, and flew back to Los Angeles, and started doing this whole eCommerce thing. I put everything in my garage and began our own microbusiness. Even though I was partnered up with my father, he didn't really do much. He was old and didn't know how eCommerce worked; it came down to me doing everything.

I created our web store, took all the pictures, and arranged visuals for each product. I put a lot of time into this, and it was really tough because there wasn't convenient software like we have today, where you can quickly build a web store; everything I did was from scratch. I was really glad I learned HTML code when I was in college because now I was coding for our microbusiness.

Top Four eMistakes

After building our business up from there, I've learned much from the process. I want to share four common mistakes that people usually make when they initially start doing eCommerce:

1. I need to sell popular products.
2. I should exclusively sell on Amazon.
3. I don't need to use social media.
4. I can't start until I have enough capital.

Mistake #1

People always think they have to sell popular products because a hot product must mean high demand, but that's actually an incorrect approach if you're a beginner. When you think of hot products, it also implies that many people out there are selling it already. So, even though it is a hot product for them, it doesn't mean yours will be hot because you're just starting out; you won't have the reviews or the capital to compete with those experienced sellers.

I believe that all beginners should start with a niche product; they are still in the vast blue ocean of the eCommerce world. Of course, not many people think, *okay, I have to sell this niche product because not that many people buy it*, but it's actually the right approach. By finding a niche product that not many people are selling, you can extend out much more quickly than all the other beginner sellers. In terms of a particular niche product, I can reveal one of the categories that I've already researched: martial arts accessories. If you only focus on accessories and not the core products, you'll be able to find your niche product. Martial arts supply is just one that I've done my due diligence on, and I know it can to be good for beginners.

Mistake #2

Too many people keep their entire focus on Amazon while ignoring other marketplaces because Amazon is so big. This is dangerous. What if Amazon just suspends your store one day? Well, your income will become zero all of a sudden. Amazon could just suspend your account for no reason, or they could find a reason without telling you why. Focusing exclusively on one platform comes with a very high risk.

You would also be missing out on a lot of great opportunities for making other income stream revenue via other platforms. eBay is still big; however, people don't really take eBay that seriously. Let me tell you, eBay still takes a lot of percentage, like 30% of my revenue; so, you should definitely consider eBay. Other options include Wal-Mart and Jet. There are also other small marketplaces like Rakuten, Newegg, and Wish.

Think about it. If you're selling about $10K per month on Amazon, if you add eBay in one of the channels, you might boost all your sales to $20K. And if you add another platform, Wal-Mart for example, then your sales might become $30K. Using a variety of platforms will increase the revenue stream of your marketplace; so, don't just focus on one. You should totally get your store or your product on as many channels as possible to get maximum exposure.

Mistake #3

Some people tend to avoid using social media for their business, but it's necessary when you have a web store – and you must have a web store because that's one of your revenue streams from different channels. If you don't do social media, again, you are missing out on many great opportunities for making other stream incomes, on many return clients, because the combination of your webstore and your newsletter is the only way you can directly communicate with your customers on your own platform and keep them coming back (by offering them coupon codes, promotions, and telling them about new products).

If it's on Amazon or eBay, there's no way you could communicate with customers via their actual emails or a newsletter. So, you must have a web store that utilizes social media to keep traffic incoming. Two of the strongest social media channels for eCommerce:

1. Facebook
2. Instagram

On Facebook, you must buy Facebook ads to get a maximum effect. One of the Facebook ads I tried that was very effective was retargeting as well as Dynamic Facebook Ad (the carousel ads that you see online where you can just scroll through different products when you see just one ad).

Instagram should also be utilized; you don't have to pay nor do you need to buy a lot of ads to get traffic/followers. All you need to do is get automatic software where you can build up your followers and include a lot of hashtags. By doing that, you will get a lot of people to follow your post, to follow your account, and you will really keep your traffic flowing.

Mistake #4

People often think that getting a business started requires a lot of money. I don't understand why so many people think that way, but I think it's because it's what our parents and teachers tell us. That advice is no longer true in eCommerce because you don't need a storefront, and you don't need a big warehouse to stack all the products; everything can be done from your computer with the WiFi from your house. You don't need a lot of employees; all you need to start is you.

I started my business with only $600; that really isn't a lot of money. Most would think you have to save $10K-$20K or maybe get a bank loan to start a business but it doesn't happen that way. I know of some people who probably don't have $600 or $1000 to start, they wouldn't have that initial capital; what I suggest is looking throughout the house and the garage, and then selling unwanted items on eBay to get some capital back. That's one of the ways I very much encourage people to take when they don't have the money.

Selling unwanted items on eBay also helps you because you are gaining more experience on how to run eCommerce, how to handle commerce rapport, how to take products, and how to write good descriptions. I stress it as one of the best practices if you want to get capital for your first eCommerce business. Don't slip into procrastination; just get started.

Million-Dollar Store, Million-Dollar Formula

If you asked me, "So, how do I get started?" I would just tell you not to wait. "Just go ahead and start. Jump in and start doing it. You will see results soon if you follow-through with the strategies I teach." And, if you want to learn more of my stories and my strategies on how to do eCommerce business, you can check out my book which became an Amazon Best Seller, *How I Built A Million Dollar Online Store from $600.*

Many have asked about my failures or mistakes from the past, so they can avoid those and grow much faster. I think my first failure was selling popular products. At first, I tried that approach by selling hot products, but it didn't work. Another obstacle that I encourage others to stay prepared for is people management. People management is always a difficult topic.

I try to keep my team small, and I do my best to keep quality people. Consider the fact that meeting the right people actually takes a lot of work and time because you don't just start with the best team at the beginning. Over time, you eventually need to let people go, and then hire new people; hiring takes a while, but that's something you cannot avoid until you find the right people with the qualities that you're looking for. My book will give you more details about my story, along with the exact strategies I used for my eCommerce, as well as how I built the million-dollar online store in four years – to be specific; I actually made $1.73 Million in revenue in 2017. If you want to learn about how you can do that, please take a look at my book.

For people who want to get more advanced techniques, where I talk about how to optimize keywords for both Amazon and eBay, as well as how to build out a huge audience base, how to pick the right niche product, and how to create your international brand, I also have a FREE webinar available: ellenpro.com/freetraining.

My coaching program is called Million Dollar Golden Formula, and it's an online program. Through this, I offer video courses where you can have access offline for a lifetime. I'm confident that my consulting service is one of the most effective offered because many other online courses out there don't involve actual interaction with instructors at all; you only get to interact with their system, and they don't have that much knowledge about this topic.

Most of my clients are beginners. One of my clients, Daniel, is from Canada. He had zero experience with eCommerce. Six months after he enrolled in my Million Dollar Golden Formula program, his monthly sales started reaching $56K USD. He's one of my top clients, and he does tremendous work. So, if it works for Daniel, a total beginner, it will also work for you.

My client, Shirley, is very experienced in online sales. She's been selling for six years to a decade, but even she couldn't get that boost. She took my course, and she saw her revenue increase 20-30% last year.

My programs work well for beginners or even for experienced sellers; it's what I focus on right now. I'm just trying to mentor and coach more people on selling online, and how to really master the strategy of finding niche product and building a national brand. The best thing about it is that I do eCommerce not only in the United States but in Canada, in Europe, and in Asia as well. I have clients from over 15 countries, such as the UK, Italy, Malaysia, Taiwan, China, even in South Africa and Ukraine. Teaching my strategies has really worked for people around the world, and I have other proven testimonials you can check on ellenpro. com/testimonials, where you can see other success stories.

In the immediate future, I just want to help more people to reach entire financial freedom through eCommerce, and entrepreneurship, as you know. Also, I would like to get on the stage to do a TED Talk. I just want to inspire others. If you want to contact me, please do so through my website, www.ellenpro.com.

25

SURVIVING THE KING

Mastering the Five Channels

By
Jason Hall

I am the CEO and founder of Five Channels Marketing. The Five Channels brand represents the online "channels of traffic" that our agency utilizes to generate an accelerated amount of business growth for our clients. Once we implement our digital marketing strategies, it's normal for clients to experience 2x-5x increase in business growth.

The five traffic channels that I am referring to are as follows:

1. SEO, or Search Engine Optimization

This source of traffic is crucial as some of your highest converting clients are searching online for your products or services. And, if they're aware of your brand, a well-managed SEO strategy is mandatory to maintain a positive online reputation. After all, most visitors never click beyond page one of the search results.

2. Paid Traffic Campaigns

When clients need positive ROI fast, then paid ad campaigns on platforms such as Google, social media platforms, and industry related websites are a must. We mastered the art and science behind paid ads. For every great ad, our clients need to deliver an amazing offer with a stellar landing page that converts cold traffic into warm leads or hot buyers.

3. Content Marketing

The power of "Attraction Marketing" is alive and well today. People want to do business with people they like – not some corporate logo. They need to hear your voice and see your face. By leading with value instead of an offer, your prospects' senses of suspicion are lowered. Continue to push content out on various platforms, and your ideal client will come to you for your services.

4. Remarketing Campaigns

Did you know that more than 80% of website visitors never make it back to a website after their first visit? Distractions, short attention spans, interruptions, poorly developed landing pages, and more pull your potential clients away from your product and services. In short, your initial marketing message has been forgotten. By remarketing your message or a similar offer back to the clients that have visited your brand in the past, they are reminded that at one point in time, they were interested in your business.

5. PR Campaigns

More and more clients are demanding social proof and the desire to work with proven leaders in their industry. By achieving premium article features and brand mentions from top journalists and editors, our clients are creating their authority that they want the public to see and not waiting for a little bad PR to ruin their page-one listings.

With all this "traffic power," my team specializes in creating a powerful increase in brand awareness, online traffic, lead generation, marketing funnels, and more – all while utilizing the appropriate marketing channels available within our clients' industries and within their budget. With diverse clients throughout the world, FiveChannels Marketing is well-connected within many industries to manage and multiply the business growth of your brand and business.

Yet, we still consider ourselves as a "boutique agency." Every client's marketing and execution strategy goes through me, and I don't want the agency to become an uncontrollable size that we lose touch with our clients. With a team of certified individuals in key strategic positions, I lay down the project milestones, and I am confident that the team will deliver results well above the clients' expectations.

But it wasn't always like this...

The King

I started learning SEO and online advertising back in '99 when I was employed at a commercial photography studio in Chicago; we needed a website, and the responsibility fell onto my lap somehow. Truthfully, I always had a passion for throwing myself into something new – even if I didn't know how everything would come together in the end.

Naturally, if you have a website, you need search engine optimization (SEO). And that's how my crazy journey (that I'm still on) began. I wanted to learn all about it. Fast forward four years, and I jumped ship to one of the largest digital marketing agencies in Chicago where I remained as the SEO Department Manager for just over seven years.

During my last year there, my eyes were opened to desperate and deceitful practices that were ordered from the top down. This agency that I'm referring to represented many companies within the same industry. Some of these companies were branded by the same parent company and located within the same major metro, so it was common to fight for top placement among the search engines wherein the majority of traffic and business growth are derived.

As my awareness increased, suddenly, the unthinkable happened. The owner – AKA "the King" – made an announcement directly to me in front of every employee. He said, and I quote, "Jason, whatever you're doing to keep your clients at the top of page one on Google, we need you to take a break. We have other clients complaining, and they want to see their rankings increase."

What?!

I couldn't believe my ears. Everyone was staring at me for a response, so I said something along the lines of, "Got it! I'll look into it." Of course, I didn't change my strategies. The clients I represented were investing thousands of dollars each month. Besides breaking the client service contracts and their trust, I knew our customers deserved better. They deserved what they were paying for instead of intentional harm to their online businesses.

I tried for most of that final year to nod my head, doing as ordered while going behind the owner's back to take care of the clients properly; that's when the "bug" bit to start my own SEO agency. I had a fire burning inside me, and I knew there was more to this all-consuming passion for digital marketing that I had. More importantly, I swore to myself that my agency would educate our clients on how their money would be spent and then follow up with proof.

Well, I left that Chicago agency, and within weeks, I found myself dead in the cross-hairs of a lawsuit from my former employer, the King. Clearly, some of the clients wanted to work with my new agency and not his big agency; the King would not allow that. My ex-employer hired one of the most expensive and aggressive law firm agencies in Chicago to bury me in paperwork. I mean, this law firm cost $20K upfront just to establish the retainer fees. Before I received the official paperwork from the King, trying to wipe me into non-existence, he left two very long voicemails on my cell phone. My mouth dropped. Actually, I sat there for hours staring off into space as I let everything soak in.

These were the type of voicemails you hear in movies when someone is about to hire a hit man to make someone disappear. I couldn't sleep; anxiety was through the roof. Massive amounts of alcohol were the only thing to keep my mind off of those voicemails. I was literally expecting a break-in resulting in a murder scene or staged suicide at any moment.

I downloaded the voicemails from the phone to my laptop, and yes, I still have them to this day as some weird type of inspiration. I shared them with a police officer, and he mentioned that I should bring charges against the King for threatening my life, but I never did anything with them. I knew his lawyers would simply bury me with court proceedings.

Fast forward about 12-15 months when I finally got served the court papers (I must laugh because I intentionally played every move possible to delay the official paperwork delivery and legal responses on my part). At first, this big, bad law firm mailed me the summons...*Now wait-a-minute, they're supposed to be the experts, so they should know better, and should deliver the paperwork in person to me instead of by mail.* I went online and researched advice for the next best steps. This is where I learned that I did not need to respond because the documents weren't physically handed to me; so, another 30-60 days passed by before the law firm's next attempt. Then, they were mailing documents to my UPS Store mailbox. *Good grief,* if the King ever learned the mistakes this law firm made, I'm sure he would have been all over them.

Finally, when an off-duty police officer delivered the lawsuit notification to me, it was time to respond; but, of course, I waited the full 60 days in between each response before I would reply. So, why did I play the delay-game? During this time, I was building up my new client list and my monthly income to support my legal representation. I literally interviewed a dozen suburban law firms to the point that they unanimously agreed I could not only defend myself against this frivolous lawsuit, but I would leave the courtroom with a victory against "the man."

I quickly learned that nobody was scared to take on the big, Chicago law firm (except for me) and they all agreed that we could defend myself against the King. However, the unanimous problem was that it would take about $100K over the course of a year to do so. My heart sank. Hope was truly lost; until this one attorney, fresh out of college, gave me the best advice ever. During our phone call, he told me that all I had to do was let everything go.

What?! He told me that I had to file for a personal bankruptcy! My ears perked up, and I listened to every word that he had to say. I had to let my car go, and I couldn't finish the small number of payments on my credit cards. Worst of all, I had to include my house in the bankruptcy which meant that I'd have to move – *Uggggh!* – I hate moving!

After we hung up the phone, and I really thought about everything. It took me forever to get over the embarrassment of filing for bankruptcy. I felt like the letter "B" was branded on my forehead from the classic novel, *The Scarlet Letter,* by Nathaniel Hawthorne. I didn't want my family or friends to find out about a possible foreclosure, or ask what happened to my car, or answer questions like, "How's the new business going?" So, I was determined to do everything possible to hide this life-consuming experience.

Then I started thinking about reality. *Well, I'm my own boss now, and I don't need to drive to work since I was still working out of my home. I'll figure something out.* I was really proud of my credit score, so not being able to send in the credit card payments very much bothered me. I wasn't looking for a shortcut or a way to make anyone else responsible for my bills. Then there was the house; three stories, two car garage, massive basement, and a fenced-in backyard. Well, during this time, the sub- primed-mortgage-housing bubble-thing was already in full effect. Sure, I was making all my payments and knew that someday it would all get sorted out – but talk about hanging a carrot in front of a rabbit!

Are you trying to tell me, I could foreclose on my home, get rid of my five-year-old car, and make the most deceitful and evil business guy of this world just go away?! You're telling me he can't touch me if I just declare bankruptcy? This was the turning point of my new life; the moment where an 800lb gorilla fell off my back. I felt relief for the first time in over a year, and I hadn't even done anything yet to make it official. *Sign me up!* I filed for personal bankruptcy with a smile on my face and my head held high.

The next hurdle I had to cross was the bankruptcy court date to make it all official.

Sounds easy right? Not quite. The King had every right to attend that same court date and make his case for disapproval of the lawsuit getting thrown out within the bankruptcy.

So, I arrived early and found a quiet little corner on the main courthouse floor which had a clear view of people walking through the security area. Every time the entry doors opened, I would bite my nails and focus on who was making an entrance. Take note, more than a hundred people walked through those doors. One might think that it would get easier and easier as more people walked through; but actually, as the court start-time approached closer and closer, I continued to think he would walk through that door just in time.

He never did.

And that's the last I heard of the King…

FiveChannels

It seriously takes a dedicated individual or an entire team to stay current on all things related to digital marketing; the available strategies that work today will soon be replaced with something new as the buying habits of your clients and consumers adapt to new technologies and consume information differently. For most business owners and entrepreneurs who are busy running their business, there is just no way of effectively self-managing multiple digital marketing strategies while remaining focused on the daily tasks at hand.

If you don't stay informed of the ever-changing and dynamic digital marketing industry, then when you're ready to launch an online marketing campaign, it can seem overwhelming to learn what's working now. Chances are, the campaign is guaranteed for failure from the start – let alone the two weeks used to test the campaign before shutting it down because you don't understand the metrics. This is why digital marketing can be so confusing, inundating, expensive, and downright frightening to business owners not actively engaging with the latest proven strategies.

Our FiveChannels of Fulfillment solution is a refreshing done-for-you service with a twist. Just like when the lawyer revealed to me that there was light at the end of the tunnel, I'm the type of person who doesn't want to pay for something and then wonder how or when I'll see results. I want to be involved and hear their actionable steps which will guarantee me results. But, as a paying client, I don't want to do the tasks. I want to understand how my investment is being applied. I want all doubts removed; this is exactly how our clients are treated.

We take the hand of the client and educate them on all of the marketing strategies available to their business; we don't mind showing them how we do what we do. After learning how we bring our strategies to life, it just reinforces why they don't have time to implement it themselves; this is why they hire the professionals to get their marketing done right, the first time. We ask our clients to tell us the end result that they expect and we then show them multiple strategies to achieve their goals. Why waste money trying to manage your own marketing on failed social media campaigns, when you can pay the professionals up front, knowing that new leads, sales, and business growth are soon on the way? Something like SEO can be read and talked about for a decent understanding, but you won't truly understand how it all comes together until you actually work with clients' websites and within multiple industries. When I started implementing SEO on my own projects, there wasn't a school to go to or a degree to acquire. I had to immerse myself into all of the online chatter, blogs, and SEO software that were being developed every month from entrepreneurs eager to fill a need within a new marketplace.

Believe me, there were many expensive failures, and I know for a fact that my team contributed to some of Google's early updates to stop spam. I learned early on that if generating traffic for my clients would be my career, I had to implement these strategies the correct way, which usually meant the expensive way. Also, early on, I discovered that clients just wanted to understand what they're paying for and what they can expect from their investment.

To this day, the digital marketing space can be used by scammers looking for a quick profit from overzealous CEOs wanting results by tomorrow. Online scams are not something of the past. Our agency is currently taking legal action against a PR agency that took us for $20K. We've learned of numerous complaints, refunds, and victims of their fraud. This agency needs to be stopped, and we need to take a stand.

If more people in our community had previously shared their horrible experience with this "publicity guy," hundreds of thousands of dollars could have been saved among my colleagues; instead, one-by-one, most people received refunds if the services were paid by credit card and companies honoring fraud and un-deliverable claims. Other individuals who paid by cash, check, or wire transfer will never see their refund – this is where I step in. My digital marketing agency will put an end to this company's fraud once and for all.

After learning firsthand how clients want to be treated, I implemented policies that "hold the hand" of every client. This is why we will always remain a boutique agency, choosing the clients that we want to work with, and never scaling to a size where this policy is lost. When clients see the proof of our work – actionable results, and goals being surpassed – they remain clients of ours for years to come.

I've discovered that by building a true relationship between our clients and our team, the client and employee turnover ratio is dramatically lowered. We have clients and employees with us from day one when I was working out of my home. It's not just another day of work; it's exciting and challenging to see what this digital marketing world will throw at us and how we can use it to grow the businesses of our clients. We very much look forward to digging into their projects and seeing which marketing obstacles we will break through.

It's actually an exciting time to be a part of FiveChannels! For the first time ever, we're implementing what we teach to our clients within our own business. For those confused by this statement, you see, we've never had to reach out for a new client before. They would always find us or be referred to us. We've never had a sales team or an inbound marketing strategy. Today, we service clients in the US, Canada, Australia, and even in Mongolia. But recently, I found an exciting calling to serve the local area that we live in and call home. We are bringing our knowledge, experience, and expertise which have been applied to national brands to our local Gulf Coast.

We're located in the heart of the Emerald Coast, and our main headquarters is in Destin, FL. The area is also known as being part of the Gulf of Mexico, as we are surrounded by the Gulf States: Texas, Louisiana, Mississippi, Alabama, and Florida. The economy of the Gulf Coast area is dominated by industries related to energy, petrochemicals, fishing, aerospace, agriculture, and tourism.

So, if you have a retail store, restaurant, home services business, legal services, online products, a book, or anything that needs your ideal customer's eyes on it, then FiveChannels Marketing can work with your brand. We represent law firms, doctors, e-commerce stores, HR companies, boat sales, auto sales, professional sports teams, solo-entrepreneurs, the real estate market, and many other different industries. In fact, targeting diversified industries is what keeps us at the forefront of digital marketing and innovation. It's amazing how a real estate marketing technique can work exceptionally well in eCommerce; or how one of our world-famous author and speaker's Facebook campaigns can be duplicated for a small local office.

I believe that if we only specialized in marketing for law firms, my team might get caught up in repetition, outdated checklists, and boredom; not the case. We love Mondays. Every week is not like the last. Sometimes we work from the office, remotely at home, on a boat, at a local restaurant on the beach, or while we're preparing to shoot video footage for an upcoming Facebook ad campaign. It's always exciting to see what's coming down the pipeline and watching our current clients reach new levels of growth within their businesses.

If you'd like to know more about FiveChannels or to get in touch, please visit our website at FiveChannels.com. We look forward to learning how our agency may partner with you!

26

OFF THE DRY TEET

A Long and Endlessly Winding Journey

By
Dimitry Boss

Hello and welcome to my world. I always knew I had an entrepreneurial spirit and an inventive drive. Since the age of six, tinkering around and solving problems was second nature to me. Eventually, I began to understand that, most of the time, if I allowed the solution to evolve and show itself, the correct and right path became clearly apparent. I learned that often the result is not the solution that I thought it would be. Continuing my story from age six would be too cumbersome, so I will resume it at college when I invented my machine and found my "Ah Ha" moment!

At 19, I was focused on fitness and body conditioning and spent a lot of time working out my mid-section. Like everybody else, I wanted shredded, ripped abs; although, I never felt soreness in areas where I wanted to improve – mostly the outer abdominals. The equipment couldn't achieve the angles that were necessary to isolate and concentrate on those muscles for a complete and truly exhausting core workout. So, out of frustration, I decided this would not hold me back – I would design a machine that would do what I wanted!

Because I was in college, I was surrounded by many talented people. I had a fraternity brother, Mark Colbert, who was working on his industrial design degree and called in a favor to explain my vision to him. I asked him to draw what I conceived in my head, and I walked him through what I wanted. He drew it all out, and he did it well. The resulting machine allowed me to hold my position at the correct angle to target, with pinpoint precision, the specific area of muscles that I couldn't reach without it.

Alas, life moves on, and eventually, I threw these drawings on a shelf where they sat for twenty-five years. After college, I really needed to focus on a business career in which I could excel and make a lot of money; so, I took a job at a local fitness center. It was an all-women's gym, where I was the only male employee – not a bad set up if I do say so myself. I met the owner of the gym, who eventually took me under his wing to teach me the art of selling. That art really translated into listening to objections and seeing how to accommodate and overcome them in order to close the sale! It's an art form for which I owe this mentor my wholehearted gratitude for making me the sales person I've become.

Through connections in the gym world, a friend of mine introduced me to an associate who was a salesperson for a local New Jersey burglar alarm company. I was fascinated to see him go on a sales call and close the deal in one hour; one worth thousands of dollars. After noting the residual income stream that followed by monitoring the alarms, I was hooked! I finished out the year working at the gym and saved up $34K; with this, I quit and opened my own company BOSS Security Systems Inc. (Best Offered Security Service) in August 1992 – and then I went to work!

I knew nothing about the alarm industry or running my own business; I just knew that I never wanted to look back and say, "What if…" or "If only I'd tried that." I just jumped in head first and forced the success of my company every single minute of every single day. I was relentless. Because of this tenacity, I have now grown my company to be among the top 20 alarm companies in Bergen County, outside of publicly-traded or national companies. Also, now that I am 50 years old, looking back on me at 25, I realize that I don't have half the energy I did back then – so I am grateful to have had that opportunity young in life.

The Boss of BOSS

After twenty years of hard work, my fortunes have allowed me to pursue some of my other endeavors. I am truly fortunate! I'm now financially able to devote both money and (more importantly) time to developing BOSS Security Systems and other projects. In 2013, five years before writing this chapter, I refreshed my college idea; I pulled the drawings and notes off the shelf, blew away the dust, and decided that now it was time to go for it!

Through Facebook, I was able to reconnect with my college buddy, Mark, who originally drew up my blueprints in 1991. When I reached him, he owned Sterling Design Group and was happy to rejoin my efforts. Because so many years had passed, new technology allowed me to expand on my original machine; the resulting invention would be for the professional and extreme marketplace. It would truly change sports statistics across the entire planet!

The combination of being able to store data in memory and adjust the conditioning through analytics and biofeedback is unparalleled. The end result is increased core strength and muscle development. It is simply a dance of four math principles working in unison and in conjunction with each other to achieve a goal. Physics, geometry, kinesiology, and an understanding of kinetic energy and its transference make it possible to chart and follow the growth of the individual or team.

I quickly realized that in order to reach the masses, I needed to develop a machine priced at a few hundred dollars, **not tens of thousands of dollars**. Thus, I simplified the originally intense Pro-elite machine into its most basic elements, and then the universal core development machine for home was born. The new idea was perfect; now all I needed to do was make this into a real product. I knew I needed a prototype and

I asked Mark to help me build one. I told him I wanted it strong and he truly delivered.

A 500-pound gorilla could use this machine, and it wouldn't break; unfortunately, it weighed 64 lbs. and was very bulky. The current unit weighs 10.5 lbs., so one can imagine how strong and thick the steel was for that first prototype. Even though it was too blocky, it clearly showed the vision and the patentability of my rotating indexing plate.

My unique plate allows the user to customize the angle in their workout to not only hit every single muscle group in one's core but to precisely set the angle to target these 29 muscle groups in ways that were not previously possible before this product came to be. There was a fascinating side effect I noticed after a few weeks of using this machine; my lower back that always bothered me felt much better. *Now, I need to market this beast!*

Marketing the Beast!

I secured a meeting with the person I believed to be the home run of home runs, Kevin Harrington. I'd seen what he achieved in the fitness world with regards to sales – billions of dollars worldwide. This was my ultimate goal...to have someone like Kevin market my product!

On January 15, 2015, I met Kevin Harrington in NYC for a one-hour uninterrupted meeting. I had the chance to discuss my ideas and gain the most valuable feedback possible. I showed Kevin my prototype and explained why it was special and how it was unlike anything else in the marketplace. His suggestion was to make it store-ready and see how the market would respond; this was invaluable information. Now that I have the finished unit in hand, it's a little embarrassing to remember what I originally showed Kevin – but it got the job done!

At the end of this meeting, I told Kevin that this workout machine was great for what I referred to as, "The post-pregnancy rebound." By being able to target the outer portions of the abdomen, the user can pull everything back inwards after her midsection was stretched out to accommodate the baby. Also, the true reduction of back pain is achievable by strengthening the muscles that surround the vertebrae. When you do this for 3-5 minutes a day, you help to reduce the pressure against the spine.

He responded, "That's your secret sauce!" I felt well on my way that I was headed down the correct path, and I was about to take the plunge with no looking back.

I prioritized everything. First, I contacted my patent agent, Quickpatents.com, to start the process of a provisional patent. Subsequently, we applied for the non-provisional utility patent; it was granted and issued early in 2017. We actually have two utility patents issued, both granting 29 claims of protection in total. Then I needed to redesign my machine to make it look and feel more complete and streamlined. Once again, I contacted Mark, and we did a complete CAD (Computerized Engineering Drawing) workup of my invention. CAD's describe every detail of a product, from soup to nuts, down to the thread size of the screws and bolts used.

By June 2015, I needed to source the prototype production off-shore to bring the price down to a reasonable level.

In discussing my invention, I guess I should finally share its name with you:

The BOSS AbBlaster System

- www.BossAbBlaster.com
- BOSS stands for Blasted Out Shredded Six-pack.
- Clearly, one can see that I like acronyms for my last name.

The Boss AbBlaster is designed to help in rehab and injury prevention, reduction of lower back pain, spine stability, core development, and of course, athletic advanced training. I knew I was onto something special, and Kevin's words of confidence were fuel to my fire. I continued pressing forward. There were then engineering problems to address and overcoming them took time and effort. As mentioned at the beginning of my chapter, I usually try to allow the evolution of my solutions to occur naturally without projecting a specific direction. I've learned that coming up with an idea and then making certain it absolutely works are two entirely different things. To date, we ended with 381 illustrations to explain concepts, 5 different sets of complete CAD files, and a total of 4 prototypes.

WBFF Fitness Pro - Zeke Samples   45° angle

What I desperately needed was to show the world that this product has merit and as always in my adult life, I knew that "sales cures all." How was I going to pull this off? I had a perfect solution to this problem; I needed POC (Proof of Concept), and Kickstarter was the perfect platform. Not only was it great for my test; it gave me the customers I needed to move the inventory.

My mantra is, "Never give up!" You may have to change directions or pivot but stay focused on the end goal. Clearly, what I was doing in the past wasn't working, and hoping to convince people that I was right by trusting me blindly was naive. All of that needed to change. As an idol of mine, Albert Einstein, once said, "Insanity is doing the same thing over and over again and expecting different results." I needed to modify my strategy. I also realized that I would need this POC for any investor to have the confidence to entertain collaborating with me on this new venture. They needed to see it for themselves. So, I took the plunge again.

I put together a campaign that was pretty intricate. I managed to get a great video development company for a reasonable price, WMV Productions. They produced two teaser videos and my main campaign video. They were an exceptional addition to the team. After this, the only thing missing was a presence on Facebook. I wasn't a fan of Facebook, so I never really went on it when I surfed the web. That all changed once I knew I would need the social media platform – I became friends with everybody!

I started to penetrate the fitness world with some pro athletes that have name recognition in their perspective fields. One person stood out, Zeke Samples, because he contacted me after seeing the potential for my invention – he wanted to be a part of it! A WBFF muscle fitness pro was now on board! Soon, our collaboration developed into a close friendship, which I hold to this day. A team player and a valued asset, Zeke helped me at a time when I needed it most; and for that, I will pay it forward. He is featured in the previous photo and as the demonstration model for our YouTube library of exercise instructional videos, www.youtube.com/c/ Bosselated

I spent $8,300 on Facebook ads and generated $33K in backer sales from Kickstarter in 45 days. We hit our target goal, and the campaign was successful. That's a 3-for-1 ROI (Return on Investment). $33K was enough for tooling and the first production run. After the campaign ended, many doors started opening; people saw that there was indeed interest in my product. Once I started to take it around to the local gyms, I knew I had a winner; everyone clearly understood the benefits. Even though the product was designed primarily for home use, these people wanted it and understood why it would be a game changer – that was refreshing.

My biggest hurdle in getting this out to the masses was that most investors and potential partners didn't see anything aside from the sales numbers and money. They aren't necessarily fitness-oriented people and don't understand the frustration felt when pro and amateur athletes alike can't achieve a goal for lack of proper equipment. Also, in all fairness to potential investors, there never really was focus on back pain reduction – until three different friends of mine said the same thing about their aging old back having never felt better after two weeks using my invention.

When I am in the right environment, the Boss AbBlaster sells itself with a quick demo. How do we get sales without spending a fortune to educate the consumer base (especially if you are not sure how to market it)? You can spend a fortune learning what works and what doesn't. Or, here's another way to solve that problem: partner with only the very best. Find a person or company to complement your weaknesses and vice-versa. I am a great sales person and working inventor; but perhaps, I am not so good as a marketer. Thus, in working with a great marketer, together, we make a complete and superior team!

The Pudding

Since I had been surfing Facebook, I started to see all these adds for this huge trade show for inventors and entrepreneurs, along with a competition for "Inventor of The Year" that was coming up. So, I did my research, found out about all details related to this show and knew that this would expose me to some great opportunities for not only the Boss AbBlaster but an entirely new patented product I invented called Genie Cone.

The show is called the ERA D2C Convention (D2C stands for Direct to Consumer). Also, Kevin Harrington was part of creating the ERA organization decades ago – (Electronic Retail Association). Since the organization running the event said that there was no restriction regarding how many inventions I could showcase, I decided that it would be best to bring both of my inventions to this competition that was just a few weeks away, in Las Vegas, at the Wynn Hotel, on Oct 2, 2017.

So, on the morning of the flight to Vegas, I looked at CNN.com at 4 am EST, and there it was – the massacre at the Mandalay Bay was just an hour old! So, there I was, flying into a lock-down zone after a terror attack (yeah, my wife was real calm about that…). Nonetheless, I needed to attend this convention/show/competition.

Well. Guess what? I can't believe it, but my Genie Cone invention took 2nd place at this show in Las Vegas. I was competing for Inventor of the Year, and I brought it with me just in case. There is something said about being prepared. The Boss AbBlaster also took top 10 honors as well. Both of my ideas were validated by the judges and the results.

The Genie Cone product line (www.GenieCone.com) is a multi-tiered hair accessory product. The Genie Cone comes in two parts. The base-cone goes into the user's hair to create the ponytail and covers that line over the base-cone. The DIY arts and crafts kit (lower left side of the picture) is for young girls to design and create their own customized ponytail holder. It has interchangeable covers that simply slide on and off the base-cone once these are decorated with the users' personal flair. This is what took 2nd place. Not too bad to be #2 out of 82 inventions. The funny thing is that I am so competitive I was a bit irritated that I didn't win – this soon faded away.

Genie Cone- Kids	Genie Cone- Adults -
Tier 1 & 2 *Fun & Casual*	Tier 3 When only the finest will do!

Tier 1 - Arts & crafts kit or 2 cover blister pack (and licensing - Disney) *SLIDE 2*

Tier 2 - Pre-designed covers of whatever is currently trending- logos, branding, casual fashion, endless choices of subject matter. Fully customizable *SLIDES 3&6*

Tier 3 Adult high end -covers feature of multiple mediums. Alloy based covers with fine jewels, textured gold flake, high-relief etching patterns, etc. *SLIDES 4 & 5*

With 3 different products one can capture the entire market. All items protected by full issued design patent in the United States.

Tier1 4-10yrs old	*Tier 2* 11-17 yrs old	*Tier3* 18 yrs & up
Genie Cone-**Kids**	Genie Cone- **Teens**	Genie Cone - **Adults**

Trending and customized

Highest of quality

We also have cover kits that are predesigned and packaged by themes. This completely opens up the market with endless possibilities. The middle lower picture is for teens with whatever is trending, casual fashion, or licensing opportunities. The right lower column is for high-end fashion. You can now wear that special outfit and match your ponytail holder to what you're wearing. We are also in development for our patent pending Genie Cone product which is a totally controllable LED version of our covers; those are going to make crowd participation at public events the hottest craze. They will be fully downloadable and completely interactive once they are completed. Genie Cone will not be a fad; it will be a staple in every woman's attire, from the age of five-years-old all the way up.

At the ERA Show I couldn't believe that Genie Cone took 2nd place and the Boss AbBlaster took top honors! So, there I was getting ready to start packing up my booth to head home – and all of a sudden, out of nowhere, Kevin Harrington tapped me on the shoulder (he happened to be walking around the convention center), and we had a chance to catch up. Since the Boss AbBlaster was with me in its finished form, I had a chance to show him what had become of his suggestions and where I was in regard to marketing it.

After a very long, hard, and arduous winding journey, things are all lining up to be fruitful after many rejections. A little bit of luck, timing, and a lot of persistence officially paid off! What am I talking about? I'll explain. We returned to our perspective lives after Vegas 2017, and I continued to work out the kinks to move things forward. I decided to reach out to Kevin right before the holidays and suggested that we take an opportunity to explore this, and he agreed. Happily, it finally worked its way out that I would fly to Florida on January 16, 2018, to sign paperwork making it official. We would both explore the possibility of really promoting my machine. I couldn't believe it was all working out.

I must say, the timing was notable…three years and one day from the very date on which I was introduced and first met Kevin in NYC. The title of my upcoming book will be the full and detailed version of the "long and endlessly winding journey" of this event. It will be titled, *Three Years and a Day*.

As the chapter for this book comes to a close, things are looking good for the Boss AbBlaster and Genie Cone – success seems imminent! I am heading back to Vegas at the end of May 2018 to attend the largest licensing trade show in the United States. I will be promoting and getting distribution channels for all of my inventions. The meetings are already set up with some of the largest players in the industry, and I can't wait! I am super excited and have all my ducks lined up in a row. I am projecting a monumental success!

Just another week in the life of an entrepreneur/inventor! Every day is filled with highs and every so often a couple of low days find their way in. The truth is you make lemonade out of lemons every day. That mentality and methodology compounds and hopefully over time, it takes root in success; not just monetary success, but success defined by that individual needs and ultimate goals. I leave that up to you as the reader to decide:

What defines success for you?

Never Give Up
(no matter what – period!)

To wrap up, if you want to be an inventor, innovator, leader, or change the viewpoint of people in the world in some way, you'd better embrace rejection – and embrace it hard! There is no other way! You will find a lot more rejections than praise or affirmation. Also, it is a true exercise in patience. It takes years to become an overnight success; however, that's a topic to be explored in the future along with the results of my upcoming Vegas trip – be on the lookout for the book!

I saw an interview with Steve Jobs and Bill Gates in which Jobs spoke of giving up and passion. I believe he said it perfectly...

"People say you have to have a lot of passion for what you're doing and it's totally true. And the reason is that [building something of value is] so hard that if you don't, any rational person would give up. It's really hard. And you have to do it over a sustained period of time. So, if you don't love it, if you're not having fun doing it ... you're going to give up. And that's what happens to most people, actually." (CNBC, 11/15/2017)

What does that say about me and others like myself? Do we do it for the love of it? Or, are we irrational and a bit insane?

As I've traveled through this experience, I realized that every rejection brings me that much closer to someone saying, "Yes!" Personally, my aspirations far exceed these inventions. It is a step toward other larger ideas ahead in my future. I need launching pads and to ultimately surround myself with other people to help complete the missing puzzle pieces. I worked for three years to get noticed and consummate a deal with the right team players. I always felt that if I could look up at my team and see that I was the weakest player/link, then I knew we were destined for greatness – that may still happen!

If you have an interest in learning more or acquiring any of our products, please visit us at www.BossAbBlaster.com or www.GenieCone. com. We look forward to hearing from you about your experience. If you think you are the missing piece to my puzzle and feel that you can further develop our platform by working with us to promote our product lines, we welcome that possibility. I am always looking to fill in the missing puzzle pieces with only the very best!

Don't ever give up the fight; embrace the success of others without jealousy or envy. Let their success drive you forward and help you put positive energy into the universe. It will come back triple fold. You must be a force for good! And always pay it forward, no matter how hard that may seem. Breathe in, exhale. Smile!

Dimitry Boss

27

RICH NICHE

*Identify Your "Niche" in Real Estate and Build
an Eight- or Nine-Figure Business Around It*

By
Cheryl Spangler

I was born in Fairfax, Virginia. Pretty much lived most of my life in Virginia other than the two years, I lived in Silicon Valley, San Jose area. I then moved back to be closer to the family when I was pregnant and started having kids. I am basically a serial entrepreneur. Consistently for the last 17 years, I have been immersed in the real estate industry, as an agent, a broker, a mentor, and an industry leader. I currently hold real estate licenses in multiple states under eXp Realty LLC.

After being an agent, buying and managing multiple EXIT Realty Franchises, and then opening my own independently, I found my calling in helping other agents build massively successful real estate businesses. I love to focus on the creation and business building, mindset, and strategy, making things simple yet efficient, creating a success path that is easy to follow, whether you are in real estate or not. My business strategies are proven and work.

I first got licensed in 2002. Before that, I was into high tech. I mean, basically, since high school, I've been a total computer geek. That all started with pulling cable through the ceiling, because it was a guy's world and they didn't really think I was serious, and then it eventually moved to where I started getting certifications. I realized that I needed to be somewhat over-educated and over-certified to compete with the men in the computer industry at the time.

I enjoyed working with computers on an individual basis and large networks and quickly became a 3rd level tech support for local area networks (LAN) and wide area networks (WAN). My bachelor's degree is in Computer Information Systems, and my MBA is in Technology Management. But what keeps me up into the wee hours of the night thinking and working on the computer (for fun) is marketing. From online to offline, I am always intrigued by marketing, so it has brought my sales careers to new levels since I do most of the creative marketing for my own jobs myself.

Ten years into the tech world, working 16- 17-hour days and newly pregnant, I knew this was not going to be the best situation for a family. So, my husband at the time decided to move back to Virginia so we could be closer to my family. We also moved so that I could start over in a career where I would utilize my computer, sales and marketing skills to the highest level.

Rough Start

I decided, after months of consideration and interviewing top agents in the area, to go into real estate. I saw men and women in the industry not taking it seriously, not treating it like a business and instead floundering around making minimal money ($30-50k per year) and never taking it to the next level for whatever reason. I was always studying this, and when I created my real estate business. I too floundered for the first 18 months, not closing even one deal, and used up practically all our savings trying everything under the sun. Everything I found told me that it would work and everything told to me said that it was the magic in getting business.

It was during that time that I realized the difference between business owners and hobbyists in the real estate industry. Business owners sit down from the beginning and map out their plan. I mean they seriously do the research about which market niche they will focus on, and they really get to know their competition. But it was more than that; the real estate knowledge and teachings regarding competition is all about finding out who in your area has the market share and who in your area are you trying to beat. It did NOT ultimately make me money, nor did it bring success in my real estate career.

The idea of having an ideal customer and knowing what makes them tick, what their challenges are, what keeps them up at night was a new concept for others around me. But I focused on this as time went on, realizing this is the most important thing I could put my energy into that would bring clients my way with less effort. The majority of real estate agents just threw a bunch of marketing out and hoped someone would call, all the while wondering why their business was not bringing in leads.

Recovering from Financial Devastation

During the time I was building my real estate business, my clientele and my niche market – which consisted of a specific geographic area of town– fell flat (or I should say, fell into the black hole of death). Realtors were selling homes before they could get a sign in the yard, and then they weren't! The market was crashing from 2006-2008. But honestly looking back, we were all so dumb about it, as if things would continue to be up, up, up forever.

311

At the height of the market with only focusing on my small geographic area, I closed around $175k-200k, made some bad decisions like not saving that money and instead buying two investment homes – one in Fredericksburg VA and one in South Carolina (this decision was one of many disagreements brewing at the home front). I was a risk-taker, and my husband was a conservative guy; we rarely met in the middle. Our personalities clashed, our mindset was different, and our household was getting unbearable, to say the least. Two kids under the age of five, three homes and a market that once brought me $30-45k per month was dwindling to $10k, $5k, and then some months, nothing. By 2008 we started having difficulty getting the rent paid on those investment homes; the money from my business was not coming in like it used to and to top it all off we purchased a brand new primary residence that was way out of our price range if my income stopped.

There was a moment where blame set in; financial stress really took its toll (not to mention we were dealing with issues at home with our ADHD son who really needed the stability of the home we were currently in). Divorce was around the corner, we both knew it; not because of the money but because we had been drifting in what we wanted out of life and who we were for some time, plus the finances, childcare, career choice, and poor decisions just made it even more apparent how different we really were.

We decided that a short sale was the only option at this point to keep the primary home and family stable and not lose everything. Those two homes were purchased in my name so during divorce I short sold the investment homes and he kept the primary. So, what does all this have to do with business? It was the beginning of my next stage of my real estate career where I focused on helping other homeowners going through the same thing and I was very passionate about it.

In aligning with this focus, from the ground up, I built a short sale business with a team of five people, with systems, processes, and fundamental business building that I frankly never used from day one in real estate. I started Virginia's Home Rescue, a name within my real estate business used to focus solely on doing short sales for home sellers.

I literally became the go-to agent in Northern Virginia, helping agents and seller's short sell their homes. This was an "AH-HA" moment for me on niche marketing, and it took me from two brutal short sales, one divorce, and one chapter seven bankruptcy in November 2010, to make over $600k gross in 2011 – and I'm not kidding about these numbers.

How was this possible? By just helping people through something I personally went through, step by step, until they understood and felt comfortable with the outcome. It was the birth of my absolute obsession with niche marketing and the concepts of building a business fast, and all of it went far beyond anything the real estate industry prepared me for. I was a sponge, learning daily things to do, and not to do, in order to expand, grow, sustain, and profit from the real estate business that almost took me down.

Three New Businesses in Four Years
(yes, really)

In 2011, I decided to purchase my own EXIT Realty Franchise, located in Manassas, VA. And in 2013, alongside my business partner, I purchased yet another EXIT Realty Franchise located in Old Town Alexandria, VA. During that time, my goal was to bring to agents what I felt was missing in the marketplace from brokers: open-minded, digital marketing knowledge, welcoming office structure (coffee shop meets real estate office), and business building on steroids. During those few years, we also opened a title company, but that was short-lived since our primary focus was on managing offices and growing agents' business.

For years, I put 300% into building the offices (by 2013 we had three locations) and the businesses, including keeping my own real estate business going. I came to realize that building the agents' confidence, skills, branding ideas, marketing ideas, sales skills, and teaching strategies could be implemented regardless of education and home life circumstances. To some degree, this worked the way I wanted, but ultimately there was a missing piece. Regardless of training and motivation techniques, the money was still not coming in, and the agents were still not as productive as I had hoped; recruiting quickly became my full-time job.

I found myself thoroughly enjoying the recruiting aspect of the job, getting to know the agents initially and putting them through what became my very successful recruiting interview and systematic onboarding process. The challenge was that I was wearing too many hats. I had two kids under age 11, I was a single mom at this point after getting divorced in 2009, and well, my roles included: office manager, agent of my own team, broker, owner of two franchises, owner of a title company, and I was my own personal admin, marketing specialist, transaction coordinator, and the list goes on. Oh yeah, and don't forget a mom, sister, daughter, granddaughter. But, family visits fell by the wayside since my life consisted of working 24/7 for real estate and barely getting to pick my kids up from school in time – and then back to real estate until the wee hours of the night.

A Spiritual Awakening in Business

I had been studying, for years, the idea of creating your own reality, mindset training, and the power of positive thinking. More than that, I started and had been studying the metaphysical world, the spiritual world, manifesting, creating and the power of focus. I knew that I created some amazing business opportunities in my life, and these things were not just by chance or luck. There is a process to creating what you want in life, and I wanted to master that; I loved it, I thrived on it, and it always brought me the results I desired.

I coached with the most amazing man, named Bill Nasby. He called himself a trainer with the company I worked for at the time, but he didn't realize he was more than that – he was a spiritual business intuitive life coach, and he taught me everything he knew about goal setting. And this was not setting goals for the heck of it; it was setting them to be manifested immediately and in tune with what is best for you.

The tools, techniques, guidelines, and process of attracting what you want in life became my everyday routine in addition to raising two kids. I worked with this life/business coach for three years on and off, expanding each time we went through a twelve-week program together. I began teaching this to agents – not the spiritual aspects, but the money and success mindset, confidence building, business building, and serving customers and clients with soul.

Serving with soul means you start your business by digging deep to identify why you started it, what you want your business to do for you personally, professionally and what you want your business to do for your clients in the long run. Everything became about providing value and how to do that with marketing, digital, video and high-tech solutions, and strategy. I know I am going on a tangent with this topic, but this is a missing piece to most real estate businesses. The National Association of Realtors (NAR) still states that the average real estate agent makes $30-50k per year and I could put money on the fact that it's because agents get licensed and the first thing you focus on is how to prospect. No one sits you down and teaches you how to really build a successful sustainable and profitable business.

After running myself ragged for almost four years with young children, no real help at home, and three real estate offices, I had a "come-to-Jesus" conversation with myself and my business partner that lasted nearly a full year. The idea of selling off the brokerages was up for discussion; pursuing a more manageable life and business model where real estate was more so virtual, and the focus was instead on the clients, not the office and overhead. Finally, at the end of 2014, we made the decision to sell the title company and real estate franchises. This decision was not made lightly, it was heartbreaking, in that my biggest concern was that the agents I had under me would continue to flourish and not be affected.

Starting Over Again

In 2014, I partnered with my mother (who was retired after 30+ years in the government). She was a real estate agent at the time in my office. We opened a Virtual Real Estate Company called FORBZ Real Estate

Group. The name was a combination of auditory recognition with the traditional Forbes Magazine, as well as the street I lived on. I always have marketing in mind when doing things, it comes naturally, and I hone this skill daily. I started over with my personal business at this point. As a broker for so many years, I lost most of my personal clientele through lack of time to nurture them.

We started our new company, where we hyper-focused our marketing, branding, and messaging around the waterfront in Old Town Alexandria, VA. Starting over was becoming quite the thing for me – not so scary anymore. I knew I could go anywhere, start anything, and within eighteen months be successful with income and market share. Because I knew how to properly align my business with my ideal customer, it further became my passion, my mission, and my drive. In fact, during this time I met with a company to create a mobile app that was like an "intuitive home buyer search app" where the home buyer would simply state things they like to do, places they like to go, and the lifestyle they like to live. The app would find the homes that would be perfect for them in a zip code, matching it with the real estate multiple listing service and all the fields that could be searched within. However, right before I sunk money into this mobile idea of mine, large companies started launching "lifestyle home search apps" like it, so I decided not to pursue it.

Getting to know the customer is what makes me a successful real estate agent. Knowing my customer's lifestyle problems, challenges, and struggles intimately, and how to solve them is what makes me a good marketer. The sales come when you simply put those two together – and add a little heart! I quickly involved myself in things that interested me like writing for Inman News as a contributor, freelance writing for the local newspaper, *The Zebra,* in Old Town Alexandria, and diving into video marketing before it became a hot button for companies to focus on.

I did online written and video blogging for various online news sites as well as my own YouTube channel for clients and customers. I prepared over 100 bloggable videos asking one question and providing one answer, each of them no more than 60 seconds long. All this, combined, was how I took our new brokerage to new levels within the first 2 years, making a name for ourselves in the industry. I became an Inman News speaker at national events, an author, and a mentor for agents.

Wealth, Health, and a Thriving Business
(yes, all in the same sentence)

In late 2014, after spending so much time on everything business related, after the brokerages were sold and the agents were transitioned, I decided to focus on some personal goals of mine. I looked in the mirror and saw a 40+-year-old woman getting a typical 40+-year-old body. One day I just said, "NO, this is not how this is going down." I went to a personal trainer to start with 2 days a week, someone to keep me accountable and on track… to teach me about how to lift weights, how to grow muscle, and lean out the fat – but a holistic approach, organic and safe, and empowering. That is when I met my first ever and now a great friend, Nina Lomax of Body Conscious Personal Training.

I met Nina at a local Women's Leadership conference and what started like two days a week quickly moved into four days a week. During this time business was building faster than ever, my weight was going down, and my muscle was increasing. But more importantly, my confidence in life, my body, and my abilities were coming back – it was pretty darn exhilarating. My family is riddled with Diabetes; my sister passed away from it, my brother diagnosed at age 39 with Type 1, and my mother was diagnosed with Type 2 later in life. I was pretty determined not to give the disease an opportunity to infiltrate my life and body, so keeping fit had to become a priority for me.

After a year of personal training, I decided to pursue a bodybuilding competition, of which I could write an entire book on the ins and outs of the International Federation of Bodybuilding and what really goes into becoming a top pro bikini competitor. I devoted my free time for four years to working out every morning, two to three hours, without fail.

I took on a routine that included a very regimented diet, exercise, water intake, and no salt, sugar, or preservatives.

I worked my way through coaches until December 2016. I hired an Olympia coach, Dan Eslinger of D4 Muscle Fit, to take me PRO and ultimately to get to Ms. Olympia as an International Bikini Pro Competitor. In June 2017, I turned PRO in New York at a national bodybuilding competition named NPC Universe. There were over 1500 competitors at this event. Only the first-place winners would receive their PRO status, and I won two categories that day, basically walking away with two pro cards.

To this day, the highlight of my life (other than my kids being born, of course, and graduating college) was winning this PRO status. Why is this? Because what it took all those years, never waning, never giving in, never giving up, always giving my best day in and day out, it taught me more about consistency than anything I have ever heard or experienced. I continued to pursue the PRO Bikini Bodybuilding Circuit until March 10, 2018, when I did my last show, placing in the top 14 girls in the world in Bikini Bodybuilding at age 46. I left that show realizing that I had accomplished what I wanted from the sport; it was time to move on. It was time to show other men and women some things that could dramatically help them in their journey of business.

Oh, yes, bodybuilding taught me loads about business and how we give up too soon, cry about things when there is nothing to cry about, and strategies that help you keep going when times are tough. I learned more about mindset than anything and how to improve a success mindset, how to turn your self-limiting beliefs around, and how to prosper in the face of failure; like when I took a dive on stage during a renowned competition, falling on my ass in front of the entire auditorium, and then returning two weeks later to take second place. It's how you respond to failure that makes you a success.

Coaches, Mentors, and Everyone in Between
(whom do you trust?)

When I look back on the seventeen years, I have been in the real estate industry, and business in general, there is one thing that has been consistent in my life: having a coach by my side. Not all of them took me to better places; some just wasted my time, my money, and my energy. But, there were a few who dramatically and completely changed my life, and I am forever grateful. They not only changed my life, but my mind, my body, and my soul.

A good coach will challenge you, inspire you, and give everything to you. A good coach will lift you up and show you who's boss at the same time (i.e., YOU are boss of your own mind, body, and soul). A phenomenal coach is one that will see the greatness in you when you are at your lowest; but, not allow you to sit in self-pity; instead, they teach you the skills you need to overcome it.

I am this coach for others now! And that is what I have learned and what I am passionate about. It is my time to teach the business building strategies, mindset work, unique skills, and both marketing and sales techniques that will change the way you grow your business and your life. The Internet, the speed at which technology is advancing is requiring us to be smarter, faster, more purposeful, more strategic, and more passionate. Doing something just because it might bring you money is not enough; you must find your genius – find your passion in something and learn the skills to build a business around it, period!

Connect with Me

Find out how I am becoming a disrupter in the Real Estate industry in a phenomenal way! I am the founder of the Rich Niche Academy, which I created to provide a ton of value at an affordable price. Whether you are just starting out, rebuilding yourself or setting yourself up to walk away from the business, this is for you! Through it, you can discover what you need to know about setting up and running a profitable and sustainable real estate business. It's all about empowering real estate professionals to 'Niche' successfully and then build an 8-9 figure business around it.

Starting a real estate business is amazing, exciting, fulfilling, liberating…and it's confusing and lonely as hell! Those last two aspects are the things people don't really talk about when they are raving how great it is to start a real estate career and quit their full-time job. The truth is that in between the closed deals where you are jumping up and down ecstatic that you made $10k or more in one day, that you own your own business, and, "Yeah baby that's how it's done!" you then have thousands of questions, frustrations and worries about how you will make it all work, get it all done, and figure it all out – so that you will actually have a LIFE, fun, and, (oh yeah, what about your…) future security! No more feeling time-strapped, tech stupid, and over-freaking-whelmed! Richnicheacademy.com is now OPEN!

REAL ESTATE SUCCESS PATH

RICH NICHE

STEP-BY-STEP | 60 DAY | SIMPLE | PROVEN

4. AUTOMATE

Step away, more time, more connection with niche, streamline marketing, content, processes, systems, team. START HERE to level-up your BIZ and regain your freedom while making more $$$.

3. GROWTH

Stuck, need assistant, get the phone ringing, eliminate overwhelm. START HERE if you need systems and processes, tech simple, automation and a die hard niche following, more $$ NOW!

2. CLARITY

Overwhelmed, feeling pressure to keep up, Niche identified but no following yet. Ready to level up. START HERE if you want better and more consistent results, branding, message to market, simple, effective plan for more $.

1. FOUNDATION

Overwhelmed, No Niche, Educated, Positive, Unorganized. START HERE if you need to define your strengths, your business goals, your ideal client.

Cheryl Spangler | 703-216-1491 | Cheryl@cherylspangler.com
IG @TheRichNiche
IG @CherylSpanglerFit
FB @LiveLovesCheryl
FB Group @TheRichNiche
LI @cherylspangler
TW @TheRichNicheinRE
YT @CherylSpanglerInspire

28

THE BEST-KEPT SECRET
IN BUSINESS TODAY...

---

*How to Use the Most Successful Marketing Strategy
Ever Created to Build the Right Business for You!*

By
Dan Olsen

During the past thirty plus years, it's been my pleasure and passion seeking out, investigating, and implementing some of the most successful investment and business strategies ever created. In those thirty years, my team and I have completed investigations on and amassed a database of close to 4,000 business opportunities, licenses, and franchises. Throughout my career, I have seen and come to understand what works and what doesn't work.

I played a significant role in building a retail service business that had only four locations in the beginning when I stepped into it. I put together a development plan for them and began working on expansion. After five years they had over 600 locations open in the USA and now have over 1,200; they are doing $1.5B per year in sales. I was also heavily involved in growing the #1 fastest growing new franchise company in the USA for 2009. At this writing, I am currently involved with a new franchise company growing at a pace faster than anything else with which I've involved myself.

It is my good fortune to be involved with several other top-selling franchises and licensing companies. I'm very grateful for having the wonderful opportunity of helping hundreds of people in becoming multi-millionaires with very secure investment and business systems – or increasing their holdings by many millions of dollars. Accumulated together, these individuals do billions of dollars per year in sales. As a result of helping these companies, there are now thousands of new hourly and salaried jobs created for our economy. Personally, I feel this is small business at its best, helping and saving the economy. The lives of many people have been changed for the better financially, and in other ways as well, because of my proprietary franchise marketing system – which you will learn how to utilize.

The success rates with companies and our clients have been extremely high. I've worked with the likes of Massage Envy, Money Mailer, Fantastic Sam's Family Hair Salon, and many others. After hiring us, one of those companies specifically was able to add millions to their net worth. Out of the 40 individuals in their organization, all were successful except for one, and unfortunately, he passed away. We were quickly able to sell their business to someone else and allow their family to continue onward, financially secure without them – while also allowing the new owner to become one of the most successful business operators on the map. All parties involved are still successful to this day.

I went to lunch the other day with an individual who told me that he scraped together his last few dollars to invest in a business with us (we don't recommend that people use their last few dollars to invest like this). He told me that I helped him create a legacy; one that he never dreamed could be possible for him and his family. And then, he told me that in the past year he made over $987K. He thanked me profusely for my help.

The companies I created and own help hundreds of others in creating long-lasting income and, in many cases, residual income that can be passed down to their families. We have defined seven different methods, any of which almost anyone can use to enter into our program, and then make a very good living and develop solid, long-lasting, residual income and increased equity – with an extremely high success rate! Our clients range from very little or, even in some cases, no money out of pocket, to a six-figure investment. It will depend on you and your willingness to follow our systems of success, which works every time when followed correctly.

Please, read the next few pages very carefully. They will unveil a fresh new way of thinking about investments and businesses. Once you are ready to embrace one or more of the seven ways of generating income and long-lasting wealth, and follow the systems provided, you will be on your way to increased cash flow, net worth, and more financial freedom!

For over sixteen years, I worked for large corporations, and I worked my way up to middle management. I believed that the way to financial security was to go to work for a large company where I could rely on them to take care of me and my family. I spent many long hours away from my family, making a lot of money for the company that employed me. My excuse was that I was doing it for my family and that the company would someday reward me. I had a fairly nice home, a couple of vehicles, a small portfolio of stocks, a basic 401K plan, and a small nest egg; still, like most people in America, I was only 90-120 days away from losing everything if there was no paycheck. During the latter part of these sixteen years of hard work, and after having developed good business skills, I began to make some changes.

Business Investments

I began to look into various business opportunities. I got very serious about it and decided to give it my best effort. My current job would not last forever – I needed to do something right then at that moment!

I looked into and tried several direct sales programs, but I didn't enjoy inviting my relatives and friends to attend meetings and buy products that were overpriced. The success rate of those who actually succeed in this type of business was so low that I figured my chances of succeeding were even slimmer if I continued. I even tried to do some direct marketing through the mail. Once again, after a good effort, and after going through some of my investment capital, I was disappointed. The success rate in direct marketing was very low and offered no safe bet for those looking for true success.

Several times previously, I thought about starting my own retail store. I had some money I could use from my stocks, and I could get a loan for the rest. When I looked at the success rates for starting a business on my own, I began to be more afraid. More than three-fourths of those businesses were no longer in business after three years. With no one to guide and support me, I questioned my own ability to start a retail business on my own.

So, if I couldn't start a business, I would buy an established business with an existing cash flow. I went to see several businesses that I thought I would like, but reality sank in as I realized I would have to quit my job and work full-time in the business. The problem was that the size of business I could afford would only pay me half the salary I was making with my current job! I couldn't put my family into that kind of situation.

Around this time, I spoke to my friend Larry about his cautions about buying an existing business. Larry purchased a retail store with a cash flow sufficient to support his life. His plan was to buy the first store, live on the earnings, and then gradually set up a second, and maybe a third store. Once Larry operated the business for over two weeks, he was looking at his cash receipts, and something was wrong. He went to the employees and asked them if the numbers he was seeing were correct; if the number of customers coming in was normal. They said it was all normal and that the flow of customers was typical.

Larry bought a business where the numbers were overstated by the previous owner! He ended up working the store himself, having no free time, and just barely scraping by. When he finally sold the business at a loss, he lost valuable time, income, and a large portion of his savings.

Buying an existing business didn't sound as good to me after hearing of Larry's experience. Besides, I didn't want to take over someone else's business with rundown equipment and out-of-date technology requiring a large investment to bring everything up to industry standards. I wanted something fresh and new that would be up to date and have a provable successful track record.

Real Estate Investments

What about real estate? I took a course on buying and selling in the industry. I looked long and hard for the bargains in real estate which I was told by my instructor were out there, but the bargains were few if any. I finally found a townhouse, bought it and became a landlord. After a few months as a landlord, I dreaded the thought of having to go collect late rent, and of then finding the property being rundown. Several times I was called to fix something that went wrong with the home. I decided I didn't enjoy being a landlord for $103 extra per month left over from positive cash flow on the property; with the market conditions slowing, it would take too much time to build any equity in the property.

Other Investments

After real estate, I had enough with businesses. I began looking into other investments like stocks. If I played the market right, I thought I could pick the right stocks, buy and sell them at the right moments, and boost my net worth very quickly. I soon found out that this wouldn't work as well as I imagined. The stock market is great for long-term growth, and while one can build a good net worth through it, this approach takes too long.

If the professionals can't beat the stock market consistently, how can I? I saw statistics showing that 70% of professional mutual fund managers do no better than the S & P 500. *So, why not put my money in an index fund and leave it at that?* After all this, I began to think that I would need to be a corporate employee for the next 20-30 years, doing my best to save money for retirement. A good strategy, but why wait 20-30 years?

A few months later, I met a man named Carl who moved into the neighborhood where I lived in Arizona. I spoke to Carl about my experiences and my goal of getting out of a job that was going nowhere while they were getting rich off my hard work and experience. He had been in the same position several years back. He once worked as a general manager for the owner of a retail location, and he got to the point where he was tired of seeing all those profits going to the owner and not being able to share in them.

Carl was already familiar with the single most successful marketing strategy ever created: franchising. On his own, he began to investigate various franchises to see which would best fit him and spent many months trying to find the best fit. He found an advertising franchise that suited him very well. He quickly built the franchise into a dominant player in the Southwestern USA. He had the freedom that comes with this type of operation – franchising had given him a great life!

I checked with other franchise owners of different concepts and found similar situations. Instead of many hit-and-miss searches for franchises on my own, I went to a franchise consultant and was quickly able to narrow my choices down to three hit options. After interviewing with the three franchisors and doing my homework, I settled on a hair-care franchise business. Over the next few weeks, I got very excited about it. Because I was starting fresh, without any previous baggage from an existing business, I could set things up right from the beginning with the latest technology. Experience in the industry was not necessary, as the franchisor trained my people for me and they also trained me how to run my business. They also helped me find my location, negotiate the lease, attain financing, understand how to advertise, and they helped me open successfully – all of this while I continued working at my current job! With minimal capital and with the help of the franchisor, I opened seven more franchises within five years. I built business assets worth over

$2M while also quadrupling the cash flow in my pocket compared to what I made from my job. So, I quit my job. I finally found the freedom and ability to build my dreams rather than someone else's.

Franchise Investments
(the best-kept secret)

There are many others out there striving to build the American dream. With a franchise, you have the help and support of the franchisor to assist in dealing with business problems. The bottom line of my story is that the quickest way to build personal net worth is through business ownership. The most sure-fire way of doing this – with the highest chance of success in building and owning a business with the least amount of risk – is through franchise ownership or working with franchises.

With a franchise, you can start out fresh and have a new business set up the way you want it. You don't have to take over someone else's problems. You start out clean. Your success rate with a franchise is the best of any business at 92%. If you find the right franchise and you are a good operator, your franchised business will be the best investment you can make for long-term gain and personal satisfaction. It's the best and lowest-risk business investment.

In a survey done by the International Franchise Association (IFA), they learned that franchising as a whole has a 92% success rate; for franchisees who own multiple units, the success rate is even higher! Increased market share equals increased profits, and franchising is the best way to gain market share. Right now, retail franchises represent only 8% of the retail businesses; but the retail sales of those franchises represent over 40% of total retail sales, making franchising the best way to capture market share and profits. And further franchise research by the IFA shows us that:

- 93% of the franchisees say that a franchise gives them an advantage
- 88% of franchisees recommend a franchise over a non-franchised business
- 83% are happy with their franchise
- 65% would purchase the same franchise over again

In short:

"Franchising is the single most
successful marketing strategy ever."

-JOHN NAISBITT, AUTHOR, MEGATRENDS

Before we look at why franchises are so successful, let's look at why so many businesses fail. The four major reasons why businesses fail according to Dun and Bradstreet and our internal research are:

1. Personal
   o The wrong personality of the owner in the business.

2. Lack of Capital
   o Not enough money to keep the business going during the rough times.

3. Lack of Marketing Knowledge
   o Improper use of resources won't bring customers to the business.
   o The company will have insufficient sales to generate a bottom line profit.

4. Inexperience
   o In other words, dumb, avoidable mistakes.

Let's further analyze each of these:

1. **Personal** – If the owner is not passionate about the business and the business is not well-suited to the proper personality of the owner, their business will be far from actually reaching its potential. Unless the owner has previous experience in a related field, they are taking a chance on whether or not they will like the business; whether their personality will fit in with the current structure. With a franchise, the owner only needs to find the right franchise out of over 4,000 that fits them best.

2. **Lack of Capital** – Most owners of normal businesses go into business without enough capital because they don't know what to expect. Once the capital runs out, they have nowhere else to turn, and they are forced to close or sell. With a franchise, the franchisor already knows how much capital is needed; they usually have ready sources for franchisees to tap into, ensuring sufficient capital. It also costs less, in the long run, to do it right.

3. **Lack of Marketing Knowledge** – If the owner of the business doesn't know how to bring a steady stream of customers in the door, they will then need to use trial and error, spending more unnecessary money figuring out solutions. With a franchise, the marketing systems are already in place, and at that, there is a proven track record on the marketing results. Franchises have the advantage of name brand recognition to make their marketing systems more effective.

4. **Inexperience** – An individual beginning or taking over a new business which they are unfamiliar with, they will often plan to make changes and improvements; but without specific experience in running the business, it is very common that it will not benefit the business in the long run. With a franchise, again, there is a proven system as well as many other owners to rely upon, to help the business owner in making the right decisions. This ongoing support from these experienced franchisors, who have a great incentive to see the franchisee succeed, will make a big difference in the chances of success of the franchised business.

Franchises have a much higher success rate than normal businesses because three out of the four major causes in business failure are practically non-existent in a good franchise; the first of which, Personality, can be dealt with if the new owner's personality is ensured to fit the type of franchise they intend to purchase. To clarify what I've shared so far, franchises offer three primary reasons as to why they are more successful than a normal business:

1. **Name Brand Recognition** – Let's face it, today we mostly buy items with a well-known brand name attached to them. Our children often demand to have certain shoes with the right brand name. We "need" to eat at a certain place because we know what to expect. Branding itself plays a huge role in both attracting and keeping clients/customers. The franchisees are able to pool together their advertising funds to create synergistic effects with exponential returns.

2. **The Franchise System** – Franchises have developed a successful operating system that allows the franchisee to beat the competition by performing the service better and more efficiently. Franchisees also have an advantage by tapping into reduced pricing on products because of volume purchasing.

3. **The Franchise Support System** – You are not alone in your business. You have help from the franchisor, who has experienced the business' various contingencies and can help you to overcome difficulties.

With these three items properly conceived and executed within a franchise system, the franchise is or will become the dominant business entity within practically any industry. These three things allow franchising to have an increased market share compared to similar non-franchised business. In addition to these three, franchises also offer the following advantages:

- A typically lower investment than a business of its type because of the system, cost savings, and less cash up front because of existing financing in place.
- The prestige of owning a name brand.
- An easier opportunity to expand into multiple units and build your own mini-empire.
- The tax benefits of business ownership.
- There are no layoffs and downsizing.

- Franchises have a quicker break-even point than independent start-ups. Therefore, less capital is wasted.

- You control your future.

Although a franchised business can help develop some of these seven keys through the system and support provided, you will need to evaluate yourself with regards to these seven keys and attaining financial independence through them. A franchisor can act as a personal financial trainer to coach you on to victory. Chances are, if you aren't achieving the financial success you desire, it's because you don't have systems to follow, and a mentor or coach to help you get where you want to be.

The Seven Levels of Franchising
(the most successful marketing strategy ever created)

Over the years, my experience as a business development advisor (BDA) unfolded within all aspects of businesses and investments, and I found a large variety of success. As a result of my experience, I've determined there are seven ways to enter into the fantastic method of doing business through franchising. Some require of these a very small amount of money to get started; others require larger investments that will launch you even faster into an extremely lucrative career and financial independence – if you work the system.

I have systems in each of these seven areas to help you succeed at whatever level you decide to enter. Here are the seven levels of entering into franchising from the lowest investment level to the highest:

1. Become an affiliate marketer
2. Work with a Business Development Advisor (BDA)
3. Acquire a single unit franchise of your choice
4. Acquire a multi-unit franchise of your choice
5. Acquire an area-development franchise
6. Master franchise acquisition
7. Become a franchisor

Level #1 – Become an affiliate marketer of franchise type businesses
This option allows the building of a very significant monthly residual income. This is the best way to start a business and enjoy a franchise based cashflow in the quickest way and at the lowest investment. The investment range is from $0 to $97. A great resource on this can be found at www.1purebiz.com.

Level #2 – Business Development Advisor (BDA) A BDA can:

- Help others find the right franchise or business and generate immediate referral fees
- Facilitate businesses to become franchisors
- Help the franchisors to sell franchises to individuals looking to acquire a franchise through our lead generation sources
- Receive residual income from royalties and equities in the companies you work with
- Utilize the power of several other small business opportunities with unique and powerful sources of residual income

There is no franchise fee required. Through our programs, you can learn more about franchising as well as helping other businesses become franchisees. We do the work of setting them up; you facilitate them through our systems while working with and learning through one of our franchisees.

After participating in our program, you can then help and coach individuals on acquiring the right franchise for them. Great income potential can be found in introducing products/services into these franchise systems that are used by all the franchisees; this can bring a huge, ongoing source of personal income. We even supply access to the products and services for you to use or introduce. Personal investment range out of pocket is $700 to $900.

A wonderful resource on this can be found at www.minifran.com.

Level #3 – Acquire a single-unit franchise of your choice.

It might be home-based at a lower cost of $30K to $60K. Or, it might be a brick and mortar location at an out of pocket cost of $50K to $100K. Using your 401k plan and investing in yourself without penalty is what many people are doing to get started.

Level #4 – Acquire a multi-unit franchise

Invest in two or more franchises to get started. This will usually include a location. Personal investment range out of pocket is $75K to $150K.

Level #5 – Acquire an area-development franchise

Own an entire area (like the region of an entire city) and gain the exclusive rights to put in your franchises there. Personal investment range out of pocket is $100K to $250K.

Level #6 – Master franchise acquisition

The best-kept secret in business today! You have the right to an exclusive territory (generally one or more Areas of Dominant Influence, a.k.a. Designated Market Areas) and can sell franchises in your territory, receiving a portion of the franchise fee, ongoing royalty, as well as distribution income, etc. Personal investment range out of pocket cost is $100K and $300K.

Level #7 – Become a franchisor.

Take your business or another business, franchise it, and expand it through others across the country or the world. Start and build your own franchise company for an investment of $100K to $500K. BDAs can also show you how to get the capital for this and have very little overhead.

And, there you have it – the best and most likely to be "sure thing" types of investments available. You can check more of this out by sending an email to i@coachdano.com. We are confident we can help you, as we've helped hundreds of others in the past.

Achieving Your Financial Goals
(making your dreams a reality)

This chapter covers and shares examples of the means of true financial independence, and those who found the way to its rewarding realm. The focus of my words is franchising, how it is and continues to be the greatest marketing strategy ever devised. Once you learn how to master franchising, outline a clear set of goals, and go to work – there's no stopping you as you cruise down the highway of financial freedom and goal attainment.

What we're really talking about here are the keys to the enrichment and enjoyment of life. Wealth and money receive a bad rap by those who misunderstand its true application in our lives. Money and wealth are energy – and when properly directed, channeled, obtained and used, great things happen; true fulfillment can happen; lives are changed for the better. It is the misunderstanding and misuse of money and wealth which is the cardinal sin. Learning how to acquire and use it properly opens doors in life that you may have never known existed!

I am Dan Olsen, and I have learned to master franchising and its doors to wealth, security, and the means to a better life. Why don't you join me and my large network of friends and associates as we learn to enrich our lives and the lives of those we love and care about – as well as the dreamers, entrepreneurs, and others who need the knowledge regarding how to transform their lives for the better, utilizing the business world's stories of success and best kept secrets. Franchising is not just about making money – it's about life fulfillment, and saying, "Yes!" to becoming all that you are and want to be.

Why not get started on fulfilling your financial dreams today? I wish you great days ahead and amazing success!

Made in the USA
Coppell, TX
07 September 2020